THE METAMORPHOSIS

OF THE GODS

BODHISATTVA. HORYU-JI, NARA, VIIIth C. A.D. JAPAN.

THE METAMORPHOSIS OF THE GODS

by

ANDRÉ MALRAUX

Translated by Stuart Gilbert

DOUBLEDAY & COMPANY, INC.

GARDEN CITY, NEW YORK

1960

"In life and painting I can quite well dispense with God. But, suffering as I am, I cannot dispense with something greater than myself, something that is my whole life: the power of creating."

VAN GOGH.

CONTENTS

PART I

INTRODUCTION

I T now is common knowledge that a new age dawned and its painting came to birth somewhereround 1860. But that, with it, there also began for art a *past* of a wholly new nature is a fact of which we have only recently grown conscious. For a long while art has ceased to mean what it once meant in the ancient East, in Christendom, in "medieval" Asia and America, even in Greece. We no longer see in it the adornment of life which successive schools of estheticians saw in it. The feelings we experience when gazing at the Avignon PIETÀ and the last Titians; at Velazquez and Rembrandt; at Moissac, Ellora and Lung-mên; at Greek archaic art, at certain Mexican, Neo-Sumerian and Egyptian statues—these feelings can hardly be conveyed by words associated with pleasure, even the delight of the eye, or with the traditional idea of beauty. It is obvious that the men who made the figures in the Royal Portal at Chartres and the effigies of Gudea did not do so with a view to giving pleasure, and that the emotions they inspire in us are of a quite different kind. What those people for whom art exists —those whom we still call art-lovers, since our civilization has not discovered their true name—have in common is not their refinement or eclecticism but their recognition of the mysterious power which, transcending history by means that are not those of beauty, makes them sense a vivid actuality in certain prehistoric paintings whose forms are not to be explained away by talk of "magic"; in Sumerian statues about which they know little more than the names; and in the LADY OF ELCHE about which they know nothing at all.

That for many thousand years art's function was to depict the gods was a fact generally accepted in the past, if little dwelt upon. By a paradox of history it was left to the first agnostic culture that the world has known, when it resuscitated all other cultures, to recall to life their sacred works. And in this immense domain where Romanesque consorts with the arts of the Ancient East, of the empires of Asia and America plunged in a never-ending medievaldom, of epochless continents, we have glimpses of that enigmatic power which unites for us, as living actualities, the statues of the earliest Pharaohs and Sumerian kings, the sculpture of Michelangelo and the Chartres masters, the frescos at Assisi and those of Nara, the masterworks of Rembrandt, Piero della Francesca and Van Gogh—Cézanne's too, and the Lascaux bison.

Let us suppose that a guardian devil (in the form of a cat) said to Baudelaire when he had just finished *Les Phares*, "Come and see," and led him into our present-day Louvre.

We can picture Baudelaire's amazement at the prominence given to sculpture—which, as compared with painting, he regarded as "a Caribbean art." The Louvre he knew was still a museum of antiquities; in the British Museum the Parthenon marbles cut the figure of "archaic" works; the Niké of Samothrace had not yet been discovered. True, Baudelaire spoke of "an ineluctable, synthetic, childish barbarism still often apparent in a perfect art—Mexican, Egyptian, Ninevite—and resulting from an urge to 'see things big.'" This remark he made parenthetically in the course of a study of Constantin Guys, and he never discussed in any detail works exhibiting this so-called "barbarism"; he is concerned solely with glorifying Michelangelo and Puget. We must not let ourselves be misled by Viollet-le-Duc or Victor Hugo; the restorations made by the former go to show that Gothic was then a province of archeology and the art of its sculpture a dead letter. The resuscitation of Gothic sculpture, like that of Egyptian sculpture, came nearly a century later; never did Baudelaire refer to Chartres.

In the rooms devoted to painting he would be glad to find that the Italianism and Academicism he despised had been excluded, and that Delacroix and Goya were given their due. But we may wonder if he would not be startled by the inscription under the PIETÀ discovered after his death at Villeneuve-lès-Avignon: "This picture is sometimes described as the most significant work of French painting." Neither Giotto nor Van

Eyck is mentioned in *Les Phares*. The place of the pictures expelled from Baudelaire's Louvre has not been taken in ours by an enlightened eclecticism (as was often predicted in his time); it is occupied almost exclusively by a proliferation of the pictures that used to hang in anterooms: those of the Primitives, which are in the same spirit as the rediscovered sculpture.

And suppose that when Baudelaire left the real museum, the guardian devil were to conjure up our "Imaginary Museum," then—from the Ravenna mosaics to Grünewald, from the Chartres Kings to South Seas figures—he would surely regard our age as one when the museum had been invaded by an art that was not an end in itself and practised for its own sake.

For the meaning of the word "art" changed when it ceased being applied primarily to works intended to rouse admiration, just as the world of art changed when it ceased being one reserved exclusively to these; when works were welcomed into it whose effect on us is manifestly foreign to the effect their creators meant them to produce. Our art world is one in which a Romanesque crucifix and an Egyptian statue of a dead man can both be living presences. Delacroix regarded them as a superior type of "curio"; though he stayed many months in George Sand's home, a stone's throw from the church of Nohant-Vicq, he was as ignorant of Romanesque art as was Baudelaire—and even Cézanne. No civilization before ours thought worthy of serious attention the art world created by artists for whom the notion of "art" did not exist.

If the emergence of thousands of religious works that no one had had a chance of viewing as an ensemble and no one admired a century ago has challenged the whole idea of art as Delacroix, Baudelaire and Wagner—and also Taine and Marx—conceived it, the reason is that all religious arts (like ours, which seems to derive a mysterious and constant justification from their forms) either reject or disdain the notion of subjecting their creations to the evidence of our senses. For the Moissac as for the Ellora sculptors; for the men who painted the Ajanta frescos, as for the mosaic-workers of Byzantium, appearance and reality had the same meaning, since all human reality was no more than

3

"appearance" as regards the world of Truth their art aspired to body forth or to suggest.

So long as the basic values of art were limited to those of the classical and baroque periods, or identified with them, this refusal to conform to visual experience seemed unintelligible. It was ascribed to the "barbarian" taste of the public for which the artists catered; to their fidelity to ancient, clumsily executed models (this fidelity was for Leonardo the keynote of Byzantine art)—above all to the artists' inexpertness. When our critics ceased attributing it, disdainfully, to the last-named cause, they decided to attribute it, respectfully, to a desire to adapt figures to architecture; more exactly, to certain kinds of architecture—for Baroque statues in Venice are no less adapted than Romanesque to the buildings in which they figure. It was thought that little by little the column-statue had been disengaged from the pillar. Yet the most famous column-statues, those at Chartres, were unrelated to pillars and stemmed from statues at Toulouse (which were, however, less elongated than they). This elongation did not synchronize with the rise of Gothic sculpture; it is also found in Etruscan and Wei bronzes, and in the bas-reliefs cut on the face of rocks along the caravan routes from Afghanistan to the Pacific. And how can the ascendancy of architecture account for the African sculpture whose discovery followed on that of Asiatic sculpture? What do the carvings in the Ellora caves owe to architecture? The figures in many Indian temples were made first, and the building was erected at a later date to house them. The Buddhist sanctuaries on the Silk Road are not buildings but grottos, and the sculpture they contain harmonizes so perfectly with their setting that the forsaken labyrinths of the Gobi Desert, like the museum-grottos at Yun Kang, awaken even in the modern mind the primitive awareness of "presence." It was not thanks to some divine inspiration that Byzantine mosaicists imparted this same sense of presence to their churches; however hard to follow is the evolution of Asiatic sculpture, its directive (like that of all great arts) was a supersession of the forms of nature. But no power, not even that of the raw material, impresses itself so strongly on this art as does the spirit of that numinous dusk in which the

gods reveal themselves, and in which man fades out, is transfigured or sublimated. The link between the sacred figures and the temple is more vital than that of any subordination to the architectural context; it is as though both architect and sculptor sought to invest the subterranean gods—and, above all, their visions of the Absolute—with lambent veils of shadow, untainted by appearance.

The word "architecture" brings to mind, almost automatically, façades or buildings situated in the open, doubtless because classical pillars and pediments are as familiar to us as our city streets. But the medieval master-builders did not give the façade of the cathedral (which was often as not in the heart of a town) the same pre-eminence as we assign to it. As strictly regulated as Greek architecture, the structure of the cathedrals was determined *from within outwards*. Western man, too, has applied his mind to the layout of empty space, to that age-old architecture whose aim is less to construct palaces for the gods than to create places haunted by the loftiest presences, whose forms they are called on to invoke. And when the architect's genius is devoted to building up an aura of mystery, it matters little whether he hews in the rock a sanctuary shrouding the worshiper in darkness, erects the Christian nave to which God welcomes him in daylight, or builds a Cyclopean pedestal encircling him with stars.

Nowhere, perhaps, is manifested more clearly the power that certain figures have of impregnating space with the divine than at Gizeh, where some of the oldest figures in the world challenge the immensity of the desert. We have only to look at them in the wrong direction for them to become incomprehensible; for the Sphinx to seem no more than an enormous knife-rest. Photography fails to bring out the accent of these figures, since it is almost impossible to photograph them at the hour when they reveal their full significance. But when, coming from the village, not from the road, we see the evening shadows lengthening behind them, while in the foreground the jagged outlines of the Private Temple stand up, already pitch-black, out of the surrounding chaos, the walls built by man grow indistinguishable from the ageless blocks of stone, across a dust-haze tinged by the

fires of sunset. We can no longer see the huge paws of
the Sphinx. Hung in air above the chasms of the Thebaid, the
head looms up, without a body, its neck replaced by the rocky
mass below; itself a rock on which some man of the earliest
civilization, sublimely arrogant, has imposed his image. The
features have been mutilated, almost to shapelessness, by the
ravages of time, and this gives them the accent of "devil's
chimneys" and sacred mountains; like the wings on barbarian
helmets, the great flaps of the headdress enclose the huge, worn
face, blurred still more by the approach of night. Towering
on high, the ruined head acquires the aspect of an hieroglyph, a
trapezoidal sign hung in the still translucent sky. Mantling
in darkness the great pyramid, twilight makes it seem like a
projection of the somber face, and into its triangular shadow the last rays weaving back and forth dissolve a still larger
Sphinx. In the distance the second pyramid closes the perspective vista and makes the colossal death-mask seem like the
guardian of a dike set up against the tides of the desert and the
encroaching dusk. Now is the time when the oldest man-made
forms give forth that silken susurration which is the desert's
answer to the immemorial obeisance of the East; the time when
they reanimate the place where gods once spoke, repel the form-
less vastness and set the rhythm of the constellations, which seem
to emerge from darkness only to gravitate around them.

Yet for that deep-toned voice which unifies the desert with
the stars—as in other lands the dazzling luxuriance of the jungle
with the noonday sun, valleys loud with the plaintive cries of
monkeys at the faint flush of daybreak, the green and grey
monotony of Chinese paddy fields with the far-flung serenity of
the sky, and Magdalenian caverns with the bowels of the earth—
for that voice to make its full effect neither the gods, nor the
cosmos, nor death would be enough. The latent power which
here reveals itself in the elemental purity of the desert was to
make its presence felt in all the cultures of antiquity, in Romanesque churches and, subsequently, in the cathedrals. What
is there, then, in common between the atmosphere of pious
communion with which the medieval dusk flooded the naves and
that massive intimation of transcendence which is conveyed by

EGYPTIAN ART. RANOFER. SAKKARA, Vth DYNASTY, C. 2500 B.C. CAIRO MUSEUM

the Egyptian architectural complexes—what is there common to *all* forms embodying an aspect of the inapprehensible? It is their revelation of the presence of an Other World, not necessarily infernal or celestial, nor merely a world beyond the grave; rather a supra-real world existing here and now. For all alike, in differing degrees, the "real" is mere appearance and something else exists, that is not appearance—and does not always bear the name of God. It is the relationship between the tidal rhythms of human life and a power that governs or transcends it that gives these forms their driving force and accent. True, the headdress of the Sphinx harmonizes with the pyramids; but all these gigantic forms rise together from the small burial chamber beneath them, and from the embalmed corpse which it was their mission to merge into eternity.

For all Egyptian sculpture is seen to link up with the eternity of death, as with that of the constellations (despite the fact that the Old Kingdom bas-reliefs had to be adapted to the dark cell of the mastabas and the Sphinx to the desert), once we rid our minds of the associations Christianity has grafted on to death. Egyptian art, though funerary, is rarely funereal; it has neither skeletons nor corpses. Now that we have ceased to regard Egyptian tombs as sepulchres, we tend to see them as country houses in the Hereafter and the mummies as denizens of a world of never-ending childhood, buried with their toys of gold or clay —a touching puerility. Yet that "country" is eternity and its time is not man's time, not even the longest time man can conceive of. Egyptian art does not set out, like Roman busts, to commemorate that which was; it gives the dead man access to the eternal, as Byzantine art gave the living emperor access to a world of holiness. It creates forms associating terrestrial forms with the mystery of the netherworld, according to the law of Maàt, goddess of Truth and Right, and thus transmutes appearance into Truth.

Less is known of the Mesopotamian cultures, and we find in Sumer no echoes of that dark compulsion which Memphis voices in its many works of art that have come down to us; in their hierarchy, cohesion, continuity. Its ziggurats have crumbled into dust and its soul has grown tenuous as the shreds of crushed gold foil, relics of the flowers spangling Queen Shubad's head-dresses, which were discovered in the death-pit, where the departure of the last living man is recorded by his footprints on the floor of beaten clay. In the amulets and jewels, in the effigies of queens who hymned on lyres of gold and silver the constellations of Chaldea, attended by a crowd of astrologers in feather skirts and by those redskin warriors whom we see in the stele of the Vultures marching below the Standard wrought in shell-inlay and bitumen—in these relics of the last phase of prehistory there lingers the Egyptian tang of sand, already laced with an Assyrian smell of blood. Those pre-dynastic, serpent-headed statuettes arose from a dark underworld more sinister than that which spawned the sleek monsters of the Egyptians. This much at least we know of the men who carved the ant-eyed goddesses of Fertility, the ferocious effigies at Asnunnak and that superb trance-bound head from Warka: that these men whose vocation it was to people a world transcending reality were accomplished artists. The Sumerian "animal-tamer" confronts the animals of prehistory with an almost human face; the WOMAN SINGING of Mari comes to us from the abyss of time, her body that of a caveman's Venus and her head that of some wild, disheveled bird. And soon, at Lagash, a sculptor of genius challenged the universal chaos by pitting against it a human figure linked up with the celestial cosmos of the astrologers. Though the figure has no architectural function, every seated GUDEA can be described as a ziggurat in human form. The hands with their rigidly vertical and horizontal fingers and the massive base formed by the limbs blazon forth a supernal, inviolable world, other than the world of man; the ARCHITECT WITH A PLAN is at once worshiper, god and temple.

True, these figures, belonging as they do to vanished cultures, lend themselves to different interpretations. But what they hint at is proclaimed in no uncertain voice by a surviving civilization, that of India.

To begin with by its failures. Those modern idols, lacking both style and cosmic intimations, that leer at us beneath the coconut palms are a cross between the Cingalese masks and

figurines sold in village fairs. Yet it is towards the myths in which gigantic heroes ruffle the locks of the Ganges palm-trees with Himalayan winds that they outstretch their pathetic little parodies of arms; for even in its death throes Hindu art still invokes the MOTHERS of Ellora. The pilgrimages persist, as do the tiny copper gods churned up like dry beans in red cauldrons at temple gates, and the great camps of covered carts, larger than that of the workers on Chartres cathedral. Every evening in the monsoon season when warm mists are rising from the pools under the streaming palms, the age-old summons of the ram's horn sounds from the blue shadows of the towers, and in the little sacred streets, where hawkers stretched on sheaves of aromatic grass are just awaking, men daubed with white ash are stepping forth and monkeys taking their first sleep, as in the age of the *Ramayana*. A stridency of chaffering weaves through the clamor of motor horns across the rain-swept dusk, and all the electricity of India is ablaze. But it is only an evening in the century of the decline of Europe—just one evening among so many others and so many declines—and once more the measured baying of the horn calls down the Vedic night to shroud alike the sleep of the sacred cows and the shrill modernity of chromium. Sacrificial blood flows in the gutters around the stone lingam and, scenting it despite the all-pervading, sickly-sweet aroma of tube-roses and red jasmine, a goat is struggling to escape, under the grimacing faces of the idols. The deserted sanctuary of the grand style is by way of turning into a curio-shop, but even in its degradation reminds us that Indian genius once discovered, greatly daring, the elemental majesty of blood.

A genius no less vital than that which engendered our cathedrals. The call of the sacred horn and the cries of the sacrificial goat bring echoes of the message of Ellora—the affirmation that a Truth exists, beyond and above appearance—and this holds good for every religious art, no matter what the faith it stems from. Though most civilizations were dominated by this feeling, it is usually far to seek in the western world of today—which reinterprets it in its own language. "Appearance" is no more illusion than it is the stuff of dreams; for illusion is antithetical to a concrete world, as the dream is to our waking hours; whereas the antithesis of appearance is that which lies *beyond* all "concrete" reality. And this other world is not merely a concept in which the idea of infinity fuses into some metaphysical Absolute. India teaches us at every turn that it can be a state of consciousness; that to the feeling of "appearance" (not to the idea) corresponds the feeling of what causes it to be "appearance." All civilizations that have experienced this *noesis* have regarded it as an intuitive awareness of Truth, absolute and ultimate. And though what Mesopotamia, Egypt and Iran now know of this feeling has dwindled to reminiscences of it in Islam, it inspires folktales of the East from Mysore to Kashmir, as it inspired the teaching of Ramakrishna in recent times and the *Puranas* over a thousand years ago.

Narada the ascetic is meditating in the solitude of the forest, his eyes fixed on a little dazzling leaf. The leaf begins to quiver and soon the whole tree vibrates as if the monsoon wind were sweeping through it, though all around the rich luxuriance of the jungle is hushed in windless calm under the sleeping peacocks.

"Choose between thy wishes," the rustling leaves murmur through the silence; it is Vishnu speaking.

"What wish should I make, save to know the secret of thy maya?"

"So be it. But, first, I bid thee seek some water for me." (The tree is a mass of blazing light under the fires of noon.)

The hermit goes to the nearest hamlet and calls at the first house. All the animals are sleeping. A young girl opens the door. "Her voice was like a golden cord passed round the stranger's neck." The dwellers in the house treat him not as a stranger but as an old friend who, after long absence, has returned. He has forgotten all about the water. And soon he marries the girl; everyone was expecting him to do so.

He has wedded, too, the black soil; the light that pounds with brazen fervor on the track of beaten earth down which a cow is ambling; the steaming rice field; the well that the villagers rouse to life by treading on its horizontal beam; the swift dusk falling on the palm-leaf roofs; the pink flowers of small fires of dried cow-dung glowing in the night. He has become familiar with

the town through which runs a highway leading to the ends of the earth; the little town where there are acrobats, a money-lender, a tiny temple peopled with childish gods. Familiar, too, with the domestic animals, the herbs that heal, the gift of sleep that nightfall brings to weary limbs, the long rest after the crop is reaped, the seasons that return as the buffalo returns from the drinking-pool at sunset. And the sad smile of the children in years of famine. . .

Then, on the death of his father-in-law, he became head of the household.

One night in the twelfth year came one of those great floods that ravage India, drowning the cattle, sweeping away the houses. Supporting his wife, leading two of his children by the hand and carrying the third, he ploughs his way through a black cataract of slime. The child he is carrying slips from his shoulder, and in an attempt to recover it he lets go the two others and his wife. All three are carried away, lost in the darkness and the elemental uproar. Straightening himself up, he is struck down by an uprooted tree. The swirling torrent hurls him upon a rock and when he partially recovers consciousness, all he sees around him is a heaving expanse of muddy water on which drift derelict trees, their branches thronged with monkeys.

And he wails desolately in the ebb of the gale: *"My children, oh my children...!"*

"My child"—a sudden, deep-toned echo of his voice booms in the wind—*"where is the water? I have waited for it more than half an hour."*

Vishnu is awaiting him in the blazing stillness of the forest, standing in front of the great quivering tree.

There are many versions of this story, ranging from that in the *Matsya Purana* to old wives' tales. In all the return to "reality" forms part of a cycle concerned with "appearance," in which a fleeting intimation of the incommunicable secret serves only to prolong the flood; and in which, in other legends, the migration of panicked ants gives the gods lessons of the nothingness of things. Even Vishnu only belongs to a higher cycle of appearance. The reason why Narada's second existence does not count is not because it was a dream, but because it was as "real" as the first. Or, as we of the West would say, "all that is subject to the rule of Time is appearance." And all that belongs solely to life is *impure*. We are familiar with the pains taken by the East to purify itself from death, but we do well to remember that the East takes no less pains to purify itself from birth. The struggle against the *sensation* of appearance—a feeling based on a deep, obsessive consciousness of Time—inspired all sacred architecture no less than it inspired the figures in the temples. The temple is no more a "house" than is the ziggurat or pyramid. The cosmic symbolism we can discern to a greater or a less extent in all religious edifices is not a schematic representation of the universe but a means of creating places in which man can shape a cosmos out of the chaos of appearances and, through this cosmos, forge a link with that inaccessible power which governs it throughout. In the Bayon temple at Angkor, facing the cardinal points, two hundred faces of the king (portrayed as a Bodhisattva)

ANGKOR THOM. BAYON, END XIIth C. A.D. →

BOROBUDUR (SEEN FROM THE GROUND), VIIIth C. A.D. JAVA

overlook the unseen sacred lake which associates their meditations with the various netherworlds. For the Westerner the
church is, primarily, a building where divine service is celebrated; but, from the age of Sumer on, there were many temples
where no services were held, though they served as places where
man could worship. Those in India are symbols of the Sacred
Mountain, home of the gods. The builder of the Borobudur
temple in Java so thoroughly subordinated what is seen to that
which *is*, that none of those who took part in the processions
that, winding their way around the temple, sought access to
the world and time of the Illumination, could discern the
mighty pattern of the whole, symbolizing the cosmos—and

BOROBUDUR (SEEN FROM THE AIR), VIIIth C. A.D. JAVA

the temple kept its secret inviolate until the coming of the first airplane. In every temple, whether a sanctuary or not, the function of both carvings and paintings was to body forth the *forms of Truth* in a place created to that end.

The sacred statue is a figure set free from appearance, as the temple is set free from the outside world. The "double" of Egyptian burial chambers resembled to some extent the dead man whose tomb he dwelt in; though GUDEA and the PANTO-CRATOR resemble men, they too are "doubles," in virtue of all that differentiates them from living men. The Elephanta sculptor could multiply the limbs of his innumerable gods, but he could not carve a Siva who was *only* a man, nor, since he carved his figures solely with the gods in mind, could he represent a man who was *only* a man. Common to the temples of Egyptian Thebes and those of Ellora, the Borobudur sanctuary, Santa Sophia and the Shah's Mosque at Ispahan, is the creation of places that transcend appearance; and common to ZOSER and the various GUDEAS, the PANTOCRATORS, the cosmogonies of Elephanta and the CHRIST OF THE SECOND COMING at Moissac is the creation of figures harmonizing the forms of life with the supreme Truth which lies behind them.

The only arts, Christian or other, which were regarded as "great" a century ago (those of Europe, from the Renaissance onward, Greek art from the age of Pericles, and thereafter the arts of Rome and the Hellenistic kingdoms) were, without exception, arts that did not tend to manifest a Truth of this order—but now we are rediscovering all the others.

The art of a culture is not merely the art that it brings into the world; it consists also of the repertory of previous figures that it draws on. What the Renaissance gave Europe was not only a new art of the living but also a new art of the dead. Our own age is contributing not only its painting but also its "Imaginary Museum," part of which is an extension of the nineteenth-century Louvre (as the Louvre was an extension of the Medici collections), but another part consists of all that is now supplanting it, as the Medici collections supplanted the "Treasures" of the monasteries.

We should have sooner become aware of the new world of art which our culture has inaugurated, had we not mistaken it for a development of the one before it; had we not seen in it a consequence of our conquests, researches and excavations in all parts of the world. Did the West "discover" African art at the time when the first bananas found their way to us? Assuredly the "discovery" of Mexican art did not coincide with that of chocolate. What our African explorers discovered was not Negro art but fetishes, and what the conquistadors discovered was not Mexican art but Aztec idols. Similarly all the objects collected by Europeans on their island voyages passed for "curios." If in the nineteenth century (which knew nothing of

Sumer) some archeologist had dug up the WARKA HEAD he would have classed it among Chaldean idols and its chief interest for him would have been its vague associations with Old Testament history. Idols became works of art only when they were given a new frame of reference and could enter into an art world unknown to any civilization anterior to ours. Europe discovered Negro art when it could see African carvings in the context of Cézanne and Picasso—not as fetishes in an ambience of coconuts and crocodiles. It discovered great Chinese sculpture by way of Romanesque figures, not by way of the *chinoiseries* dear to our forefathers. And it did not discover Romanesque art at the world's end but on the walls and capitals of our churches—as in the past it had rediscovered the art of antiquity in the ruins of ancient Rome, and in Flanders and Italy the works of so-called "Primitives" that had remained *in situ* since the day when they were painted. To begin with, the metamorphosis of the past was a metamorphosis of our way of seeing; had there not been an esthetic revolution, the sculpture of early periods, mosaics and stained glass would never have come to rank beside the painting of the Renaissance and the age of the great monarchies. Never would our ethnographical collections, however much enlarged their scope, have crossed the barrier between them and the art museums. Europe's dominion of the world would have served no purpose if it had not called forth the painting which removed the cataract from western eyes and revealed for the first time the "formal dynamism" of works whose distortions had formerly been put down to ignorance or clumsiness. True, modern art is not enough to account for these rediscoveries; but by subordinating appearance to creative vision, it has given access to a world in which a Mexican god becomes a statue, not a mere fetish, and Chardin's still lifes join the Chartres *Kings* and the gods at Elephanta on a footing of equality : the first world of a truly *universal* art. And far more different from its predecessor than at first sight it seems.

In the Louvre, the Uffizi, the Pitti—in the palaces—pictures and statues have retained that quality of precious objects which they had in the royal galleries of earlier days, and in the most modern European and American art museums they still compose "collections." The museum transforms the work of art into an "object"—if proof be needed we have only to compare its Gothic rooms (and even the Cloisters in New York) with a cathedral. But our new "Museum without Walls" adds to every real museum not only the contents of all the others, but the cathedral too —not to mention the tombs and caves that none of them could ever house. And it is not the showplace of an exalted form of luxury, a palace of "high art" regarded as a decorative asset, to the exclusion of African and Oceanian sculpture (though the delicately sophisticated painting of the Far East is welcomed in), as Gothic art was once excluded. Our art world is not limited to works that are readily accessible—the KORÉ OF EUTHY-DIKOS, ever-present in the memory of artists, has reposed for fifteen years in the cellar of the Acropolis Museum—but neither is it a world of "objects," for ever since the days of Romanticism the world of works of art has been less and less identified with that of *objets d'art*.

Moreover our imaginary art collection, the "Museum without Walls," whose local habitation is solely in the mind of each of us, does not set up to be a national heritage, like the Uffizi or the Prado, or even the repository of a widely eclectic culture, like the Louvre or the National Galleries of London and Washington. In our imaginary museum the great art of Europe is but one great art among others, just as the history of Europe has come to mean one history among others. That illusionist art which the West once prized so highly is no longer regarded as the climacteric of art's eternal quest or as providing the art historian with one of his surest criteria of values. It is now by way of being assigned to a particular phase of painting which lasted from 1400 to 1860, in the same way as idealizing illusionism now is seen to be a characteristic of the art of antiquity and the arts deriving from it. To the thinking of a traditionalist Far-Eastern painter, Greek Aphrodites are no less arbitrary than Sumerian statues; Leonardo and Courbet no less arbitrary (though in a different way) than the Egyptian fresco-painters and Byzantine mosaicists. But the Chinese or Japanese painter we have in mind has studied the histories published by the universities of his country, in which the western arts bulk large—and, when confronted with these, the art of Nara and that of the Sung dynasty seem hardly less arbitrary and empirical. Everywhere traditions are losing that omnivalent authority which codified the relations between art and appearance in the great European kingdoms as it had codified them also at Byzantium, though on very different lines. It was on the strength of a museum art, seemingly grounded on appearance, that, to begin with, modern painters were attacked, and for a long time art historians believed that in the case of newly discovered or resuscitated works of art a convenient yardstick for all alike was provided by museum art. But these new comers, far from falling into place within that frame of reference, tended to give the lie to it.

The word "art" conjures up for every individual, if imprecisely, his own ideal art museum. LES PHARES tells us what was Baudelaire's, and that it included no work previous to the Renaissance. We, however, include in ours the effigies of ZOSER and RANOFER, the KORÉ OF EUTHYDIKOS and the LADY OF ELCHE, some images of SIVA and Buddhist figures, the EAGLE KNIGHT of Mexico and the Dogon mask in the Musée de l'Homme in Paris, the KINGS of Chartres, the BEAU DIEU of Amiens, the Bamberg EVE, the SAVIOUR of Sts Cosmas and Damian in Rome and the THEODORA at Ravenna, NOTRE-DAME-DE-LA-BELLE-VERRIÈRE at Chartres and the Avignon PIETÀ. And when to these—and to how many other figures!—we add Vermeer's LACEMAKER, Chardin's HOUSEKEEPER and Courbet's ATELIER, we can admire in these three pictures the creative power which links them with the above-named earlier works—but not the "artistry" which assimilates them to a woman making lace, a housekeeper or a painter's studio. For we know that what we admire is not the imitation of these scenes—though Vermeer, Chardin and Courbet put their hearts into imitating them. The scene may have been indispensable for the creation of the picture, but a picture's value becomes independent of its theme, once that ideal museum of ours is no longer devoted to illusionist art. We also know today that what we admire is not only the representational technique or *facture* of a picture, but the qualities which differentiate it from its model; which differentiate

23

Manet's OLYMPIA and Cézanne's portrait of his wife from Victorine Meurent and Madame Cézanne respectively; and the Egyptian "double" from the dead man it represents. It is not our modern sophistication that leads us to see both in the masters commonly described as realists and also in their adversaries—in Caravaggio, Vermeer, Chardin and Goya as in Michelangelo and Rembrandt—as in all sacred arts (and in our own) an allusion, sometimes overt, sometimes enigmatic, to a "something other than appearance." Nor is it our superior "enlightenment" that leads us to discern in the great artists of extinct cultures that power, sometimes deliberate, sometimes held in leash, sometimes unconscious (and unnoticed for many centuries), which gives their works their contemporary appeal; rather, it is because we are now confronted by the art of the whole world. And, as a result of that confrontation, appearance has come to seem no more than the inexhaustible libretto of an interminable opera.

The rich diversity of works of art with which since the beginning of this century our memories have been stocked does not include either those charming trifles, the Tanagra statuettes —which, as it so happened, preluded a rebirth of Greek art— or the little effigies of boatmen, soldiers and artisans which rendered the same service to Egyptian art (both types of figure were made to be placed in coffins). What we remember are figures associated with the gods, bearers of offerings and worshipers or votive statues: the KOUROS hardly distinguishable from Apollo himself, the KORÉ so closely resembling the DEMETER of Eleusis, the painted processions in the Valley of the Nobles and the Valley of the Kings. All alike mirror the human and ephemeral—appearance—yet carry intimations of the Other World. The "dialogue" between art and appearance, so misleading in the days when the HOUSEKEEPER or a Velazquez portrait was compared with its model, a VENUS by Titian with a naked woman, or the Attic Maidens of the Parthenon with a picturesque procession of young girls—this dialogue becomes much less deceptive when with these Maidens we compare the KORÉS of the Acropolis; with an Episcopal Council the

CONFESSORS of Chartres; or with a royal cortège the depiction of Theodora's retinue at Ravenna (or that of any monarch of the ancient East)—when in renderings of divinities and ancestors, of priest-kings, immortals and the dead, we see a company of figures invested by an artist with the function of liberating man from the human situation and from Time. Once we cease to regard such works as clumsy imitations of their models, we realize that the power through which they make their impact on us—what we now would name creative power—was initially the power of giving form to that which made the human animal become a man and freed him from the chaos of his beginning, from his instincts, from Siva the destroyer. If man had not set up against appearance his successive worlds of Truth, he would not have become a rational being but another ape. The artist created images of Truth in the same way as man created his gods and the world they illuminate; the images of Horus were not imitations of Horus (whom nobody had seen), nor were they likenesses of men who, in virtue of some hieroglyphs, configured Horus. The RANOFER is not an imitation of Ranofer the priest or the RAHOTEP an imitation of General Rahotep; they are representations of these mortals as they were to be in the realm of immortality. When we contemplate them, when we overhear their silent dialogue with the oldest historic civilizations and social systems, we make the same discovery as when we contemplate those ancient temples whose symbols, wrapped in lianas, arise in forests given back to the tribes of monkeys of the ancient legends—and this even when the temples have been restored. All these temples, all these images, tell us that for thousands of years the major aim of all artistic creation—and this anyhow is something we feel familiar with, even though it undergoes a metamorphosis in transmission—was to reveal or to uphold the forms of Truth. "Men give the gods their names," an Indian tells us, "but the gods accept or disregard them as they will." The greatest artists created the forms of their gods but the gods accepted them only if men recognized them as such. And so began the reign of *style*.

Our discovery of the significance of sacred styles does not imply that we regard the sacred as sole criterion of art. But it calls in question the criteria of an earlier age and makes us aware that our histories of art have failed to take into account the existence of this sacred element, and even its nature (which, however, they assume to be common knowledge). It may be that in various ages artists depicted what they saw, aimed at making their work lifelike, and found pleasure in so doing. For the *means* of art have been employed for many ends, from graffiti to portraits, before being used for the embellishment of drawing rooms. But, though making pictures is a natural human instinct, it was not "natural" that certain men should make those we have in mind, which rank as works of art; works that are as far removed from representations dominated by appearance, or intended solely to give pleasure to the eye, as is a poem from even the most vivacious tale in prose. Similarly, it is not "natural" that these works of the past should take on a new life or a Velazquez portrait should "speak" to us, like a living presence, precisely in virtue of all that differentiates it from what a photograph would have been, had photography then existed—an appeal that is not accounted for by his "exquisite taste"; for if Velazquez' language is not that of a great photographer, nor is it that of a *grand couturier*. What appeals to us in his art is the same quality that fascinates us in the "likenesses" of King Gudea, of the Pharaoh Zoser and of Theodora, in the Arcadian landscape art of Venice and the flowers of the Ajanta frescos; the quality which appeals to us in all art we admire, our own included. That worldwide art which, for the first time, is coming on the scene does not merely reveal what distinguishes every style, each masterpiece, from visual actuality; it also reveals that which likewise distinguishes them from appearance in the metaphysical sense.

Great as is the number of works we now are rescuing from oblivion, we have a feeling, unclear but certain, that our present admiration of the great religious works of the past somehow links up with our admiration of Michelangelo, Grünewald and Rembrandt. Nor does it seem strange that we rediscovered simultaneously Romanesque art and El Greco and, soon after—as though this discovery had led up to it—the sculpture in the grottos whose recesses, haunted by otherworldly presences, open on the immemorial vastness of Indian forests and the sluggish waters of Chinese rivers. But Baudelaire was still alive when to the galaxy of artists in his *Phares*, contemporary painters added Velazquez *and* Chardin—pending our rediscovery of Vermeer.

Undoubtedly Vermeer's MAIDSERVANT POURING MILK and Chardin's HOUSEKEEPER do not belong to a world of Truth that they aspired to body forth as did Egyptian statues, the Chartres KINGS or (by other means) the Isenheim Altarpiece; nor to that sublimated reality which in the art of Michelangelo and Rembrandt took the place of revelations of the eternal. The maker of ZOSER sought to endow a Pharaoh with eternity; Vermeer did not try to eternize a maidservant. Yet that word "eternize" may give us pause—was not Vermeer, also, trying to withdraw *something* from the thrall of Time?

When he invented forms that differed from appearance, the sole concern of the Old Kingdom sculptor of "doubles" was to assure eternity to the men they stood for. And that of the statue was bound up with it, even though the sculptor saw it solely as a vehicle of magic. Nor were these forms invented as a means of "beautifying" the model; true, the finished work resembled him, but the *sacred style* was no less essential than likeness to the survival of the "double" : a "double" can never be mistaken for the effigy of an Imperator.

Though, in creating forms set free from Time, the maker of the ZOSER had not the same aims as Rodin, he, too, willed this deliverance, and no less strongly, no less consciously. As did all the creators of great sacred and religious works. To create figures that manifest the world of God is to create figures immune, to some extent, from Time. Not with an eye to recognition by posterity; nothing could be more remote from Egyptian thought than "posterity" as Greece conceived it; nothing more alien to Romanesque Christendom than "posterity" as the Renaissance understood it. The art of the static civilizations of the East was made for an equally static future, a non-historical continuum in which generation followed generation like successive generations of blood-horses. Our medieval artists (like the Greeks) were alive to an historical evolution. Nineteenth-century art historians were to declare that the KORÉS were outmoded in the age of Pericles, and Romanesque VIRGINS in the nineteenth century. But when the Athenians, at the threat of a Persian invasion, hid their KORÉS underground, and when fifteenth-century Christians buried some fourteenth-century effigies of Our Lady of Pity, this was not because they had ceased to please; it was because they had "entered into Time" and thus lost the quality of eternal life manifested by the works that followed them. Nonetheless they had once possessed it. The MÈRE-DIEU of Amiens would presumably have been buried, had not its engagement in the portal preserved it from this fate; yet we cannot doubt that its maker intended this image of the Eternal Virgin to outlive the vicissitudes of time and place, as the Egyptian wished his "double" to act as the dead man's counterpart through all eternity. We shall see how the creators of Christian forms, when they ceased to relate their work to the world of God immanent in Romanesque churches, and then to the City of God immanent in the cathedrals, ceased relating it to the eternal; and how Christian art came to locate in Time the scenes that Byzantine and Romanesque art had placed in Eternity. But we shall also see what was the nature of the relationship of Flemish art to appearance; and also how Christian art lost its vision of Eternity only when Italy "discovered" immortality—just as the ancient world lost the former only when the latter was "discovered" by the Greeks.

For the access of the work of art into the realm of the immortal played for Michelangelo and Titian the same part as that which its access to an eternal world had played for the maker of ZOSER and for the Chartres sculptors. Posterity had entered into the artists' field of vision and Michelangelo felt sure he could reckon on its approval since beauty is immortal—genius being the power of creating things of beauty, and immortality being one of their prerogatives. Gradually, however, that word "beauty" acquired a new accent, new applications, and ceased to be the means whereby a work of art could stake a claim on immortality. What was there in common between what Michelangelo called beauty in his DAVID and in his BRUTUS and, subsequently, in his RONDANINI PIETÀ? And between what

Titian called beauty, when he was painting his PROFANE LOVE and his MARSYAS or the Venice PIETÀ—which foreshadows Rembrandt. The fable, the historical scene, the portrait, landscape and still life successively became major art forms once they made their entrance into that uncharted realm whose limits they extended, and which absorbed them one by one. Landscape entered into Rubens' painting when he asked of his trees what he asked of his nudes; "non-significant" subjects made good their place in art when artists took to asking of them what formerly they asked of gods, and of man made in the image of the gods. (Gods, men and sacred animals were almost the only subjects of the early periods, and Chinese landscape painters impregnated the ephemeral with hints of the eternal.) Though Vermeer had no intention of imparting to his MAIDSERVANT that morsel of eternity which the Egyptian sculptor imparted to his ZOSER, he may well have wished his picture of this girl to enter into a world akin to that of the Pharaoh's statue. The sculptor's creative activity—the arrangement of forms by which he conferred eternity on his model—was directed to defeating the tyranny of Time; and this was also true of the painter's creative activity. If Vermeer painted his MAIDSERVANT in this way and no other, it was neither with a view to perfecting Dutch illusionism nor to inventing a new technique, but solely with a view to enabling his work to win a place in the world where all great works survive, defying Time, and thus to share in their survival. The Egyptian sculptor believed he was immunizing his *model* against Time; Vermeer set out to immunize his *picture* against it. Perhaps he made the YOUNG GIRL merely as a portrait of his daughter; and every illusionist portrait vanquishes Time in its own manner, simply because it records forever the features of a living being. For the YOUNG GIRL is also exempt from Time in the same way as Egyptian "doubles," since it too belongs to a timeless world —not as would a portrait painted by a clever but uninspired Dutch master, but as does the LITTLE STREET IN DELFT.

Still, Vermeer did not break, consciously, with illusionism: that deceptive verisimilitude which used to "justify" his paintings. Not until our discovery of a universal art and their differentiation from models that they appear to imitate so closely—like that differentiation of the ZOSER from a model which it imitated at a further remove—did all such works become invested in our eyes with the same power. But with the appearance of OLYMPIA (contemporary with the death of Delacroix) great artists had inklings, vague at first, of this new value and turned it to account by rejecting both illusionism and the "justifications"which had meant so much to their predecessors. Then, at last, our art and the world of our art arose; our modern masters and the "Museum without Walls" won through.

When this art came on the scene—with Baudelaire's *Phares* and the Louvre—it was the painting of the "unreal," which was born in Florence and died with Delacroix in Paris, that had wiped out the great figures of Christian art and the lineage of images laying claim to immortality. In Chardin's case the justification of his art by "the feeling behind it" was patently absurd; but this was not the case with Michelangelo, Titian, Rubens, Poussin, Rembrandt, Watteau, Goya and, finally, Delacroix. All the same Chardin looked to his *subjects* to justify his work, whereas Cézanne found that justification in his art alone. In the same way as the VENUS OF URBINO, while ostensibly a nude woman, belongs to a world of dreamlike unreality, so the MONTAGNE SAINTE-VICTOIRE, while representing a mountain, belongs to what Cézanne called *la peinture*, an autonomous realm that Titian had never dreamt of and which, deriving perhaps from Vermeer's art world, had been emancipated from it since the appearance of OLYMPIA and the subordination of illusionism to the specific language of painting. This is a realm manifested exclusively by the painter's personal "Imaginary Museum," to which his pictures must win their right of entry, as RANOFER won admission to the world of Horus, Pheidias' ATHENA to the world of the gods and the Royal Portal of Chartres to the world of God.

Were it only a matter of "colors arranged in a certain order," why should Cézanne have sacrificed all else to it? It is certainly not because he held that nature should be treated "on the lines of the sphere, the cone and the cylinder" that we see in him the heir of the Greek archaics and Piero della Francesca. Like all the sacred arts, Cézanne's rejected appearance and, given the fact that so many centuries had rejected it in favor of a Truth that they proclaimed, we may well wonder whether Cézanne, too, did not reject it in favor of a Truth of which he was unaware, but to which he dedicated himself whole-heartedly.

He had witnessed the death of works that Michelangelo had thought immortal; he knew they had been forgotten for over a millennium and that the art of the cathedrals had been regarded as "barbarian" for five hundred years. Yet, if God had told him that his painting would not outlast his death, he would probably not have believed Him—but invited God to come with him to the Louvre. If, however, he believed the divine announcement, he might perhaps have stopped painting, though this is unlikely; for even if one of his aims was that his name and works should live on in men's memory, his supreme desire was that his art should win admittance to that world in which, to his thinking, Poussin had a place beside Tintoretto; the world where masterpieces are more than the milestones of a one-way past, since in it Poussin is not a "successor" of Tintoretto any more than Cézanne is one of Poussin. It is the world in which, for us, the ARCHITECT WITH A PLAN forgathers with the KORÉ OF EUTHYDIKOS and with the KINGS of Chartres, the Avignon PIETÀ with the Ajanta frescos, and Vermeer with Rembrandt; the world of the presence in our lives of what should, normally, belong to death.

We sense the existence of that world, but do not know its nature. We are aware of it as one is made aware of the presence of a huge, frameless mirror by the images reflected in it. We are beginning to see that the West discovered that world at the same time as it discovered the world of history, and that these two entities, akin yet adverse, have been haunting it ever since the creation of figures inspired by Faith, by the unreal or by an ideal of beauty, ceased as a result of their joint influence; ever since a sequence of philosophies, voicing that "sense of time" which seems to be an obsession with our present age, bereft of Eternity, has taught us to see in Time man's chief antagonist.

Perhaps the first worldwide civilization will give birth to the first complete history of the human race. But a "continuous" history, whether it describes man's conquest of the elements or man's creation of himself by himself, premises a constant progress, broken though it may be by tragic setbacks. In the world of art, however, the statues in the cathedrals do not culminate in Michelangelo's NIGHT; for it does not mark any "advance" on them, or on RANOFER. If it did so, they would cease being masterpieces, or even great works of art; and so long as the idea of an evolutionary progress obtained, they did not rank as such. A work emerges in its time and from its time, but it becomes a work of art in virtue of being *outside time*.

The history of civilizations, as formulated in the present century, is discontinuous and answers to a feeling profoundly different from that of the continuous history which preceded it. In the latter Egypt used to be identified with "the childhood of humanity"; whereas in the eyes of the modern historian Egypt represents a form of humanity that has had its day. Now that the fantasies woven around the noble savage, the Persians of our eighteenth-century plays and the Chinamen of lacquer screens, have given place to an intellectual discipline, the past is subjected to an objective, dispassionate analysis. For the Egyptian (unless his name were Akhenaten) "believed" in his civilization as in the gods presiding over it; even when he modified it, he remained immersed in it, like a fish in an aquarium. We can study Egyptian culture as a stage in the march of history but we also see in it one of the various forms humanity has assumed, one of the many human "possibles." The Moon King ritually strangled during the satellite's eclipse, the Khmer king painted gold and borne in procession on a pedestal of gladioli and the Chaldean astrologer watching on the night sky a stately progress of huge heraldic lions—these fascinate us no less than the strange genius that conjured up the Magdalenian bison. In our investigations of man, as in our world of art, what seems most alien to us links up with what is furthest away in time; those we once called savages are now called primitives. We ask of the history of dead civilizations, as of the ethnography of dying races, that it should tell us what man is like when most unlike ourselves.

But also in what ways he resembled us, aside from sex and hunger, fear and laughter. From the realm of the distant past which we are now exploring we learn that man has always had two "constants": his instincts and his spirit of enquiry into the outside world. Every culture is the special form in which a race coordinates them with a view to ensuring an harmonious relation between its members and the universe, and this is no less true of the Sumerians and the Maoris than of the Greeks and the Dogons. The concept of Truth on which the Sumerians and Greeks based this correlation has passed away with them (this is not the case with the Maoris and Dogons). We see ourselves as the heirs of Greece, not of Sumer, Egypt, China or Mexico; yet their works of art are now by way of acquiring for us the same actuality as the Athenian statues. That ineluctable "Nevermore" whose shadow falls across the history of civilizations is challenged by the magnificent enigma of these undying presences. No trace survives of the power which called forth Egypt out of the prehistoric night; but the power which brought forth ZOSER from it speaks with a voice as compelling as that of the master-builders of Chartres and that of Rembrandt. With the man who made that statue we have nothing in common, not even his feelings towards such major issues as love and death—not even, perhaps, the same way of seeing his work. Yet when we contemplate this statue, the accent of a sculptor forgotten for five thousand years seems as invulnerable to the rise and fall of empires, as ageless, as is the accent of maternal love.

Cézanne knew that great works which seem dominated by appearance are less so than they seem, but he did not know that the West was about to discover a "Museum without Walls" in which the Nara frescos, Chardin's still lifes, the statue of the Pharaoh Zoser and his own pictures would be found to express a power common to all four. That upon the face, friendly or forbidding, of human history, art was about to cast a gleam of that eternity which, it seems, belongs to art alone. In each successive civilization it elicited from the chaos of appearances certain cosmic figures with which man could feel in harmony, or which served as embodiments of his loftiest dreams. And, following their rediscovery, we see with new eyes all those works in which the artist, whether overtly or covertly, replaced the data of visual experience with a new vision of the universe. The man who carved the effigy of Zoser epitomized in stone the spirit of Egypt; the maker of the portals of Chartres, that of medieval Christendom; Vermeer had catered for a group of connoisseurs many of whom saw in him no more than a successful rival of Pieter de Hooch—only in the present century has he found his "true believers." When the Avignon PIETÀ entered the Louvre it seemed as if destiny were deputing the greatest of the ancestors of Cézanne, then on the point of death, to prepare his place for him in that august assembly, for the PIETÀ entered it as an envoy of the art which was now to combat the invincible hegemony of Time with an invincible communion.

Thousands of Europeans crowd exhibitions of Mexican or Etruscan art; hundreds of thousands flock to exhibitions of the art treasures of Vienna and Rembrandt's works; as many Japanese pause to admire Braque's canvases, and millions of Americans those of Picasso and Van Gogh. The pilgrims to the "art cities" of the West are more numerous than those who visited Rome in Holy Year. And though, when gazing at the figures of Florence or Venice, they can associate art with happiness, beauty, the delight of the eye, it is not so when they contemplate the figures at Chartres or Luxor, Mexican or Etruscan statues. Neither happiness, nor traditional beauty, nor the pleasure of the eye accounts for the making of a film whose hero is Van Gogh; for the fact that the ceremonies commemorating Rembrandt's death were presided over by Europe's last kings; that our exhibition of stained glass was opened by the last Asiatic emperor; or that the populace of Soviet Russia flocks to the Hermitage Museum. People of all lands, hardly aware of what it is they have in common, seem to be asking of the art of all time to fill a void they dimly sense within them.

When the Japanese made "pilgrimages" to Chartres, it was not *quâ* Buddhists that they visited the cathedral, but neither Sesshiu nor Hokusai would have gone there *quâ* artists; yet some of their successors go there today in the same spirit as we go to Nara. The many art worlds of the past were self-contained, mutually exclusive, as are religions; our modern art world is an Olympus where all the gods and all civilizations welcome all who understand the language of art (as the sciences, all who understand their language). Each civilization had its "high places"; all mankind is now discovering its own. And these are not (as the nineteenth century took for granted) regarded as successive landmarks of art's long pilgrimage through time. Just as Cézanne did not see Poussin as Tintoretto's *successor*, Chartres does not mark an "advance" on Angkor, or Borobudur, or the Aztec temples, any more than its KINGS are an "advance" on the KWANNON at Nara, on the PLUMED SERPENTS, or on Pheidias' HORSEMEN. All are, for the first time, united in a world in which the dying fetishes are given a new lease of life such as they never knew before; in a world where, also for the first time in history, Time is vanquished by the images that human hands created to defy it.

In this book I attempt to make that world intelligible, and to analyse the power, old as the "inventions" of fire and of the tomb, to which it owes its being. My aim is neither to write a history of art (though the very nature of artistic creation sometimes obliges me to keep pace with the progress of time), nor a study of esthetics; it is to try to discover the significance of the fact that throughout the ages man has always sought an answer to the problem set him by the spark of eternity latent in his being—a problem which has assumed a new complexity in our modern culture, first of all cultures to realize and recognize its ignorance of man's significance.

SPHINX, MIDDLE IVth C. B.C. ACROPOLIS MUSEUM

PART II

THE DIVINE

KORÉ OF EUTHYDIKOS ("POUTING KORÉ"), EARLY Vth C. B.C. ACROPOLIS MUSEUM

There can be no doubt that the problem posed by the very fact of art's existence would have been broached much sooner in Europe had not a belief persisted over so many centuries that the source of all art worthy of the name was to be found in what was then regarded as its acme, the art of Greece, the reason being that this art alone seemed to have perfectly mastered the rendering of appearance.

Nor is it so easy for us, even today, to regard Greek art as just one art among others; a Japanese who saw in Chinese art but one art amongst others might well have difficulty in understanding his own. "Sole true goddess"—thus Renan apostrophized Pallas Athene, meaning that her godhead was unique. The sacred had trampled ugliness and beauty in the same dust; God alone had counted, all else was vanity. By liberating man from his humanity Siddhartha had become the Buddha. It was in Greece that for the first time a voice was heard (through the mouth of Euripides) proclaiming: "I love not the gods that are worshiped by night." And then began the fragile art of gods who lived in daylight and had to perish with the nightfall.

Gods, however, whom the Romans—but not the Hellenistic kingdoms—were destined to forget. We are getting to know better than in the past all that differentiated Greece from Alexandria and, above all, from Rome and from the world of allegory sponsored by our Roman heritage. True, from the early fifth century on, Greek art impresses us as being freed from the clotted darkness of an East haunted by death and the eternal; against the pyramids, against Queen Shubad's tomb and the Etruscan tumuli, Athens set up the luminous future invoked by Pericles. Yet in Greek art we find not only "sweetness and light," but also the quest of a secret lying deeper than the realm of Reason. And in the same way as we have retrieved the quivering drapery of the Parcae under the dead folds of their antique copies, we are now rediscovering on the sad lips of the pouting *Koré* an enigmatic echo of the voice of Antigone.

There had been Mycenae, but the names of the Atridae

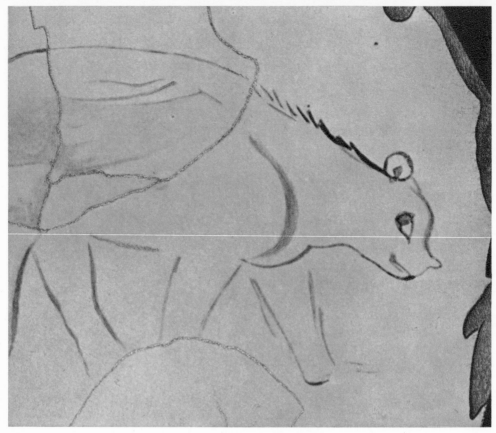

OSTRACON, NEW KINGDOM. COPY BY Mme VANDIER. CAIRO MUSEUM

on the gold masks cannot blind us to the fact that Mycenae
was hardly less oriental than Cyprus. There had also been the
Minoans. Alongside Evans's bold reconstitutions and the bulls
of the Euphrates we find works such as the "Harvesters" vase,
the famous "Parisienne," and the larnax of Hagia Triada where
there is assuredly a touch of caricature in the witty freedom of
the line. The Egyptian sculptors, too, made humorous sketches
on their ostraca, but these they threw away; whereas the Hagia
Triada sarcophagus was painted to last for ever. At Knossos
there are neither palm-trees nor the desert; but our familiar trees
and a purple flood of bougainvilleas covering the relics of a seagirt

culture whose dolphins already prefigured Amphitrite. True, it was the first white civilization, but it was also the glittering lagoon of a Maori world. In some Ionian *Korés* we find the tip-tilted nose of the Cretan goddesses; and those acrobatic figures, those deities so blithely floating up on swings are at a far remove from Egypt's cataleptic majesty. All the same (though here we find as it were the childhood of the smile) there is difficulty in associating the Iliad, or even the Odyssey, with these courts in which naked princes wearing ostrich-feather headdresses bowed their lances before Phedra-like *grandes dames* exhibiting their breasts above chastely billowing flounces of fine linen. And though the links between the palace of Knossos and the Acropolis are evident, they are tenuous at best, despite all that Athens inherited from the earlier culture; the Lion Gate at Mycenae is far from symbolizing liberty.

Then there had been Achaemenid Persia. Only the change that came over the term "barbarians" in the course of centuries leads us to think the Greeks looked on the builders of the vastest monuments of the age as one huge tribe of savages. They knew that Cyrus had put an end to the Assyrian reign of terror and announced that he would rule the vanquished with justice; Aeschylus wrote the threnody of Xerxes in the same tone as Homer wrote Hector's last farewell. True, Persepolis did not point the way to Athens; yet its figures differ from those of Nineveh as a chivalrous knighthood differs from a horde of killers. These figures humanized that crushing, brazen light with which the desert floods so many Eastern arts; like the Greek coast, the high plateaux of Iran are morning lands. In the last holy place of Persia, Behistun, we sense the same virile fraternity as on the high cliffs of Taygetus. On the horizon line looms up a tidal wave of mountains cataracting down to valleys where a wind from the Zagreus furrows the tall grasses like the waters of a strait; at one point of the range we half expect to see another *Niké of Samothrace*, but the sheerest promontory in the world is its own statue. All that shows on its flank is the seal of Darius, struck on the mountainside by the father of the man who dreamt of chaining up the sea, and eagles circle, mewing like cats, around

NAXIAN SPHINX, FIRST HALF VIth C. B.C. DELPHI MUSEUM

the huge heraldic hawk. At the little inn beside which a mountain spring has conjured up a garden like that of a French parish priest, a child hands the traveler a bunch of roses, crushed in his tiny fist; roses he has picked beside the bridle-path where Cyrus' lancers and Alexander's infantry saluted with the same awe-struck silence a masterwork of the gods.

At Delphi we find the same roses—but fewer— and the same forever wheeling eagles. Delphi is better known, though most photographs give a false idea of it, as seen from the ruins halfway up the mountain side. Like the grass of Behistun, olive groves make a river of the valley. Here are the two Cyclopean buttresses that shore up the towering cliffs of the Phaedriadae, the narrow ruins—like debris of a diadem—of the Sacred Way, and the prophetic gorge where shrilling eagles invoke the voice

CATTLE STEALERS (THE DIOSCURI), TREASURY OF SICYON, VIth C. B.C. DELPHI MUSEUM

of Aeschylus' Prometheus. For it was not on the Caucasus
but on this rugged, sun-scarred throne, between the Phaedriad
pinnacles, that the mighty specter listened to the consolations
of ancient Ocean and mused on the gift of fire. Delphi is the
tomb of Uranos but it is as a dead conqueror that he haunts it.

To Pheidias the *Dioscuri* must have seemed no less foreign
than the gift-bearers of Persepolis. For these pseudo-Greek
warriors were blood-brothers of the Hittite warriors. But
something here is blurred: not so much the accent of the East
as that chthonian, aboriginal accent which art history has not
yet succeeded in particularizing and which makes its presence felt
from Asia Minor to Etruria—the accent of the "white barbarians." It tallies with the figures on the Geometric vases but
not with the lighter forms of Cretan art; we find the last traces of
it, after the *Naxian Sphinx*, in some *kouri* draped in a curiously
Romanesque manner.   But there is nothing in common between
the *Siphnian Caryatid* and the *Naxian Sphinx*; any more than there
is between its ample modeling and the art of the East, between
its stylistic innovations (so little in keeping with the porch where
it belongs) and those other styles which have all the intricacy
of hieroglyphs.   When this *Caryatid* made its appearance, round
about 550 B.C., all arts were hieratic. Buddha's sermons,
the works of Lao Tze and the Upanishads had been known for
nearly a century.   And Western Europe had reached the end
of the Iron Age. Half a century later came the *Fair Ephebus*
and the *Koré of Euthydikos*—a bare fifty years had sufficed to
overwhelm the art of three millennia. But during those five
decades man, for the first time, had broken with the sacred.

At the time when Greek art discovered the smile—and
also a new poise of the body—it was still linked up with Egypt.
But it would be impossible to mistake the *Kouros of Milo*, even
without its head, for an Egyptian statue. The figure's elongation, the thinness of the torso, arms and spindle legs, and the
length of the neck (twice as long as that of the "Scribes" of
Memphis and much more vertical) make it seem as light as a
clay vase—a lightness that is never found in even the least static

Egyptian figures, in *Tui* or *Karomama*. In all Eastern sculpture there is a curious and constant ponderosity, as if it always were clamped to the ground by the foundation pegs used in many Chaldean bronzes. It is as though the artist felt obliged to root all that he represented in the land of the dead; inventor of winged beings, the East refused to let them fly. The birth of Greek art marked an end of this subjection to the Eternal. Art historians of the past have found trouble in accounting for the change; assuming as they did that the problems of the creation of forms were always problems of representation, they set it down to "the discovery of movement"—an equivocal, if suggestive explanation. For the movement of Assyrian horses is no less convincing than that of the horses of the Parthenon; it is simply of another nature. We see this difference most clearly in the treatment of the human figure. The depictions of Egyptian dancing girls record a movement, those of Greek dancers *suggest* one. In the seventeenth century movement meant that quality which so much impressed sixteenth-century observers of Raphael's *School of Athens*; the term that rises, to the modern mind is, rather, "unconstraint." It is an absence of stiffness, the opposite of hieraticism and, strictly speaking, means the independence of the figure. Until the nineteenth century it was regarded as a step towards more faithful representation, almost as a technical discovery: a liberation from the "dark ages" and what passed for clumsiness—the common characteristic of idols, Pharaonic statues and Gothic saints. But every hieratic art involves a rejection of the profane, paralleling the use of sacred languages: Sanscrit or Church Latin. The free-standing figure in Greek art did not announce the discovery or victory of imitation but art's liberation from the sacred.

Never had any major art of the East set out to imitate a human figure, even in representations of Gudea; even when the sculptor Tutmosis made plaster casts of living men's faces. The Amarna reliefs are the most famous examples of so-called oriental realism; yet those first strokes of the sculptor's boaster which transformed Akhenaten's mouth and eyes into sculptural planes pointed the way to the procedure that was to convert his mask into the faces of his colossi. Never had the "doubles" *imitated*

MASK OF AKHENATEN, C. 1360 B.C. BERLIN MUSEUM

the dead, whom they had nevertheless resembled for two thousand years. Such was the dexterity of the Egyptian sculptors that they could have achieved the most convincing realism had they wished; just as they could have exactly copied any Greek *Discobolus*. And, also, suggested the independence—even something more than the independence—of their figures, as they did

in certain statuettes. But surreptitiously—for in sacred arts representation always means translating into the language of a supramundane world.

In Mesopotamia, as in Egypt, that language had been built up in terms of a closed, hierarchically ordered system. But in the minor arts of the East, particularly in ceramics and terra-cotta figures, we often sense a latent tendency to whimsical effects. It is no more than hinted at; even in the toys the humor hardly makes us smile—they seem to have been intended for deadly serious children! The hedgehogs and wide-eyed bears, the rams of Susa with their crazy horns, which suggest the beginnings of a style, appear and then die out like the "Sunday painting" of the nineteenth century. Nobody would have guessed that the Egyptian artist had a spark of wit had not some of the pebbles on which he made his preliminary sketches been discovered. But what the ostraca prove is that, though these painters and sculptors were not without a sense of humor or an idea of the interest of the independent figure, they deliberately ruled out both, and for the same reasons. The arabesque moving freely in space was no less alien to the purpose of Egyptian art than was the comic spirit. One can hardly imagine the *Discobolus* in a tomb. The Eastern conception of the sacred involved not only a profound awareness of eternity but also a system of forms, charged with numinous power, against which cataclysms were impotent (the Hyksos invasion was a mere parenthesis in the history of Egyptian style).

Undoubtedly the Greeks practised a religion; for they had recourse to prayers soliciting divine favor or protection. Otherwise, it seems, only hymns figured in their ceremonies. Ulysses did obeisance to Mother Earth, but that was a survival of a primitive cult; we can hardly imagine Pericles doing obeisance to Athena, still less praying with clasped hands. The ritual gesture symbolic of Greece was the presentation of offerings. But the interventions of her gods were as capricious as her oracles; the laws that governed them were never codified in any holy book. No religious teaching was given in the temples and

Greece had no priestly caste. The Christians were quick to differentiate from other unbelievers these pagans who had no clergy, no theocracy, no Creator, no Judge and no eternity.

Even though we do not ascribe to Dionysus (anyhow the fifth-century Dionysus) the importance Nietzsche gave him, we must be chary of aggrandizing Reason. Robespierre saw in Reason the arbiter of all the gods, and Renan the "soul of Athens"; Pericles saw in her merely one goddess among others. It was no more reasonable to represent the goddess of love as a naked woman than to believe, like the Jews and Persians, in the absolute impossibility of depicting the divine; and it was quite unreasonable to represent successful battles by winged women. Greece had not the monopoly of picturing the gods in human form. Her gods stemmed from the folklore of the past, from the sirens of the islands and, tradition notwithstanding, it was not Man alone that she glorified, anyhow to begin with. On sixth-century vases we see ridiculous specimens of humanity, like Karaguez puppets, posted beside the majestic curves of the "great-hearted horses." The dreams of Athens and her art are peopled with Centaurs, and it is on the face of a Sphinx

BLACK-FIGURED HYDRIA (DETAIL), FIRST HALF VIth C. B.C.   LOUVRE

at the Acropolis that the first enigmatic smile makes its appearance.

True, the feelings of Sophocles when he made an offering to Athena Parthenos can never be recaptured. But at least we know the vast background of myths from which the gods emerged. We no longer confuse these myths with divine biographies (though Christianity is based on the life of Jesus), nor the gods with their effigies. We realize that Pallas Athene and Aphrodite were no more women than "La France" is one; that the gods personified certain powers beyond man's control —within himself and in the universe. But their existence seemed no less manifest than was that of the "libido" to Freud, who resuscitated Aphrodite. Cultured Athenians did not believe in their existence as a Christian believes in Christ's, but sometimes in much the same way as a Christian believes in the reality of Satan. They were conscious of these presences in themselves; certain gods cohabited within them—like sins, like instincts, like the compulsions of psychoanalysis. And in the same way they inhabited the universe, and continued to inhabit it until the end of the ancient world; even Caesar, atheist High Priest, compromised with these obscure forces, no longer dominated by the sacred, but beyond the mind's control.

"Polytheism," wrote Victor Hugo "is the waking dream that obsesses the minds of men." For the Greeks the cosmos was no less haunted than it was for Orientals, but of the powers, secret or manifest, inhabiting it, they made gods very different from those of India. When it is said that Greece "divinized" springs or the principle of fertility, this is usually taken to mean that she made them into allegories—but in practice she also made them into goddesses. To the oriental mind the spirit-of-the-waters dwelling in the spring belongs to the world of the sacred. Not so the Naiad; but she does not dwell in the spring as a secret, fay-like presence, she sublimates it. Demeter is not blind fertility; she is fertility ennobled. For Greece the sacred in its full sense did not exist, but neither did the wholly "profane"; since immanent in every form of life was a spark of the divine enhancing it.

Nothing is explained by the term anthropomorphism; the nature of the gods of antiquity derives from a basic ambivalence: they are humanized but not human, and they live neither in time nor in eternity. That they were not given fantastic forms in art and poetry does not mean that Greece regarded them as mortals. They differ from men primarily by the range of their powers; else, they would be merely heroes. Simple folk saw in them somewhat unreliable protectors (it was only a step to their becoming patron saints); others saw in them capricious powers of the cosmos. But the feelings which prompted the deification of Aphrodite did not imply merely a relationship between her and the cosmos; the fact of making offerings to her implied, apart from a wish to win her favor, that she was esteemed a goddess, in the special sense that Greece has imparted to this word. She is neither an abstraction—though the Greeks dealt freely in abstractions—nor altogether a sacred being; rather, a luminous figure inseparable from her radiance. Isis was not born of sunlight rippling on the sea, and the Aphrodite Freud invokes is not "she whose smile illuminates her immortal face" or the Aphrodite of Praxiteles. We speak of the sensuality of her effigies because we compare them with Christian effigies; but what if we compare them with those of India? Some have regarded them as symbols of sexual pleasure. Yet for a century the Parthenon Aphrodite was mistaken for one of the Parcae! The last thing the goddess resembles is an erotic figure of any kind whatever, and no sculptor before Praxiteles had shown her naked. But it was no woman he depicted; it was a goddess.

Along with Achaemenian relics and the treasures of Persian art, the Museum of Teheran contains a Greek statue discovered at Persepolis, brought there (an old legend has it) by Xerxes. It seems as much out of place in Teheran as that "savage" crucifix of Perpignan would seem in the Acropolis Museum. We no longer stress the distant affinities between the Iran of the Achaemenidae and the Hellas of Aeschylus. The undulations of that captive drapery, estranged from its environment by the passage of time, confront oriental immobility with something the East has never even hinted at: wind-borne movement.

GENIE.   NIMRUD, 885-860 B.C.   LOUVRE

GREEK STATUE (? BY TELEPHANES) FROM PERSEPOLIS, vth C. B.C.   TEHERAN MUSEUM

As seen from Asia, Greece is a whirl of fluttering veils. To Greece we owe the dance (what we call "the dance"—not ritual ballet). Does the glamour we still attach to that word come from the waltz and the carmagnole and not, rather, from the figures of Greek bas-reliefs and vases? And if the word "virgin" carries echoes foreign to its sexual and its Christian referents, is this not because it conjures up inevitably the maidens of the Panathenaic procession and indeed all that Athens stands for? Young people had not free access to the temples of Sumer, of Egypt, or of India—or to any holy place of the patriarchal East. In what palace of Babylon (in its last phase), where in Egyptian Thebes or in Nineveh, could the priest-kings and the living-dead of the East have dreamt of the poignant majesty of Sophocles' retort to their defunctive gloom: "When men have slain joy, I do not think they are alive!" Greece did not invent joy or youth, but she was the first to celebrate their glory.

The sacred of the archaic world was not only the supreme value, not only the predominating value; it stood for the whole realm of values. All that was unrelated to it was worthless and what pertained to it derived value from it alone. It recognized no "heroes" other than its own. Though admiration seems to us a feeling that has always existed, where else was it given the form and function it had in Greece? A Greek did not admire Achilles in the way an Egyptian admired Rameses. An Egyptian did not admire his gods, he worshiped them; nor did he admire any real or fabulous being as a Greek admired Achilles. And when Greece found her Rameses in Alexander, he aspired to be another Achilles.

For, as against Zeus, Achilles did not cut a wraithlike figure, as did the warriors of India with regard to Krishna, or even Roland with regard to Christ; Zeus had not created him and was not to be his Judge at the Last Day. That quality of the divine to which the hero owed his luster came into being after the notion of an indivisible oneness of the human personality, in which *veneration* sponsored admiration, had passed away: there could no more be an Achilles without an element of the divine than there could be saints without Christ. The Greek hero was a brother of Heracles—not of Napoleon—and the object of an admiration that might be warranted by his deeds but was not limited to the admiration due to these alone. This comes out clearly in the case of the "heroines" of Greece; were Helen's beauty only that of a very attractive woman, the Iliad would degenerate into an early version of *La Belle Hélène*. The divine is reflected in the poem and illuminates it. Just as the Pythia of the Delphic Oracle was "possessed" by Apollo, so Greece was "possessed" by a romantic myth. For though the Greeks had no sacred book, this race, which became a nation only at rare moments, had a national book: the Iliad. Dwellers in fifth-century city-states knew their Homer as the English were to know the Bible. And we are familiar with the role Herodotus assigned to poetry. "It was Homer and Hesiod who gave the Greeks a theogony, the gods their names, their capacities and fields of action; it was they who made known to men the faces of the gods." The art of the Greek poets met a need unknown to Babylon and Egypt; Homer was a revealer of the Divine as the Hebrew prophets were revealers of the Truth. The Old Testament God and the immortals were not born of the same mentality; the immortals and the heroes who vied with them could be born only of a soul knowing nothing of such a God.

The sacred had imposed its order on the seething chaos of the world of ancient myth, as kings, its vice-gerents, had imposed their order on the turbulence of contending clans. Such was its authority in the archaic age—drastic as that of Original Sin in the Middle Ages—that the glorification of a rebel hero then was inconceivable; even Aeschylus' Prometheus would have been accounted sacrilegious. Never did a laugh break the august silence of the sacred until the "peals of inextinguishable laughter" of Olympus resounded over Hellas. Nor would the art of the sacred have countenanced Hector's farewell or even the portrayal of Helen, that lonely figure walking on the Trojan ramparts whose memory has outlived three millennia. The poetry of Greece differs radically from that of India, Babylon and Israel because it represents a wholly different world; for, though Homer's epics are the fruit of his personal genius, Homer's world belonged to the memories from which it stemmed, memories shared by all the Hellenes. These epic poems, meant to be recited and sung, and bound up with the dance, at once built up a *chanson de geste* of the gods out of the primitive myths, and preserved it from lapsing into mere narration; for every Greek art aspires to the condition of poetry. It was not the poet's task to "give their names" to the gods of the sacred, but he enabled the Olympians to triumph over the teeming confusion of their predecessors. Those ever-changing gods, whose only "constant" was their luster, born with the earth or with man's first appearance on it, were not "the origins or sources" of the divine, but its representatives—and a sense of the divine, like that of the sacred, is fundamental to the spirit of man. It does not originate from gods and heroes, it calls them up, thrives on them, and welcomes or forgets them, as the oriental world of Being welcomed its successive gods (but disdained "heroes").

The multifarious deities of India equaled in spirituality the One God of Islam. It is not polytheism, but the replacement of the sacred by the divine, that makes Zeus so incompatible with Brahma and so radically differentiates Heracles from Gilgamesh, despite the similarity of many incidents in their legends; and by the same token makes it impossible to confuse Ares with the gods of Assur. Homer did not transmit the "history" of the gods to the Greek city-states in the same way as Akkadian poems transmitted to Nineveh the tale of Gilgamesh; nor in the same way as the mythologies transmit both to us. What he transmitted to the Greeks was a vision of the divine, an inspirational theogony; much as Plutarch bequeathed the legends of exemplary lives to the age of the great monarchies, and the Old Testament bequeathed the sacred lore of Israel. But visions of this divine were not limited to the epic poem; even less to those transmitted by Homer. It was the world in which Sirens forgathered with Zeus, and Centaurs with Apollo; a world in which the Sacred Mountain of the great cosmogonies became Mount Olympus, the fierce Erinyes became the Eumenides (the kindly), and the final version of Medusa's face showed her as a sleeping goddess.

Had the Greek myths not undergone this metamorphosis we would speak of them as we speak of the Celtic or Polynesian myths, their progeny. The divine elements of the cosmos, for the Greeks, were natural forces, those powers which lie beyond man's control. All that quickened the sense of wonder (not the awestruck obeisance of the Orientals) shared in this divine element, and everything it permeated called for admiration. Admiration played in Greece a part akin to that of adoration in the East; to the role of compassion in Buddhism, and of love in Christianity. In earlier times the nymphs had been malefic spirits. The Greek super-world contrasted with that of the East not only in its nature but in its climate; never before had men experienced the feeling, profound as the awareness of the sacred, which led them to apply the same word ("cosmos") to the universe, to its order and to its beauty.

Never-changing, ever-changing, as the sea, this sense of the divine dominated Alexander no less than Pericles; Homer was as "contemporary" for them as for Herodotus—at once archaic and a present actuality, as the Koran is to Mahometans today. Yet we can see more clearly than Pericles what linked him up with Homer and what differentiated them. Greece challenged the authoritarian sameness of the East with her restless spirit of enquiry: an interrogation directed far more to the cosmos than to man. For, despite the inscription at Delphi and Socrates' injunction, the individual Greek "knew himself" but little and little wished to do so. What he set up against the hierarchy of the absolute was not man, the individual, but the prestige of the imaginary. And what then arose for the first time (but not for the last) was a culture in which man, greatly daring, based his supreme values on his loftiest ideals and concentrated his efforts on all he could *do* to harmonize himself with them; not on what he ought to *be*, so as to attune himself to the eternal. "Future generations," Pericles proudly assured the Athenians, "will say of us: These men built up the most glorious and the happiest of cities." What Oriental king would not have been surprised by this fraternal pride? His eyes were fixed on eternity, and in eternity "the future" counts for nothing. But Hellas brought something new into the world: that appeal to Justice which, superseding the Wrath of Achilles, was launched by Aeschylus; that appeal which, answering Akhenaten's *Hymn to the Sun* and the *Book of Job*, is voiced not by Helen but by Antigone. For a dramatic change was coming over man's outlook on the scheme of things; he now was seeking within the hierarchy of his admirations and in the mysterious workings of what he regarded as the divine element in the universe, a power enabling him to do away with the sacred. This divine element was preserved and transmitted by what Greece named "the Muses" and we call "art," in so far as art signifies *creation*. For, though any epic poet could narrate the events of the Trojan War, the revelation of the divine in them was a creation of Homer's genius; and though any sculptor could depict the Panathenaic processions, it was through Pheidias' creative genius that their share in the divine was manifested.

The Olympians who figure in their chariots on archaic vases, the lame god Hephaestus admitted on tolerance into their company, Zeus and Demeter, Aphrodite and Dionysus, Heracles and the Hamadryads, the tribal gods of the Dorians and the immemorial deities of the vanquished were on an equal footing in so far as each personified a special power and expressed a divine element of the cosmos. It was this that art aspired to isolate and body forth in forms emancipated from appearance. That is why we find the same process of sublimation in depictions of Zeus and Poseidon, Artemis and Aphrodite, of the gods of Homer, of the shepherds' gods, of those whose mysteries were celebrated by initiates, and in the statue of Athena queening it on the Acropolis. That, too, is why the oldest goddess of the underworld was transformed into the young *Demeter* of Eleusis.

All Greek gods were ruled by Fate (who had no temple), and also by that nameless god who unified them under his ineluctable control, and made his presence felt as secret overlord of the universe when the sacred was replaced by the sublime, the supernatural by the wondrous, and Fate itself by tragedy.

Greek tragedy always stages a human sacrifice. Yet,

DEMETER (DETAIL), C. 450 B.C. BAS-RELIEF, ELEUSIS. NATIONAL MUSEUM, ATHENS

however closely associated with the festivals of the Dionysia, it did not originate from a sacrificial rite but from the art of poetry. It was a poem in itself; the masks, the music and the prosody redeemed the *Oresteia* and *Oedipus Rex* from that insistence on the gruesome which Europeans read into it in the age of western melodrama. Not only was the audience familiar since childhood with the legends enacted, but the stylization of the Greek theater, far from heightening the effect of horror, tended to diminish it. Those hieratic figures, whose high buskins gave them superhuman stature, did not create an atmosphere of "blood and thunder," shocking as were their deeds. Sophocles did not write *Oedipus Rex* with a view to striking fear into his public, but in order to give the Athenians access to a world worthy of Homer's world. And what the populace admired in their tragic poets was not their skill in staging horrifying scenes, but their revelations of a divine "something behind everything," akin to those that they admired in Homer.

The poetic emotion which Aeschylus aimed at evoking derived from the contagious presence of his true hero: the doom of the Atridae. And the tragic content of the poem is its revelation of human bondage, man's total subjection to his destiny. Yet when the Athenians were so profoundly moved by performances of the *Agamemnon*, *Oedipus* or *Antigone*, what they felt was not despondency but a passionate sense of enthusiasm: the selfsame thrill as when they listened to the Iliad. From the Hellenistic period on, commentators failed to understand the nature of that exaltation, since they looked for its cause in the *subjects* of the dramas. Its true origin lay far deeper than any participation in the tragic action of the ancient legends; it was the discovery that poetry—the poem itself, not the tale the poet told—could challenge Destiny on equal terms. When Orestes stepped forth upon the Athenian stage there took place a dialogue yet more momentous than his with the Erinyes; a dialogue between the City of Athens and the last, tremendous echoes of Uranos. In a world where man was imparting so many forms of beauty to powers beyond his control, Greek tragedy deliberately gave form to those which crushed him to the ground, but, *in it*, he ceased to be their victim.

Why, indeed, should we appraise the works of Aeschylus in terms of their subjects, when we do not appraise the work of any poet, in any civilization, from this angle? Does the genius of Shakespeare consist in the fact that he tells, better than any other, the tale of Prospero? The tale of Orestes was known to all Athenians and that it should be related in a poignant manner mattered little. What mattered was that in the Aeschylean tragedy the power of poetry challenged something that no human power had ever challenged hitherto. The novelty was the revelation of a world in which tragedy was for the first time transmuted into poetry; a world in which man could fraternize with Destiny, ruler of the gods, as in Homer's world he had fraternized with the gods, rulers of man.

Nineteenth-century Romanticism was to "discover" (belatedly) barbarian Argos and contrast it with classical Hellas. And, in contrasting the tragic poets with the Greek Anthology, to contrast tragedy with the sculpture of the age. But Greek tragedy did not imply submission to the tragic but a victory over it. By introducing Destiny into the theme of the poem, the poet relegated it to the company of the gods, on an equal footing with the rest; thus Destiny became a subject of art ("subject" in both senses of the word). There is nothing in common between the presentment of blinded Oedipus on the stage and that of Athena upon the pediment of the Parthenon; but everything in common between Sophocles' creation and that of Pheidias. For both alike revealed to the Athenians a world where men had escaped from their basic relations with the gods and with Destiny. Greek tragedy is the sculpture that would have figured in temples of Destiny, if the Greeks had built temples dedicated to it.

The sculptor's approach to the gods, viewed as minor manifestations of Destiny, is of the same nature as the tragic poet's; it links them up with Man. But, of all the divine Powers, Destiny was the only one beyond the pale of human admiration; that is why it had no effigy. The gods were at once other than men and admirable; but were they merely "other," they would not be the Olympians; and merely admirable, they would be no more than heroes. Thus beauty is not one of their adornments but belongs to their essential being, and though human beauty may pass for godlike, *their* beauty does not liken them to men. For it is peculiar to themselves. Aphrodite is not more beautiful than Hera in the way that Aspasia was more beautiful than her rivals. The beauty of the goddesses is intrinsically divine and points their difference from, not their resemblances to, mortal women; just as they wield a power different from that of any earthly monarch.

There was a domain in which it was incumbent on the artist to express that beauty; the domain of representations of the gods. It once was thought that the Greeks aspired to make their gods resemble human beings; but the whole evolution of Hellenic art proves the contrary. This art proceeded from the gods to man, not from man to the gods, and in all the arts deriving from Athens, though human figures were made to resemble gods, the gods were never quite like mortals. What was meant by "beauty" in fifth-century art had nothing in common with what it meant in later periods. It revealed man's awareness of the essentially divine nature of the gods and its basic difference from the human—a power of apprehending the Divine in the same way as spirituality had enabled apprehension of the Sacred. For all Athenians the *Parthenos* was a revelation of Athena.

But no one would have dreamt of "recognizing" Athena in the most beautiful living woman in Athens; only in the realm of art was the divine (no matter what name it bore) made manifest. And it was manifested by all that differentiated from appearance Greek goddesses in gold and ivory, bronze athletes, polychrome Korés with red eyes; by all that differentiated the sculptor's creations (in a metaphysical sense) from appearance and enabled him to body forth the "otherness" of the divine in figures compelling admiration.

A *Koré* is not the portrait of a young girl; she signifies the "first young maiden" of the ancient myths, but pledged to a Greek, not to an Oriental, god, and thus she has a place in the Greek theogony in which she becomes a sister of the *Goddess with a Diadem*.

64

GODDESS WITH A DIADEM, EARLY Vth C. B.C.   CYRENE MUSEUM

Similarly, the statues of athletes are not portraits, but votive offerings in the grand style; in much the same spirit as Philip Augustus after a victory presented a saint to a church, victors at the Games presented these statues to the temple. The Olympic Games were ceremonies very different from their modern counterparts (despite a superficial resemblance) and much more akin to the stage play (which they did not resemble). The glory of the victors crowned with leaves of the sacred wild olive was an aspect of the poetic romanticism which then pervaded Greece, as historical romanticism was to pervade Europe in a later age. As hymned by Pindar, the victors participate, if obscurely, in the nature of heroes; the Games played the same part in the world of the Divine as great religious festivals played in that of the Sacred. They stand in the same relation to the Egyptian processions as the *Charioteer* to *Ranofer*. And the *Charioteer* certainly differed from the man who posed for it (assuming there was any resemblance at all) even more than from the Chatsworth *Apollo*. Thus, too, it is an open question whether the many copies of the *Doryphorus* are likenesses of a victorious athlete and not, rather, of the last *Kouros*, a successor of the *Fair Ephebus* and in the lineage of the Olympian *Apollo*.

Whether he made the statue of an athlete, a Kouros or an Apollo, the Greek sculptor always sought in what he selected from appearance a means of expressing the divine. If some art historians have spoken of the *Palatine Apollo* and the *Doryphorus* (whose muscles give the effect of a cuirass) as "illusionist nudes" —idealized perhaps, but certainly illusionist—this was because they were so much struck by the independence of these figures and by the vivid rendering of movement in the *Discobolus*. (Actually the "illusionism" of the *Discobolus* was a case apart; it had no sequel until the Hellenistic age.) Yet to Chinese eyes, all these statues appear more arbitrary than *Ranofer* or *Karomama*, and the *Doryphorus* and *Discobolus* have the same significance as the *Apollos* and the *Persephone* of Selinus.

Supposing we could see a film in which the *Persephone* was shown after a sequence of the masterworks—from Memphis to China—that had preceded it, we should certainly not get the

CHATSWORTH APOLLO, C. 460 B.C.　CHATSWORTH COLLECTION, BRITISH MUSEUM

THE PERSEPHONE OF SELINUS, TEMPLE E, 460 B.C. PALERMO MUSEUM

impression that it testified to the intrusion of appearance into art, or to idealization, as we should, were we shown, instead of it, a Roman bas-relief. Rather, we would find in it the same revelation as when, at Teheran, we contemplate the statue brought back by Xerxes. Perhaps more intensely, since what is there in question is a face. And that face is *not one of a woman* —a spectator without any feeling for art might call it "crude"— nor yet a symbol of Persephone (for it was long thought to represent Hera). Tradition notwithstanding, the symbolization of cosmic forces played a relatively small part in Greek art; it has not yet been decided whether the *God of Histiaea*—ranking beside the *Charioteer* as the largest fifth-century bronze figure— represents Zeus or Poseidon. What strikes us in the *Persephone* is that the face is one that can never have existed, and if we leave out of account its majesty (foreshadowing the art of Pheidias), what remains is a quality it shares with the *Goddess with a Diadem*

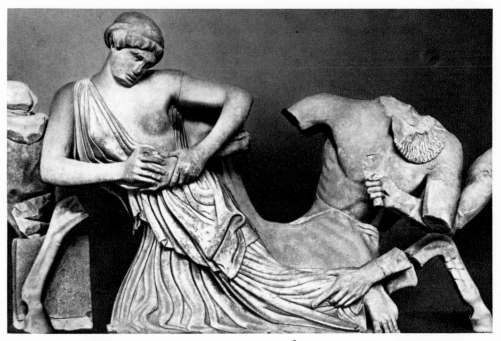

BATTLE OF CENTAURS AND LAPITHS, 470-460 B.C. OLYMPIA MUSEUM

69

ATHENA, 470-460 B.C.   OLYMPIA MUSEUM

and the *Athena* of Olympia, and the *Athena* shares with the
Lapiths in the same temple—a quality whose presence would
certainly be felt more strongly at Olympia were not the works
of sculpture there so badly damaged.   The men who made them
did not aim at decorating a building or telling the story of the

Lapiths to a public who already knew it by rote, or at representing pretty young women or an ideal Apollo. They were trying to do what their fellow artists aimed at doing and what Pheidias was to aim at. The so-called miracle of Greece, the revolutionary change in art, was not that the sculptor subjected to appearance forms that formerly had been subordinated to the Sacred; it was that he now created forms expressing the Divine, as his predecessors had created forms manifesting the Sacred.

We may leave it to specialists to decide what Pheidias may have owed to Paeonius or the latter owed to him; and even to decide which works were by Pheidias' own hand. Even if he did not make the centaur's head (thought to be a self-portrait), it was certainly not made by any of the other sculptors who worked on the metopes, since it differs so much from the heads of the other centaurs. The name of Pheidias is a symbol for the whole vast enterprise he planned and supervised; for the accent which distinguishes the figures on the Parthenon from all that had preceded them; for the overall conception which harmonizes the vertical draperies of the processional maidens with the grandiose arabesque of the horsemen—all that makes the Panathenaic frieze one of the peakpoints of sculpture. Let us, then, resign ourselves to speaking of him as we speak of Homer.

The young girls of the Parthenon frieze have inherited at once the nobility of Olympia, Ionian elegance and even the incisive, almost geometric accents of a calligraphy common to the designs on vases and bronze and terracotta tablets. The masters of ceremonies and the gods seem to be welcoming in all the Korés of the Acropolis Museum and combining their diverse styles into that of the maidens, weavers of Athena's robe.

The Korés—but not the young girls who walked the streets of Athens. For this frieze is as unimaginable in the world of the living as is an Egyptian bas-relief, and it was even less imaginable when the Athenians first set eyes on it, ablaze with its three colors. Looked at from ground level, amid the tumult of the real Panathenaea, the procession on the frieze must have produced the effect of a cortège of painted pillars. When we compare the head of the *Hipparchus* with Achaemenian heads,

SUPPOSED SELF-PORTRAIT OF PHEIDIAS, C. 440 B.C.   PARTHENON

440-435 B. C.   PARTHENON FRIEZE.   LOUVRE

73-74.   PROCESSION OF ATHENIAN MAIDE..

ASSYRIAN TRIBUTARY, VIIIth C. B.C.   KHORSABAD.   LOUVRE

perhaps contemporary with it, or with those of Khorsabad, we are surprised, not at finding so much imitation in the *Hipparchus*, but (like Canova) at finding so little of it.   The hair of living beings has not the snail-shell coils of the hair in Assyrian bas-reliefs, nor does it take the form of volutes.   Here the arabesque plays the same transforming—not illusionistic—

HIPPARCHUS, 440-435 B.C.   PARTHENON FRIEZE.   BRITISH MUSEUM

role as do the straight-falling, parallel folds of garments in the case of the Athenian maidens. If we placed the photograph of a similarly dressed, bearded man alongside one of the *Hipparchus*, the effect would be ludicrous. For Pheidias' work does not aim at imitation (even of an "embellished" nature) but at winning a place for itself in a world beyond appearance; it is no more a representation of a ceremony than the *Antigone* is a "news item." Starting out with effigies of gods and their earthly representatives, the monarchs, the styles of Nineveh and Memphis had transposed all their figures into the Other World, as sacred languages translate all that they express into the world of the Sacred. Pheidias transposed all his figures into the world of the Divine, and we would be unable to distinguish the processional maidens from the goddesses awaiting them, could we not identify the latter. Is this because the goddesses have been given the aspect of young girls? Yes, but the aspect of young girls transmuted into sculpture.

It is sculpture that affiliates the *Hipparchus* to an effigy of Heracles—or even Zeus—but it does not liken Zeus to an hipparchus, that is to say a cavalry officer; or goddesses to weavers, even though these are beautified. The girls who wove the robe have not been made prettier or nobler than ordinary girls, nor are the goddesses made to look like beauty queens. Spiritualization did not give the queens of Egypt the faces of mummies. The Greek figures owe their kinship with the divine to their translation into an *Other World:* a world apart, whose style precludes the intrusion of appearance. The most skillful counterfeiter could not succeed in inserting an "illusionist" face within the Parthenon frieze. The beauty of the Athenian maidens is not that of the girls who may or may not have posed for them; it is a beauty of the same kind as that of pillars, of music, of everything that expresses the divine. For the maidens are approching the *Parthenos* herself, who awaits them in her shrine; it was to Her that Pheidias attuned them.

For his statue of the *Parthenos*, Pheidias did not take a lead from any recognized style. Nor had the Old Kingdom sculptors done so. As far as can be judged, Egyptian sculpture moved on from the pre-dynastic figures to that of *Zoser*, in the same way and by the same process as Greek forms advanced from the primitive Korés to the figures of Olympia; that is to say, both eliminated clumsiness and imposed order on appearance. But the Greek sculptors, untrammelled by the dictates of a priesthood, were equally immune from the dark compulsions of an underlying mystery to which the oriental priesthoods ministered. Their religion had no Holy Book, no custodians of the Scriptures, and this gave Greek artists a liberty hitherto unknown, limited only by a certain deference to a flexible tradition, which (like the poets) they were free to modify. Thus we find remarkable differences between the gods of Delphi, Aegina, Olympia and Selinus. The Athenians were familiar with them all and had already come to regard some of them as "ancient"—for they had made the discovery of Time. They had several sculptors to choose from, Myron, Polycleitus and Pheidias, and their choice fell on Pheidias. For to Athenian thinking, every god could have several aspects.

The sacred style had seemed like an emanation of the sacred, the divine seems to emanate from its *form*. Sacred art carried conviction in the same way as the sacred itself. Had Akhenaten's monotheism prevailed, it would have given Egypt a new style, but not creative freedom. This was ensured in Greece by the Hellenic zest for competition; while acknowledging the same rulers of Olympus, the city-states expected of their sculptors ever "truer" simulacra of them; the divine is also the inaccessible. The forms the artist now was called on to invent corresponded to that constant spirit of enquiry into the scheme of things which was basic to Greek thought. That absolute Truth which every sacred style had aspired to voice ruled out artistry; Isaiah was not admired for his literary gifts and Ranofer did not admire his "double" for its merits as a work of art. Egyptian and Sumerian statues were accounted valueless before their consecration, and they once more became mere blocks of stone if it was withdrawn from them. But the *Parthenos* would have been a reflection of Athena and the *Zeus* of Olympia one of Zeus, even if they had never been cult statues. Whether or not a *Horus* created by a man of genius was more truly godlike than the others, the Egyptian appraised it as if its creator had not been responsible for it, and the god had manifested himself through it. To ascribe to art a *power* over the sacred would have been sacrilegious. Greece, too, consecrated statues; but from the Greek viewpoint a work of art, consecrated or not, and whether it represented mortals or immortals, could participate in the divine in virtue of the artist's genius, since for the Greeks, and for the Greeks alone, genius was nothing other than an expression of the divine. The gods took form through art, as light through all that it illuminates.

Thus mystery lost that dark compulsion with which it was invested in civilizations dominated by it. In the Orient it was designated "the Apart" and man dared approach it only on bended knees. The East sought to uncover in the world of Being the secret of that which is other than the cosmos; the Greek to discover in it the secret of the cosmos itself: the never-changing ground behind the flux of appearances, that element of the divine implicit in all life, in the same way as Man is the divine element common to all men. "Man is the measure of all things." That is the usual truncated version of the dictum; what Protagoras actually said was far less categorical. "Man is the measure of all things: of existent things, that they exist, and of the non-existent, that they do not exist." A reservation is implied. For the measure of "the non-existent" is not man but his dreams, set free from Being. And when "cosmos" signifies at once the universe, order and beauty, its true image is not man but the statue which re-creates him in the likeness of Apollo.

Destiny is indefeasible; Aeschylus and the master sculptors of Olympia were dead, Sophocles and Pheidias were soon to die. Yet Pericles believed that the Oresteia and the Parthenon would never die. After a dynasty of arts with a precarious foothold in eternity, this race, whose gods were merely immortals and for whom the only afterlife lay in a world of shades, conceived the notion of an immortality allotted to great human creations, by reason of their participation in the divine they body forth. Always, since the first groping efforts of the earliest culture known to history; since the dim aspirations of prehistoric man, and perhaps since the discovery of fire, the divine had been the sacred. After Delphi the only sacred in Greek art was the divine.

Hence that momentous change: the end of "the gods who are worshiped in darkness." No longer solemnized inside the temple, religious ceremonies now took place in front of it. The façade of the Parthenon became the backdrop as it were of a gigantic open-air theater, where the whole populace took part in dramas that were no play-acting but a homage to Truth. The gods of the East had been secluded in their sanctuaries, but homeward bound Greek sailors rounding Cape Sunium could salute from afar the shining helmet of Athena welcoming them home. The sanctuary, night-soul of art as of the city, had oriented creation and imposed unity on all forms, even those outside it. The *Discobolus* might be described as the first god of the space laid open to the gods once they had stepped forth from the shadows of the temple. And this new freedom led to a metamorphosis of art, affecting even Byzantium and lasting nearly a thousand years.

At Athens the word temple did not signify the place where the goddess dwelt but the Acropolis itself. Such "high places," dominating the tumult of the nearby "lower city," often inspire a sense of civic pride and satisfaction; even the humble citadel of Cairo rising above its city of the dead and the stronghold of Aleppo with its dried-up fountains share this prestige. But what high place of the East is not a place *set apart*, reserved for sacrifice or a display of power? The Acropolis of Athens is a vast offering; its temples are unlike others by reason not of their architecture but of their amazing visibility. Crown and scepter of the city, the Acropolis proffers its share in the divine to all that is divine within the universe. Certainly Pheidias' Athena has not that leonine majesty with which the Sphinx claws down its prey of stars into the desert sands; yet, hardly less than the monuments of Gizeh, the Acropolis is charged with portentous meaning. In the same manner as the Asiatic high places are gigantic pedestals for vanished apparitions, the Acropolis is the high place of the death of *Being*; of that intellectual venture which

THE ACROPOLIS, ATHENS

made it cease to be the primal object of thought. Heretofore mystery—as hard to stare at fixedly as the sun and death—had governed every form of meditation as strictly as death governs life; but on the Acropolis the sacred lost its instancy. Last posterity of the Delphian Caryatids, those of the Erechtheum took their stand on the slab that seals the tomb of the Erinyes. But it was not Man whom the colossal Athena Parthenos proffered to the sky on her uplifted hand; it was a Victory, six feet high.

However obsessed they were with an absolute, the ancient empires also had a cult of power. Those of the East loved to celebrate their triumphs and, to their thinking, victory could be symbolized only in terms of human suffering. Thus on an Assyrian bas-relief we see an archer herding the captives —the "displaced persons" of that age—towards a land of exile;

CAPTIVES, VIIth C. B.C. NINEVEH. LOUVRE

RAMESES TRIUMPHANT (DETAIL), C. 1160 B.C.   CAIRO MUSEUM

a King's chariot rolling over the vanquished, prisoners impaled, a Pharaoh holding by the hair a batch of severed heads, and kings constrained to grovel at his feet.   Marathon and Salamis are the names not of victories but of liberations; yet surely

NIKÉ OF SAMOTHRACE, C. 190 B. C.   LOUVRE   →

the hideous fear the Great King whose empire stretched from the Indus to Nubia had inspired, might have justified some decapitated Persians' figuring on the bas-reliefs. But no, the art of Greece invented a woman's form, winged and poised for flight, and gave it that superb movement of a galleon in full sail which has compelled men's admiration through the ages. To give the name of "allegories" to these creations, which relegated to the Orient the Sphinxes and winged bulls of other arts, is to render them unintelligible. They stand to allegories in the same relation as the laughter of the living to the effigies in graveyards. The figures of Olympus rise above the turmoil of terrestrial life as *Niké* transcends the carnage of the battlefield; and we would understand Greek art better if, disregarding its statues of athletes, we saw its symbol in this heroic being who sublimates the carnage as grandly as the genius of Aeschylus transcends the butchery of the Atridae.

II Long before the fall of Athens, Socrates, Euripides and the Sophists had undermined the prestige of the gods of the city. But the divine outlived the glory of the Olympians. Alexander fulfilled the dreams of those he vanquished; for the triumph of Dionysus was no Asiatic victory but that of the fantasies which Greece, and Greece alone, had woven around a legendary East. Obsessed with Athens, a city he had hardly seen, the conqueror proclaimed his sovereignty over her by incarnating the hymns which Homer's Athena sang to the Argive warriors. The shield of Ilian Athena, found at Troy, saved his life on a memorable occasion, the storming of a city of the Malli. He claimed to be a son of Zeus, captured the stronghold of Aornus (which Heracles had failed to take), converted his return from the India campaign into a Bacchic progress and, when he died, was preparing for the conquest of the West. He claimed to participate in the divine, as Saint Louis was to claim authority from Christ. It was this element of the divine that linked him with the visionary princess who was his mother; with his far-flung conquests in Asia; with his hero Achilles and his teacher Aristotle, for whom the aim of art was "to depict the hidden meaning of things, not their appearance: for in this profounder truth lies their true reality, which is not apparent in their outward forms," and for whom, moreover, "poetic creation is truer than methodical investigation of that which is." Would not Pheidias have said the same thing of the creation of divine figures? But Greece had recognized Athena in the *Parthenos* and Apollo in the *Apollo* of Olympia. She did not recognize him in the *Apollo Belvedere*, when "makers of gods" were by way of becoming makers of statues.

If we are to understand the metamorphosis which then took place, we must discard that concept of Pheidias' work which once made it a subject of debate, championed or attacked by successive schools—since praise and blame alike were based on the assumption that its purpose was to *represent*. Implicit in it, nonetheless, were the germs of our romanticism no less than of our classicism. A tradition of modeling in the round had grown

STUDIO OF PHEIDIAS. HORSE OF THE SUN, 440-432 B.C. PARTHENON

up from the Siphnian Caryatid to the lyrical plenitude of the
horses of Helios and Selene, which preceded some of the more
"classical" elements of the Panathenaic frieze.   True, Goya owed
nothing to Pheidias, yet if by Romanticism we mean that
lavish orchestration which gives the nineteenth century a sono-
rity so different from that of the medieval Masses, with which
it claimed a vague affinity, and if among the objects of the
Romantics' admiration we select Michelangelo rather than the
sculpture at Chartres (of which they knew next to nothing)
—then surely Romanticism began with Pheidias' *Centaur* and the
horses of the Parthenon.   In no earlier civilization do we find
this lyricism; no previous sculptors had employed such bold
relief, and neither Michelangelo nor Rodin would have found it

easy to carve the head of a horse having no resemblance to the horse of Selene. Four of the qualities traditionally assigned to Greek art—balance and measure, serenity and simplicity—can hardly be accorded, unequivocally, to the pediments of the Parthenon. Pheidias did not aim at creating a style but, like Homer, at "giving the gods their aspects" and at giving man an aspect worthy of the gods.

His great predecessors had made the same attempt. Why did no *Dionysus* follow on his *Zeus*? Though Athena died along with the hegemony of Athens, the "loosener of care" and master of the Maenads—and some other gods—were very much alive. Mystery took root in Greece, with a vigor we can hardly credit, since we believe only in mysteries whose dwelling-place is darkness. Like the Dionysus of whom Alexander dreamt, the Aphrodite (so different from Pheidias' Aphrodite) who haunted the dreams of Praxiteles mingled her sunlit splendor with the unfathomable shadows where Demeter and Persephone resumed their role of deities of the underworld. Doubtless the greatness of Praxiteles lay in his attempt to express that mystery, and if we knew his works in the original we should probably discover on the faces of these goddesses something of that enigmatic smile which Leonardo da Vinci was to recapture by very different means. Praxiteles was the last maker of goddesses in an age when the makers of gods were dying out. We must not let the countless progeny of the *Cnidian Aphrodite* mislead us; the goddess of love was an exception, the only deity whose divine nature could henceforth be validated by the attribute of beauty.

Aphrodite was an intruder in the ranks of the Greek theocracy and, like Demeter, reverted to her origin when she regained her mystery. But the "legitimate" Olympians were not gods on whom mysteries could be grafted; nothing was more foreign to Zeus than the Ineffable or the Increate; nothing more foreign to Pallas Athene than the revels of the Maenads. One of the injunctions of Olympus was the exercise of self-control. Thus the orgiastic and ecstatic cults whose rise to favor led to a resurrection of the chthonian divinities involved a return to the pre-Olympian world of the sacred: a world lacking the spiritual ethos of the East but not its sense of Otherness. Man participated in it by abandoning what made him Man. Admiration did not play the same part in the Dionysiac mysteries as in the Apollo cult. And the mystery gods, both the purest and the impurest, would certainly have evoked images like those that were to be "invented" by the Parthians and by India, if their cults had permeated the Greek social order as Christianity was to permeate the Roman. But Greek culture, no less inflexible and authoritative than in the days of Pericles, while assuring the cohesion of the aristocracies born of the Macedonian conquest, ruled out such images or disdained them as fit for slaves. For Dionysus to qualify as another Zeus he would have needed to begin by becoming an imperial god. His processions took place at night and dispersed with the first rays of dawn. Thus none of the new cults could substitute an order of its own for the order which the Olympians had imposed on the Hellenic world, and the gods of empire who had owed to Homer their Olympus still owed to him its maintenance.

They were no longer gods of a religion, but the gods of a culture; as they were to be in the art of the great Christian monarchies. And the other gods, including the mystery gods, resembled them, as Christ was to resemble them. Dionysus, once an old bearded god—but "rejuvenated" by Pheidias—was to impose his traits on effigies of Apollo. Art was no longer servant of the divine; the Olympians in their decline served art.

But "art" was now regarded from a new viewpoint. For the first time the religious significance of great works of the past was seen as a conjuncture of *forms*. The sacred images had lived on what had made them sacred; now they were dying with its death. To a Roman the sacred images of Egypt came to seem primitive and pointless; those of Byzantium seemed hardly less so to Michelangelo. But the sculpture of the Parthenon appealed to the Macedonian overlords in the same way as Michelangelo's religious works were to appeal to his atheist admirers. As a result of the part played by admiration in the creation of the great Olympian figures and of the slightness of the difference between the methods of representation practised

by the masters of the classical style and those of their successors
—of, in a word, their genius— the ebb tide of Olympus left
high and dry an array of figures, exemplary but no longer numinous. And to what could these relate, once they had ceased
to relate to the divine—if not to appearance? What did the
Parthenos become when, ceasing to be Athena, she signified no
more than an idealized woman? And what could the *Koré
of Euthydikos* and the *Discobolus* signify on ceasing to be votive
offerings, except mere representations? For now appearance
became the arbiter, respectful but critical, of divine images
stripped of their divinity, as it was to become disdainful arbiter
of sacred images stripped of their sanctity. It was now that those
Hellenistic canons of art criticism were drawn up which, taken
over by the Romans, were to become the "Bible" of the estheticians of classical Europe. And these preposterous Greek
savants treated the austere style as a stage in the progress towards
illusionism, and the inspired works of the sculptors of Olympia
as clumsy attempts at representation—much as the art of Chartres
was treated in Fénelon's esthetic.

Taking their stand on Pheidias' art, they brushed aside or
disparaged the austere style, failing to see that his achievement
was of the same order as that of the sculptors of Olympia (though
not resembling it), and not of the same order as Hellenistic
art forms feigning to resemble it. That earlier art had become
unintelligible to them, as Romanesque sculpture was unintelligible
to estheticians of the seventeenth century. Pheidias had ever
before him his vision of Athena and, despite his admiration of his
predecessors, he had the sensation of a huge lacuna, which his
genius bade him fill; like the pediments of Aegina and Olympia,
those of the Parthenon seemed sudden revelations owing nothing
to the past. He had no masters, nor could he have had any, for
a great artist does not discover the divine in others' works.
Hence the originality of these fifth-century sculptors—who aimed
at it so little. Within a century (from 530 to 420 B.C.) Greek
art made greater progress than "antique" art was to make
thereafter in six hundred years. For the master of the temple
of Bassae (Phigalia), as for Scopas—in the heads found on the

site of the temple of Tegea—and for Praxiteles, creation still meant a break with previous forms, the discovery of an unknown world, or of a divine image. Pheidias dreamt of a Zeus diviner than the Zeus of Calamis; Praxiteles of an Aphrodite diviner than all others; but after his death sculptors dreamt only of statues "better" than his and those of Pheidias. Hellenistic sculpture took its stand on the official Olympians and its past was peopled with *statues*.

A statue was now a god or a votive offering treated as a representation and an "object." So far as representation went, the *Cnidian Aphrodite* unquestionably excelled the *Koré of Euthydikos*; and Lysippus' *Apoxyomenus*, the *Diadumenus* of Polycleitus, who aimed at making the spectator forget the athlete it represented, so as to reveal beauty at its purest, inasmuch as he still regarded beauty as an expression of the divine. It was not due to chance that Hellenistic esthetes saw in Lysippus their greatest sculptor; with him the creation of the divine came to an end.

What used always to be admired in the *Apoxyomenus* was an advance in illusionist portrayal and the "discovery of space." Yet how does its relation to space differ from that in the *Discobolus* or the *Diadumenus*? What we have here is not a new sense of space but that conception of the free-standing statue which goes back to the very origin of Greek sculpture: the opposite of "rigidity." Archaic sculptors had done away with the stiffness of the sacred, and what Lysippus sought to do away with was that of the divine. He was not attempting to invent a Baroque art or to conquer space by movement. Almost all his figures were practically motionless, indeed the *Apoxyomenus* symbolized repose. He was trying to overcome the rigidity of bronze and marble by suggesting *the possibility of all sorts of movement*—which is life. This statue makes us think "He's going to move," as some famous portraits of a later age, "He's going to speak."

But this infinite possibility of movement related to human movements only; the life in question was solely that of mortals. We cannot conceive of a god, whether a god of the sacred or an Olympian, resembling the figures of Lysippus; were that so, he would have lost his divinity. No trace remains of the new gods

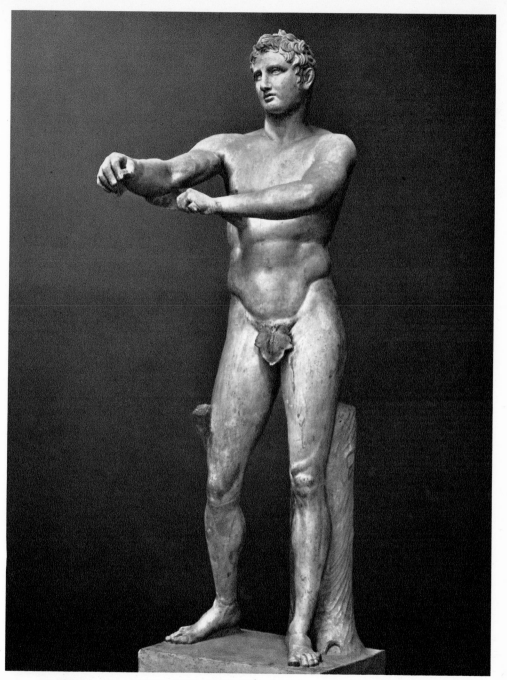

LYSIPPUS.   THE   APOXYOMENUS,   LATE   IVth   C.   B.C.   REPLICA.   VATICAN   MUSEUM

93

POLYCLITUS.   THE DIADUMENUS, 420-410 B.C.   REPLICA.   NATIONAL MUSEUM, ATHENS

made by Alexander's sculptor; but so far as can be known, they were much like his athlete figures, whereas *Athena Parthenos* was relatively monolithic.

" I make what I see," he said—long before Courbet. Courbet saw what he needed to see, so as to paint; Lysippus saw what he needed to see, in order to make statues. His aim was not to represent with the utmost fidelity an athlete at rest; but to breathe new life into the sculpture he admired and thus to pit himself against the masters: to animate the *Charioteer* and the *Diadumenus*. He drew inspiration from his model, but equally from beauty —and beauty was by way of acquiring a new meaning.

For the beauty Lysippus had in mind no longer stemmed from the artist's vision of the divine, nor from the beauty of the model, nor even from an embellishment of the model in terms of appearance. It derived from that mysterious process by which the model became a statue and aroused an admiration no longer directed to him or to the divine but to a transmutation of a wholly new order. What the spectator admired in the *Apoxyomenus* was not what he had admired in Pheidias' *Athena* or the *Charioteer*; sculpture had discovered a new power—and by the same token the first world of esthetics. *Athena* had been a divine figure, the *Charioteer* a votive offering; but from now on the figure of a *Youth in Prayer* was to rank as a "work of art."

No more than that of Polyclitus and Pheidias, was this new beauty that of living beings, the common measure of selected models. It was now a quality suggested by the statues that Hellenistic connoisseurs admired; and, from the artist's viewpoint, all that added to this quality the illusion of life. Had sculpture's sole concern been that of beautifying the female form, Aphrodite would not have culminated in the Venuses of Alexandria or the coquettish young women of Myrina, but in the wax dummies of our hairdressers. To "beautify" a woman meant sublimating her into a fictive world, the world of statues—and this spelt the beginning of idealization.

Along with idealization, appearance entered into sculpture. Hitherto, with some rare exceptions, sculptors had confined themselves to animals worthy of the gods or destined to be sacrificed. At Alexandria they now included dogs, and indeed everything that had formerly been banned from sculpture. Idealization could justify the use of any and every motif, and it reached its climactic point in Hellenistic realism. These servant girls, knife-grinders, fishermen and drunkards belong to a world that can be recognized at a glance, and it is not the world of reality, but that of the warriors, fauns, gods and satyrs who figure alongside them. They do not become more and more illusionist, and they do not culminate in wax dummies, but in de-luxe figures. Athens had reserved "luxurious" presentations to her gods. Did the later artist, when he carved an old fisherman with bulging veins, really wish to imitate his model or not, rather, to "make a statue" of him? Rome was to produce copies of such works in polychrome marble. They were intended for the art lovers who collected them, not for the slaves whom they depicted and they belonged to an esthetic world—that is to say, to a "fiction" of a new, unprecedented order.

One has the impression that from the end of the fourth century until the decline of Rome the theatrical was supplanting the divine. True, its figures owed nothing to the stage—and this despite the fact that the theater was in high favor throughout the period; their faces are the exact opposite of masks. Nevertheless, they owed all to the imaginary theater that, from childhood up, every Greek maintained within his bosom, a theater without actors that, in an age when the novel hardly existed, was the playground of the romantic spirit, a spirit which found expression not on the stage but in epics like the *Argonautica*. Narrative now bulked large in sculpture, and its themes ranged from the legends of Marsyas and Laocoon to the anecdotal. The tragic sense of life and the comic spirit played an active part in these creations, which revealed both the afflictions of the human lot and its picturesque or playful aspects: childhood and laughter—but always translated into something other than themselves. Thus anecdote and folktale, the genre piece of the drunken woman or the startled nymph, incidents of history and the lives of the gods, entered into art. And, parallel with this,

BUST OF HOMER, IInd C. B.C.   REPLICA.   LOUVRE

there now arose the cult and the portraiture of the Great Man.
That art of admiration which had "given their faces" to gods
and heroes, now created the famous bust of Homer (twenty-four

replicas of which are extant), the *Demosthenes* of Polyeuctus and Silanion's *Plato*. As they receded into limbo, the gods of Olympus transmitted a last gleam of the divine to the great poets and philosophers of the past, and it was in this new Pantheon that the creative spirit of the third century achieved its most original expression.

Nonetheless it was from the gods, and not from men, that the sculpture of the following century was to derive its final accents. That modeling in the round which had begun at Delphi came to an end at Lycosura, and the combats of giants of the earliest Greek art terminated in the *Götterdämmerung* of Pergamum —the first "opera" known to history. Pergamum had not lost its sense of the Cosmos; the city was one vast Acropolis. Did it owe its "Baroque lyricism" to Asia? But such a description hardly tallies with the essentially hieratic art of the East, from that of the Sumerians to the Parthians'. Perhaps it was rather that the Pergamum sculptors had heard, for the last time, the voice of Dionysus; it was they who created *Night*— and the *Victory of Samothrace* was meant to crown the tomb of Alexander.

This art*, created, one might think, to captivate Alexandria

* If I confine myself to briefly citing the most famous work in the Hellenistic style, this is because its world-wide fame seems to me largely unconnected with its style. None of the Victories has come down to us intact; the wings of Paeonius' Victory are broken and the Victories in the temple of Athena Niké have lost theirs completely. Structurally, the wings took the place of arms; thus the Victories should in practice have been armless. Angels have familiarized us with winged human figures, but the mutilation of the *Niké of Samothrace* demonstrates in the most striking and conclusive manner the form the perfect angel—and, for that matter, the perfect Victory— should have taken. Nevertheless the arts to which we owe both Victories and angels would not have tolerated or even conceived of them in this form, and the *Niké of Samothrace*, as it has come down to us, is not a wholly human creation; Destiny has had a hand in it. This Victory we know belongs to all time and to no time; it is more akin to Michelangelo's "unfinished" works or Rodin's *Balzac* than to any other Greek statue. And the very absence of the head, giving it a continuous movement, unparalleled in antique sculpture, from the lowest edge of the drapery to the wing tips, enhances this strange timelessness— which is why it has been so often represented as art's eternal symbol. Aware of this, the conservators of the Louvre have very rightly given it a place apart, isolated from other Hellenistic works.

ALTAR OF ZEUS AT PERGAMUM, EARLY IInd C. B.C.   BERLIN MUSEUM

Eschata (Furthest Alexandria), was not unknown to Egyptian Alexandria, but there it was regarded as outlandish, not to say barbaric.   Like all large cosmopolitan cities of that age, Alexandria preferred the sculpture Rome was to make world-famous: not the rugged poetry of Pergamum, but the polished art of its *Galatians*; not even the accent of Magnesia-ad-Maeandrum (which foreshadowed that of the Gandhara schists), but a statuary of sinuous, curly-haired fauns—in short, the representation of scenes having an appeal to the emotions, though the artist's task was not to imitate such scenes exactly, but to metamorphose them into "something rich and strange."   What was then called form was the means by which this metamorphosis was effected. The creative art of the fifth century had come to be regarded as archaic.   Those historiated vases which for three centuries had

99

portrayed characters in legends and fables even more persistently than medieval art was to portray saints, but whose accent was incompatible with illusionism, disappeared altogether. The Master of the Reeds was the last great artist in this field. And despite a semblance of continuity, there now took place a cleavage as drastic as that when the divine supplanted the sacred.

In the world where Caesar met Cleopatra, "Roma" did not replace Athena, nor did Caligula's horse replace consuls or the gods. Rome conquered Greece and Olympus but she did not conquer the divine; she was now to invent, unwittingly, a parody of divinization. She symbolized what Renan called the "religious nullity" of the West. The Romans were superstitious, but superstition can go as well with atheism as with faith; they sacrificed to unknown gods, but never entered into communion with them. But for Greece, their gods would have had no images; yet that sense of a soul within the Cosmos which called Apollo and Aphrodite into being meant nothing to them. Fifth-century sculpture had been motivated by the divine as Negro sculpture is by spirits; Rome "conversed" with Greece much as European imitators of Negro sculpture "converse" with it. Pheidias did not father the creative processes of Roman sculpture; they were of a quite other nature.

Relatively near, however, to the art of the last Hellenistic sculptors. Aristotle had spoken of imitation (though also of "the secret of things which is not in their appearance") and thereafter art was commonly regarded as imitation, or idealization, of appearance. But in the work of art the Romans justified the art by the object represented, and the object by its function. The depiction of the victory of the gods over the giants on the altar of Zeus at Pergamum was a votive offering, dedicating to the gods the victory of the Greeks over the barbarians; Rome erected triumphal arches so as to remind the vanquished of her conquests, and pillars to remind herself of them. When triumphs supplanted Victories there was little scope for veiled allusions; whereas, even when serving merely decorative ends, Hellenistic works always hinted at something beyond their obvious themes. Their esthetic content was sufficient in itself; hence the

MASTER OF THE REEDS. LECYTHOS, EARLY IVth C. B.C. ATHENS MUSEUM

impression of independence, even of free fancy, they produce. Compared with the Roman rooms in our museums, the Alexandrine seem filled with bric-à-brac left over when Cleopatra was moving house. That world of fiction into which the sculptors of Antioch and Alexandria transposed reality meant nothing to the Romans, except when they had recourse to it for decorative purposes. We speak of "reality" with reference to Roman sculpture, but in the case of Hellenistic we prefer to speak of "realism," using the word in the sense in which it is applied to the Rheims statues, to Velasquez' portraits or to the plausible verisimilitude of the novel.

In the age of the divine, the portrait rarely figured in Greek art; making the likeness of an ordinary person seemed to the Greek sculptor a task for artisans, as compared with the demiurgic power of giving bodily form to the gods of the city. Like the art of the sacred, that of the divine disdained the individual or, when it had to take him into account, dis-individualized him. Hellenistic portraits, on the other hand, are lifelike and characterized. Our caricatures, though they too are lifelike, do not for that reason belong to reality; for though each resembles a model, none is the true likeness of a man. Similarly the aim of the Hellenistic sculptor was not to *imitate* his model, but to give him a place in that conclave of the eminent where he could forgather with Homer and Demosthenes. Any other reality was foreign to his art.

But not to Roman sculpture. Though portraiture was not a Roman invention, the Romans invented their own type of portrait. What it owed to Etruria, to wax casts, to effigies of ancestors matters little. Before Rome took over the Hellenistic portrait, her own tradition in this field was well established, and it is impossible to mistake a republican portrait for an Etruscan effigy, even one of a late period. No previous civilization had venerated dead men who looked like living men. What was at issue was something more than a tradition of the portrait, for this new type of portraiture stemmed from a conception of reality that all the arts had eschewed for three thousand years—a conception not to be accounted for by the term "realism" and one

ETRUSCAN HEAD, MIDDLE IInd C. B.C.   LOUVRE

FRAGMENT OF THE PARTHENON FRIEZE, C. 440-435 B.C.   BRITISH MUSEUM

which makes its presence felt, intrusive and imperative, in even the most thoroughly idealized Roman sculpture.

When we compare a Roman bas-relief, even one as skillfully

FRAGMENT OF THE SUOVETAURILIA, 1st C. A.D. LOUVRE

executed and ambitious as the *Suovetaurilia*, with the fragments of
the Parthenon frieze which it deliberately resembles, we cannot
fail to note a *difference in kind* between them.   In spite of all that

TANAGRA WORK.   VEILED WOMAN, IVth C. B.C.   LOUVRE

the Roman work may claim to owe to the Greek and despite its idealization, it is differentiated from the latter by an emphasis on the "real" that is not due to mere illusionism: the same difference that we find between the Ludovisi *Juno* and any Athenian *Hera* or the simplest, least ornate *Veiled Woman* of the many produced at Tanagra; the difference between all Roman replicas and their Greek prototypes.   "Reality" is our name for a correlation of the elements of appearance that accord with the normal human viewpoint; hitherto every art had adjusted appearance to the requirements of the gods or the divine, whose

ROMAN ART. VESTAL VIRGIN: "LA ZINGARELLA." NAPLES MUSEUM

service was its function.   Even if Rome had aspired to over-rule appearance, what gods could she have invoked?   For the first time a major art accepted the order of appearance as the order of the scheme of things; for the first time appearance ranked as *the real*.

This is why, though there were many artists in the Roman world, there was no Roman art in the true sense, the sense in which we speak of the arts of Egypt, China, Mexico, or the Middle Ages.   Art aimed no longer at superseding appearance, but at embellishing it.   The bust became an apotheosis of the face and deified emperors were portrayed in the style of the gods of Olympus no less scrupulously than Byzantine saints were portrayed in the manner of icons.   Gods served to decorate gardens, and were "owned" often as not by private individuals. The nameless deity presiding over their images was not Minerva but the most majestic decorative art the world has seen.   Rome contemplated the glamorous art of Alexandria with the condescendence of a race that flocked to watch gladiators and executions rather than tragedies enacted on a stage.   Battle scenes, official propaganda, pomp and circumstance, treated with the superficial stylization that Roman artists foisted on appearance, were the order of the day.   The only forms of art to escape this servitude were those which were not taken quite seriously: private portraits, stuccowork and paintings used for interior decoration.   True, Pompeian painting shows a certain freedom and it often disdained illusionism, but its mythology —that of the painted screen—and even its quality hardly answer to the traditional conception of the epithet "Roman."   But for the tyranny of reality, Rome might have developed a massive architectural sculpture, hints of which can be seen in some fragments of the Arch of Trajan and Provençal monuments.

But the mighty arabesque of that strange symphony in stone, the Pergamum altar, is as alien to Roman realism as to the Panathenaic frieze; it would be no less out of keeping on the banks of the Tiber (except as a trophy) than would be the bas-reliefs of Persepolis, or the Sphinx.   If Augustus wished to make Greek art the official art of the Empire and the culture it stood for, this was because he thought to see in Pheidias the originator of the spurious art of his successors. Thus Rome (far later, long after Athens had launched this rather puerile movement, in the first century before our era) was to toy a while with the archaizing type of statue. However, the imperial art of Rome, rejecting the austere style, started out from the masters of illusionism, from Hellenistic recipes, and embarked on a progressive conquest of appearance. It took over all the gods and much of the legendary lore of Greece. But in so doing it incorporated them in its own "reality"—a down-to-earth reality in which Anubis, transformed into a watch-dog, figured alongside exotic sirens and harpies inherited from Alexandria. The form in which Rome adopted and adapted the Egyptian gods is much more revealing than the way she assimilated the gods of Greece, though she used the same methods and for the same ends. Thus the dog Anubis, sirens and

SIREN. ALEXANDRIA. CAIRO MUSEUM

harpies were given Roman animal forms, just as Pheidias' bull became the bull of the Suovetaurilia. Every Roman replica of a Greek masterwork is to some extent a "siren" in this sense.

While Egypt demonstrates all that Greece owed to the vibrant radiance of her glorious dawn, it is Rome that shows us best all that she owed to the nightside of her culture, the primeval gloom of Erebus, the doom of the Atridae.

All that survived of Greece, of Egypt and the East in the precarious splendor of Roman pomp and pride was a motley horde of gods empty alike of the sacred and of the divine. Yet meanwhile portraits were being painted on the winding-sheets of the Fayum, and the capture of Palmyra dispersed its funerary sculptors throughout the Roman empire; darkness was falling on the western world but the eyes of the sacred were kindling once again within the shadows.

PART III

THE AGE OF FAITH

JUPITER SERAPIS, IInd C. A.D. (?).   COTE-D'OR.   SAINT-GERMAIN MUSEUM

I At the apogee of imperial art the whole Mediterranean world formed part of the Roman dominions; by the sixth century only the regions governed by Byzantium retained the semblance of an empire in the all-pervading anarchy. And this new empire replaced gesturing statues with static, spectral figures; shadows of the Catacombs and Santa Sophia blotted out the sunlight bathing the public squares where a noisy populace had walked and wrangled under the lordly gestures of marble tribunes and majestic effigies of emperors. For the images of personages or events of Holy Scripture were not meant to figure on the terrestrial plane but in a place withdrawn from earthbound life; the sanctuary had reappeared.

Hence the kinship between Christian and oriental forms. It had begun in the age of the Catacombs. When, in the Catacombs, "Good Shepherds" and pagan figures, drained of significance and used as signs, were replaced by representations of Praying Women, the East had made its entry along with them. The "West" meant Rome alone, for as yet there was no question of the "barbarians"; the East was all the rest, the world which the legions had failed to conquer and with which religion was now associated, as once had been the splendors of oriental luxury. By the third century that world existed *within* Rome as at Antioch and Alexandria, and Christian figures arose wherever there was an upcrop of the subterranean presences that had formerly been kept under by the Roman imperium.

In Rome herself—even in portraits—certain forms appeared which were later to be accounted for by "clumsiness" (though actually there was no dearth of expert artists), and which we find again in the triumphal arch and effigies of Constantine. Lying as they did on the fringes of imperial art, the provinces retained, intractably, an accent in which were oddly intermingled Celtic vestiges, heavily modeled, snake-limbed giants and hybrid gods, the almost Asiatic drapery of the Mother Goddesses and the racy schematism of bas-reliefs depicting "crafts"—an accent which seemed to presage that of the great invasions. In the East, under the Antonines, there developed a "Flamboyant antique," very different from Hellenistic Baroque, that seemed

BIRD-SOUL, IInd-IIIrd C. A.D. MEROE. CAIRO MUSEUM

—for example in the *Tyche* of Prusias—to point the way to the
death of the classical models which inspired it. Meanwhile
Egypt was commingling, in terms of a defunctive magic, all
the bas-reliefs of the Mediterranean littoral, confronting with
her geometric bird-souls the harpies and exotic sirens of her

WOMAN'S HEAD, IInd-IIIrd C. A.D. HAURAN. DAMASCUS MUSEUM

neighbors, and recapturing her genius for the funereal in the
Fayum portraits. Barbarian sculptors proliferated in the Hauran
region and overran Syria. Grecian in its temples, Palmyra
is Parthian in its tombs. Forms of the underworld were beginning to invade imperial art, and the "Imaginary Museum" of
the fourth century is an assemblage of insurgent arts, among
which Christian art seems merely the most successful rebel.

FUNERARY RELIEF, IInd-IIIrd C. A.D.   PALMYRA.   DAMASCUS MUSEUM

HEAD OF PARTHIAN KING, 1st C. A.D. HATRA (COURTESY OF H.E. NADJI AL-ASIL)

SASSANID KING HUNTING, IVth C. A.D.   PHILADELPHIA MUSEUM

Classical historians used to treat the regions outside the Empire as a hinterland of barbarians and nomads. Military historians saw in the Parthians successors of the Scythians, who defeated Crassus and whom Trajan failed to conquer—and this though their capital Seleucia on the Tigris was the third largest city of the world. But we have only just discovered their art. A realm of forms has been disclosed at Hatra, vaster than that of the Achaemenids and amplified a little later by Seleucia and Vologesias. Many of the unclassical forms of the Empire, ranging from the stelae of Macedonia to the effigies of the "Antaios" gods of Egypt, by way of Syria and the Hauran, have vague affinities with this art. To it belong the bas-reliefs of Palmyra and Dura. Those of the Sassanids are as clearly its successors as Shapur is the successor of its tiara'd kings. The continuity of the forms created in Sumer remained unbroken, except for a period of less than a century. The Roman East was not a sealed-off province, a self-contained world, but one of the marches of the Empire facing Seleucia. And Rome was in close touch with Palmyra, where she recruited her best cavalry. During the centuries when Christian forms were in the making, men's eyes were often drawn towards the East, soon to be the lodestone of Byzantium, and when those forms developed into a style, it was in terms of the rejection of appearance congenital to the East. A large dose of western nationalism would be needed to see in Santa Sophia a successor of the classical temple, rather than a direct descendant of the oriental cupola and a prototype of the mosques of Islam. And it would be hardly less short-sighted to regard Byzantine forms as the progeny of Rome, rather than as stemming from the world—not only of forms but of colors also—that made a tentative appearance in the Fayum and Palmyra.

So little of the painting of antiquity has survived that we know next to nothing of its large-scale works; but more is known about the colors it employed. In the first centuries of the Christian era two varieties of painting co-existed within the Empire —as was the case in eighteenth-century France: a traditional type and a strictly decorative type which, as such, could indulge in a certain freedom. Van Loo and Huet's *singeries* parallel the great mythological scenes and the fantastic art of Pompeii. Though the ornamental figures were often painted on a dark ground, all these artists arranged their tones with an eye to harmonious effect; the traditionalists more markedly, since white was often the dominant hue in their compositions. The Egyptian palette, like the color-schemes of Mesopotamia and Iran, was based on ochres and blues (allusions, perhaps, to earth and sky). Greece had contributed white—as she had contributed marble. A color orchestration much like that of Italian Trecento frescos prevailed for six centuries, from the lecythi to the mosaics of Piazza Armerina. Finally, in decorations of public baths, as in the *Battle of Alexander* and the *Baker's Wife*, most Roman paintings and mosaics were executed in a monochrome of ochres, perhaps deriving from Greek vases. Common to traditional painting and decorative figures was the use of color-scales planned with an eye to consonance. Hellenistic art and the art of the Empire in its death-throes had intermittently made use of color-schemes in which the possibilities of *dissonance* were exploited—as, likewise sporadically, they indulged in forms that clashed with appearance. In descriptions of Hellenistic painting its use of "discordant" colors is often mentioned. But this was something that in both Hellenistic and Roman art owed nothing to Greece or to Rome; rather, it stood for a revolt against them. True, the Fayum portraits were sired by Roman portraits—but they were parricides. To suggest by using the epithet "Hellenistic" (which in point of fact relates to a period rather than to an art form) that Roman busts and the figures of Palmyra, the *Bathers* of Piazza Armerina and the synagogue scenes at Dura-Europos, belong to the same art has the effect of making the nature of these contemporary but conflicting trends unintelligible.

On the eve of Constantine's triumph all the arts concerned with the Other World, whatever god they venerated, disdained the decorative and realistic arts of the age, and in the rare cases where we find the trance-bound gaze of ecstasy in a pagan work, this was borrowed from figures only yesterday its enemies, and was a departure from the norm. Colors which painters of the classical age would never have dreamt of were combined with forms that were equally hostile to illusionist idealization. In Coptic portraits the clash of colors corresponds to the broken accents of Coptic sculpture; the painting at Dura echoes the busts of Palmyra. Though no

BATHER, IVth-Vth C. A.D.   PIAZZA ARMERINA, SICILY

THE ARK OF THE COVENANT, IIIrd C. A.D.   DURA-EUROPOS.   DAMASCUS MUSEUM

great importance should be attached to Dura, it is there that
we find the earliest "likenesses" of Christ as a beardless youth,
while the Dura *Prophets* combine faces resembling those of
late Egyptian portraits with drapery as pre-Byzantine as that of
the Palmyran stelae. Beyond that outpost on the desert's
edge stretched the far-flung Parthian world. Yet it was less
this world, or its Sassanian successor, that challenged the art of
antiquity, than the versions of the "Temptations of St Anthony"

123

FUNERARY FIGURE, LATE ROMAN EPOCH. EGYPT. CAIRO MUSEUM

whose bizarre forms throng the "Late Epoch" rooms in Cairo Museum. These curiously amorphous figures, which provoked smiles only a century ago, were magical in purpose and the mosaic art which disseminated them from Spain to Mesopotamia, by way of Tabarka in Tunisia and the Gilboa synagogue, was not spontaneous but purposeful. And the "graffiti" were painted on winding-cloths. Everywhere a vast religious fermentation was at work below the surface, sapping the vitals of the Empire, and the forms and colors of those for whom terrestrial "reality" was all were being rejected by those who held that life was but appearance and "reality" a mystery.

FUNERARY CASKET, LATE ROMAN EPOCH. EGYPT. CAIRO MUSEUM

The Libyan desert teemed with the dead, as the Syrian desert teemed with gods. The painting in the Temple of the Gods at Palmyra (dating from the first century of our era) is hieratic; and the colors in the Dura synagogue would seem hardly less surprising in third-century Pompeii than would those of the Ajanta frescos.

But they would occasion no surprise in Alexandria, where the basic colors—salmon-pink and violet in particular—are those of Roman Egypt in its death-throes. They pervade the frenzied figures of the last sarcophagi and dominate the palette of the Fayum painters. We find echoes of them in that masterwork of sixth-century Christian art, the apse of Sts Cosmas and Damian in Rome; also in the Bawit frescos, Nilotic icons, Christian manuscripts of the East, Cappadocian painting, and in most Byzantine art not under the direct control of Constantinople. But sometimes, too, even in "official" Byzantine mosaics. The colors of the Ravenna *Theodora*, very different from any classical color scheme, are akin to those of the Fayum portrait illustrated in *The Voices of Silence*. While colors inherited directly from the art of dissonance continued, to some extent, to be used in the "underground" arts of Byzantium, the Peace of the Church was bringing into being a form of art that soon made good throughout the Empire.

This, the so-called triumphal art, derived its accent primarily from the Christian basilica. The clandestine church had now become a public place of worship in which the gaze of all was drawn to the great arch which celebrated the martyrs' triumph and overhung their relics. Magnificence was ensured by rows of pillars (henceforth *within* the church) and the splendors, now put to Christian uses, of the ancient temple. In many ways the basilica is a temple turned inside out. The ancient temple had been linked up with its environment, Polis or Urbs as the case might be, by its façade; the basilica, heir of the secret Christian sanctuary in this respect alone, had no façade.

The rows of pillars bring to mind processions; they had to point the way to Christ, and it was owing to His presence that the Christian triumphal arch differed from its Roman predecessors and these churches ceased to resemble imperial basilicas. For the Christian basilica required an imagery of its own.

But though the Church had a clear idea of what it wanted of the architects employed on the nave of Santa Maria Maggiore and could strictly supervise their work, it was unable to control the creations of the mosaicists. The patron could commission edifices suited to his personal taste, and depictions of appearance; but it took an artist to create images that were emancipated from appearance.

At the beginning of the present century only artists realized to what extent these latter were "creations." Even for art historians icons symbolized a *style*, the Byzantine; and when they ceased describing as Byzantine all such images as were no longer antique and not yet medieval, there developed a practice of describing as antique all such as were unlike icons. Thus, after being assigned to an ill-defined Byzantinism, the mosaics in San Lorenzo of Milan, in Santa Maria Maggiore and Santa Pudenziana were assigned to an art period known as "late antiquity." Yet they are poles apart from the art of classical antiquity—even when, as in *Christ and the Apostles* at San Lorenzo, they show the Apostles wearing togas. This work brings home to us the limitations of the type of art history which is confined to the history of forms. True, these Apostles form part of the heritage of antiquity, but whereas the Roman mosaics depicted gods, Christian mosaics manifested Christ.

It is easy enough to isolate certain figures in pre-Byzantine mosaics and to stress the points they have in common with the productions of traditional Roman *craftsmanship*; just as it is easy to stress the resemblance between some figures on Christian sarcophagi, isolated from their contexts, and those on pagan sarcophagi. But, for the analogy to hold, the antique figure needs to have lost its antique accent and the Christian to have failed, as yet, to acquire its Christian accent. The antique forms we find in Christian art are not those of Praxiteles, nor even clumsy copies of them; they are, exclusively, forms that now had ceased to have significance. For, had they not "lost their souls," the Christians could not have used them as signs.

The figure of Christ in Santa Pudenziana may resemble an effigy of Jupiter—but a Jupiter no Roman artist would have dreamed of; and though the Prophets and Apostles in Santa Maria Maggiore may look like Romans, they would certainly have startled the painters of Pompeii. For this Christ, these Prophets and Apostles were created to figure in a world whose very existence was unthinkable in Augustan Rome; though the mosaicist gave them the same white hair, the same beards, the same togas and sometimes a bodily structure seemingly of the same pattern, he denied what the Roman painters affirmed and what he affirmed was something quite unknown to them. When the whole function of art has changed, any talk of a continuity of forms is pointless.

It is common knowledge that the earliest Christian art was executed in mosaic. And since this is usually regarded, primarily, as a technique, some have spoken of its "evolution" from the Roman thermae to Ravenna. But the creations of the Christian mosaicists no more represented a phase in the evolution of a Roman craft than our machine-made colored windows stand for a development of the stained-glass window as it exists at Chartres. The Romans saw in the mosaic "a painting made to last forever, a work of man that man alone can destroy," and from the fact that it was impossible to wear out, drew the practical conclusion that it made an ideal floor surface. Sometimes, too, they used it on walls as a substitute for painting and, oftener, as a form of decorative mural art resembling that of the pavements. There was a time when Christian (in particular Byzantine) mosaics were considered purely decorative; but that was when contemporary Europe had ceased to understand the first thing of their idiom. The distortions in the *Africa* mosaic at Piazza Armerina, which depicts an allegorical goddess enthroned between a checker-work elephant and a richly dappled tiger, are as different from the distortions of Christian mosaics as is the color scheme of the "Bathing Women" from that of the mosaics in Santa Maria Maggiore. And the colors of the noblemen in the Hunting Scenes beside the Bathing

Scenes (though here the palette curiously resembles that of Dura-Europos) have nothing in common with those of any portrait of a saint, from the *St Ambrose* at Milan to those in the Orthodox Baptistery of Ravenna.

If the mosaicists, while shutting their eyes both to decorative Roman painting (which they disdained) and to traditional Roman painting (which they disapproved of), created an art that often reminds us of the best fourth-century Egyptian portraits, this was not due to borrowings from the latter—for they borrowed nothing—but because of that special use of color which was common to all religious painters of the age. The effigies of souls in Coptic coffins had to belong to the Other World, as did the scenes depicted by the mosaic-workers, who, like the painters, called even more on color than on form to translate all they represented into an otherworldly ambience.

It would seem that antique art discouraged the "irrational" no less in painting than in sculpture; its colors were accorded to its illusionism. But the forms rejecting illusionism led to a "disincarnation" of their models; and so did their colors. It is in this respect that the mosaics resemble Coptic paintings. But the Church did not relegate its images to tombs; they were intended to be seen by generations as yet unborn.

The mosaicists did away with the space perceived by our senses. Did they then replace this by another? Not altogether. We occasionally find in mosaics, from those of Santa Maria Maggiore up to the last Byzantine cycles, hints of a third dimension, but not of real space; like the carvers of bas-reliefs, the mosaicists did not try to associate their figures with *depth* but merely with a *ground*. The whole conception of this ground was diametrically opposed to that of space, its function being to ensure a unity feasible solely in terms of the art creating it. For the artist's purpose was not to produce the illusion of a real scene but to conjure up a vision of the supramundane; and space was irrelevant to the Other World he was creating. Thus, like the stained-glass windows, the mosaics take no account of space. Hence the need for inventing grounds that, while purely arbitrary, could be vaguely assimilated to the sky or to sunlight:

the neutral blue of Santa Maria Maggiore, the deep blue of Ravenna, the night-blue of Sts Cosmas and Damian, and, lastly, gold—colors that "went with" the scenes only in virtue of their basic unreality. The overall gold ground *suggests* the light of God, but does not *represent* it; when our Primitives took to leaving only a strip of gold, by way of representing sunlight, Byzantine art had had its day. The gold grounds stood for the light of heaven, not to be seen outside the church, a celestial radiance with which the artist had to harmonize the figures he depicted. In this respect all the grounds of Christian mosaics, whatever their color, resemble the gold ground, and since the artist's concern was not a more or less illusionist depiction of a sacred scene, but a presentment of the sacred, he could harmonize his figures with this pre-existent ground (or create simultaneously both ground and figures) only by using forms and colors foreign to appearance. That is why the tesserae in religious mosaics were systematically left visible. Roman artists occasionally did this for decorative ends; but whenever Roman mosaic art sought to vie with painting, the cubes were of the most minute dimensions. Christian art refrained from these—until the fall of Byzantium—and the Christian mosaicists employed *visible* tesserae (just as sixteenth-century Venetian painters left their brush-strokes visible) not because of inexpertness, but because they did not practise an illusionist art. And they handled color in the same way.

We are sometimes told that the mosaics of Santa Maria Maggiore owe their style to illuminations. Their subjects, yes; but not their style. Though Utrillo sometimes took his subjects from post cards, he did not owe his pictures to them. While there is no question that Christian mosaics linked up with the art of Late Antiquity, by way of the illuminated book, this link concerned only the element of representation, and the mosaics broke with it once they became works of art, that is to say original creations. Just as it is vain to seek to trace in pagan forms the spirit of the *Bearer of the Cross* in the Mausoleum of Galla Placidia, so it is vain to seek in them the *invented structure* which in the "Abraham" mosaic (Santa Maria Maggiore)

PARTING OF ABRAHAM AND LOT, IVth C. A.D.   S. MARIA MAGGIORE, ROME

brings to mind Masaccio and Seurat and stems not only from the
religious significance of the work but also from the solid bulk the
artist gives the figures so as to unify them with his background;
and also from the liberties he takes with color.

Each figure in Santa Maria Maggiore was conceived for one
purpose only, that of glorifying God; but in this act of homage,

rejecting as it did appearance, the artists exercised a freedom denied to antique painting, except in decorative art. Nevertheless there is nothing fancy-free about their work. True, this glorification of the Almighty did not oblige the maker of the "Abraham" mosaic to depict walls like violet and yellow flags hung above doors resembling other flags in violet and green; nor to make the face of the girl in blue tell out against a yellow nimbus and the monumental figure on the left stand out against the orange-red garment of the man immediately behind. All the same it imposed on him the duty of making the city in the background harmonize with the figures, in a world that was not the world of appearance. Forms are emancipated from appearance not by faith alone (the paintings in the Catacombs are proof of this) but by "invention," and the mosaicist does not invent forms as does the sculptor; what he invents is a system of forms involving color schemes foreign to illusionism (since it is an Other World he is evoking); foreign also to the caprices of free fancy (since the world in question is a sacred world). Even the decorative painting of antiquity, "free" though it was, derived its accents from volume, light and movement—allusions to appearance. But Christian mosaic art first subordinated, then ruled out, all three, so as to stress its allusions to the super-world of Truth.

The master artists of Santa Maria Maggiore (the others were mere story-tellers) aimed at locating the Annunciation in the world whence came the angel herald. If we forget this fact, their art seems incomprehensible—as indeed it was for some five centuries. And this was also indispensable; without it the effect produced by the basilicas would have been no more than an imposing vastness. As Pheidias had brought the Greek gods to the city, so the great mosaicists brought to the Christian congregation a vision of the world of Truth.

But they did not bring Jesus to it.

Though they represented Him, their art did not aspire to *portraying* Him, as Gothic art was to do. Nor to making the Virgin a real presence. It seems that in art—and probably in religion too—Christ tended to become the more Jesus, the more God the Father receded into the background. But through-out the fifth century God remained the dominant presence.

We never think of dissociating Romanesque or the art of the cathedrals from the faith which they express so clearly; yet we tend to speak of fifth-century art as if it were a province of arche-ology (sometimes, indeed, of modern painting). Undoubtedly the body of believers in a State religion differs from that of a persecuted religion. Yet all the writings of the age imply that faith was deeply rooted in the masses; as for the Church, any assumption that its spiritual life was negligible in the time of St Augustine would be rash, to say the least. What our age understands best in the faith of the Romanesque and Gothic epochs are those elements of it which do not properly pertain to Faith: such as love of one's neighbor or the mildly ration-alized imagery of St Bernard and St Francis—all that tends to assimilate the charity of a saint to the devoted care of a phys-ician, the building of a cathedral to that of a gigantic dam, Crusades to Revolutions. What we now appreciate in medieval Christianity is its insistence on brotherly love, not its vision of transcendence. But in the short-lived empires of Milan and Ravenna, as in the Eastern empire then in the ascendant, transcendence was the main directive of Christian art and thought. Though the Revelation which had changed the face of the world and now was clothing Christendom with a robe of churches brought a message of love, that love was something more than an appeal to human fellow-feeling. It was God the Father who gave his Son for man's salvation: "God so loved the world that he gave his only begotten Son, that whosoever believeth in him should not perish, but have everlasting life." Besides being a pledge of winning through to heaven, salvation means a spiritual rebirth, a new awareness of God and a love which, through Christ, reciprocates God's love. The martyrs did not accept a brutal death in the arena merely to earn an endless holiday in heaven. Eternal life has nothing in common with the immortality promised man by many old religions. Basic to the Christianity of those days was not the hope of Paradise, which it seldom represented in its art; nor the morality

133

preached by Jesus; nor even the Crucifixion. Its quintessence was the secret of the Godhead, as revealed by Christ: the Revelation summed up in three momentous words: "God is Love."

But not human love. God's love is sacred love, and partakes in the central mystery of his Godhead. The Revelation did not bring elucidation of this mystery, but communion with it. To "explain" the Cosmos was no longer the chief aim of human thought. Though God was love and though man had access to Him through love, the ultimate mystery of his being remained inviolate. The Greek for "revelation" is "apocalypse," and the tomb of St John at Ephesus was hardly less venerated than the Holy Sepulchre itself.

All Holy Scripture, including the Gospel narrative, centers on manifestations of this mystery; God had manifested himself in Christ's life as, formerly, in the Burning Bush. And evocations of this mystery, antecedent to appearance and, like the gold grounds which were soon to prevail in every church, making God's presence felt behind appearance, now became art's supreme concern.

These artists never attempted to depict Jesus and Mary as individuals or even to standardize Christ's physical appearance; indeed their depictions of his face, from Milan to Ravenna, differ greatly. Yet in one respect—their otherworldliness—all these figures of the Saviour have a striking uniformity, and this is equally true of the biblical scenes over which they preside. For these scenes do not depict events that once took place on earth, but episodes of the sacred.

The prestige of fourth-century Rome still dazzled the Mediterranean world; that of sixth-century Rome, an easy prey to invaders, tended to be overshadowed by the splendors of Justinian's new capital and empire. Yet the art we call Byzantine was built up in *all* parts of Christendom and perhaps the influence of Rome in her decline weighed no less heavily in the scales than that of the monasteries of Egypt. But the characteristic accent this art owed to the Western Empire (to Constantine, not to Augustus)—the note struck by the Christian basilicas—had been given its death-blow. Even in Rome the apse of Sts Cosmas and Damian relates to the Apocalypse and foreshadows the "Christ Pantocrator" of Byzantine iconography; less than ten years later Santa Sophia proclaimed the victory of the East.

"I have conquered thee, O Solomon!" Justinian boasted, seeing in his great church the proud successor of the Temple of Jerusalem, not of the Pantheon; while he did not ignore Rome's grandeur, he molded it to his ends. Like the basilicas, Santa Sophia has no façade. But the basilicas, majestic rather than evocative of the supernatural, owed their atmosphere of mystery solely to the images within them. The earliest churches of Anatolia had been crypts raised little above ground level; Santa Sophia is a gigantic crypt and Justinian called on the genius of his architects to impart to it a numinous immensity worthy of an emperor who saw himself as Roman, combined with the secrecy and silence of an early Christian shrine.

Santa Sophia was the glorious resurrection of the Catacombs. Thus mystery was given an architecture appropriate to it; as compared with Santa Sophia, the basilicas seem relatively pagan. Their layout resembles that of a palace, even a private house; it is a geometrical, "human" space. Santa Sophia does away with this by that characteristic invention of the East: the cupola. For us today the cupola suggests a dome; but Santa Sophia no more has a dome than it has a façade. Its architects did not even try to mask with decorative facings the maze of cupolas overhead; they sought to reinvent a space adumbrating the sacred.

It was not a new *form* which Anthemius of Tralles, that architect of genius, imposed on space, but a sort of music. Though photography does justice to the interiors of Santa Maria Maggiore and San Paolo fuori le mura, that of Santa Sophia defeats the camera. For the emotive impact on our sensibility produced by the solid blocks of shadow in the cupolas comes from the fact that a special mode of lighting gives them a curious formlessness. The effect of the flooding light of St Peter's in Rome and the vertical lighting of Agrippa's Pantheon, on the other hand, is to bring out the architectural space within the domes. The lighting of the cupolas at Byzantium—by contrast with the West, one is tempted to say their "darkening"—makes the space within them seem like a haze of dancing motes or an evening mist tinged by the rays of sunset. This Byzantine lighting replaces the geometric void of the basilicas with an amber-golden glow that thickens as it dies out into darkness. We talk of the "boundless space" of the great cathedrals, but this would apply more properly to the concept of space that differentiated Byzantium, *toto caelo*, from Greece. For the builders of the Parthenon paid no heed to space and the only depth they knew was that of perspective vistas: marching ranks of pillars and the cult statue seen in recession in the cella, as if at the far end of a street. The Byzantines visualized a divine space permeating earthbound space as the light of a taper permeates the darkness. This divine space was vaguely associated with the universe, since the East imagined the firmament as an enormous cupola. Santa Sophia stood for more than the discovery of a style; it was primarily a place set free from the thrall of appearance, even under its most august aspects.

The various techniques by which churches were converted into outposts of an Other World matter little; it was through a *style* befitting it that the mystery of transcendence found expression. The mosaics were no less unified with the sanctuary than the Egyptian "double" with the tomb. The Ravenna mosaicists and (it would seem) their contemporaries in Constantinople carried their predecessors' work a stage further; it was as though they *spoke* the language that the latter had been seeking for. In the Orthodox Baptistery color was employed (in "portraits" of Apostles) as it had never been employed before. The *Last Judgment* in Sant'Apollinare is represented by the figure of Christ seated between two angels, one blue and the other red, signifying the "separation of the sheep from the goats," while for the first time in monumental art the Last Supper (hitherto merely symbolized by its prefigurations, usually the Marriage at Cana) is pictured as the First Communion. But in the form of an hieroglyph of the supernatural. Though the "Bible of the illiterate" was intended to remind beholders of "what actually took place," it also reminded them that this took place in an Other World; for the function of every sacred style is to express

APOSTLE, C. 458. ORTHODOX BAPTISTERY, RAVENNA

THE REDEEMER, 526-530. DETAIL OF APSIDAL MOSAIC, STS COSMAS AND DAMIAN, ROME

the sacred. While San Vitale was being built, the most grandiose vision of the Christ of the Apocalypse was figured forth in Rome herself, on the apse of Sts Cosmas and Damian: the great *Redeemer* (precursor of the Daphni "Christ") which made all the art of the Peace of the Church seem like the work of novices. Twenty years later Christian imperial art found its supreme symbol in the glorious mosaics of Justinian and Theodora and their Retinues, dispatched from Byzantium to Ravenna.

When we look at the portrait of the great Emperor of the East we cannot but be reminded of those of his great western predecessors. Yet here, what trace remains of the hierarchy governing the art of classical portraiture? The portraits of Constantine and even Constantius Chlorus had already ceased to be those of men invested with imperial dignity; the imperial style of portraiture was now extinct and the only "privileged" likenesses were those of saints. The Fayum portrait ended in the icon, and the Palmyra bas-reliefs in apostle figures.

Despite all it owed to color (a debt that sometimes the lavish use of gold enabled it to disregard), the mosaic stepped into the place of sculpture, not that of painting. It meant to the church what statues had meant to the colonnade during the preceding epoch. The art of the mosaic was now the major art. Rome would have depicted the San Vitale processions in the form of bas-reliefs. But the vast heritage of the forms of antique statuary belonged to the pagan past; they were associated with façades of temples, with the agora or forum, and now belonged solely to the world of decoration. The *Athena Promachos* and the *Cnidian Aphrodite* were used to decorate the racecourse of Constantinople. In the fifth century it seemed as if another sculpture were coming to birth. Here and there, instead of conventional figures like those on the sarcophagi of all the Christian lands, we find apostles whose curiously haggard faces neither resemble those of the saints in contemporary ivories, nor foreshadow those of the ivories of a later period. Such indeed is their emotive power, and so full the modeling, that they seem to prefigure their Romanesque successors. But Romanesque sculpture was transposed from the interior of the church to its outer walls, for all to see;

SARCOPHAGUS, IVth-Vth C. CHRIST AND THE APOSTLES. LOUVRE

SARCOPHAGUS (DETAIL), IVth-Vth C.   LOUVRE

and it was homiletic, a sermon in stone. Byzantine apostle figures, while pointing the way to western art far more emphatically than any contemporary figures of the West, were doomed to extinction by reason of their very emotivity; emotion is an attribute of man, not of God. Had it contained statues, the Byzantine crypt would have lent itself to idolatry rather than to edification; well aware of this, the Eastern Church had the wisdom to prefer pictured representations of saints to their statues, and henceforth all portraits conformed to this conception, as the "heroic" busts conformed to effigies of the Olympians. Even the bust of the Emperor. Even that of Theodora.

It is not hard to visualize what the Empress looked like in real life. No one questioned the gaunt but very real beauty of that long, sad, pensive face; not even the local ballad-mongers who, doubtless out of Christian charity, said no worse of the Augusta than that in her youth she had been a "bear-leader." In any case her exact appearance was not in issue, for though the artist has individualized her—differentiated her from the ladies of her retinue—the Theodora of the mosaics resembles the Virgin. Not too closely; she is more like a female saint. And in creating the Empress's "double," the artist harked back to Egyptian frontalism. In short, we have here a Fayum portrait —imperialized. But now the huge eyes of Fayum art and its faces rapt in ecstasy were no longer relegated to coffins, nor was the hieratic art of Palmyra reserved to burial places. All the intimations of the otherworldly that had been conveyed by the underground arts of early Christendom were now aligned to a "grand style" worthy of the Empire. Though the round tesserae representing Theodora's pearls may be no more than schematic, the dark red streaks along her eyelids and the line of the same red as the rim of the aureole marking the shadow of her nose, patently conflict with the evidence of our senses; and the same is true of the vermilion contour lines around the fingers of "the daughter of Belisarius," showing up against the golden yellow of her garment, while her mother's fingers are outlined in black against her pale grey cloak. These colors are no less arbitrary than the blue-black of Justinian's hair or the multicolored rocks in *Moses*

THE EMPRESS THEODORA AND HER RETINUE (DETAIL), C. 547. SAN VITALE, RAVENNA

receiving the Tables of the Law. In all cases the choice of colors has the same purpose: a *disincarnation* as deliberate and far more drastic than the idealizations of an earlier art—a means of giving human beings access to the world of Truth. It matters little whether or not the religious scenes depicted at Byzantium owed something to the rites and ceremonies of the Sacred Palace, for the artist's vision of the world of God was not inspired by the

143

Court of Constantinople; his purpose was, rather, to reveal Justinian's and Theodora's presence, not (as some have said) in a world of dreams, but in that divine world to which they belonged in virtue of their rank of consecrated sovereigns.

This art is not a representation but an annexation; it has imposed on these images an order of their own, befitting them—and some have seen it as a revival of the old order of Roman monumental art. Yet surely Cato would have felt ill at ease in the Great Palace of Byzantium, whereas Xerxes or Shapur would have felt at home there; the effigies at Ravenna remind us less of converted Caesars than of Christian Sassanids. But the religion of the Sassanids banned images, and this art of supramundane majesty, which in Justinian's churches achieved what the triumphal art of the Romans had failed to achieve in Constantine's basilicas, is the sacred art of the Empire, whose profane art, so far as can be judged, was uniformly decorative. Such fragments of the mosaic pavements of the Imperial Palace as have survived are more like Roman mosaics than like those in the Mausoleum of Galla Placidia. In the works of the court illuminators we find much use of Hellenistic motifs; the lost hunting scenes played, it seems, the part of our western tapestries, and Byzantine taste in these fields owed much to that of Persia. But Christian creative art, even in its most gorgeous manifestations, always functioned on a plane above the mundane luxury of Byzantium—in a world that, releasing man from his earthbound self, enabled him to commune with his Maker.

Its sole function was the revelation of that world, however various were the forms revelation might take. Constantinople never succeeded in overcoming the religious chaos of her dominions, and imperial art was not (as has been said) "an expression of the Empire," for the Empire had no unity. Nor was it an expression of eastern Christianity, in the sense in which medieval art expressed the faith of western Christendom. The provinces which were not Graecized developed (chiefly in their monasteries) an art as remote from the State art, as was the art of Armenia or Georgia. And Egypt, too, persisted in retaining Coptic forms in her sculpture, frescos, decorations, icons and illumin-

CHRIST AND ST MENNAS, VIIth C. EGYPT. LOUVRE

ations. Nor were Anatolian frescos and the Gospel Books of
Syria any less different from the imperial mosaics. The Rabula
Gospels and the Louvre *St Mennas* symbolize the art of eastern
Christendom no less than the "Processions" of Ravenna and
Constantinople. We rarely find imperial art—and never the
art of the poor—in the productions of the monasteries. But, as

145

Justinian is shown presenting the bowl of gold at San Vitale, so the Sacred Emperor placed at the service of the Eastern Church the only power that still survived in that anarchic age, for the greater glory of an art that was to persist, indefeasibly, for over a thousand years. It was a State art—but its forms were to outlast the government that sponsored it; and also an ecclesiastical art—but at the service of the Church only in a strictly theological sense. Here, again, the show of opulence may mislead us; but any notion of glorifying God parsimoniously was distasteful to the East, and even the art of Islam did not keep long to its austere simplicity. More than an instrument of propaganda, the Byzantine sanctuary was a manifestation of the world of God, and the purpose of the mosaics was to reveal the mystery of its Otherness. It was with this in view, less than on behalf of the authority of Church and State, that the creations of imperial art waged war on heresy.

Pentecost and Easter were Christianized versions of Jewish feast-days; Epiphany and Christmas, of the Greek and Roman celebrations of the winter solstice; the ritual of Holy Week, of the Phoenician cult of Adonis—and the imagery in the churches served to crystallize and consecrate these ancient rites. The Church combated the great heresies with the same weapons; each was countered by the celebration of a passage in the Gospels under the form of a feast of the Church and by a standardization of its imagery. These commemorative rites associated the believer with sacred Time—the Christian Year— and the images acted as visual links between him and the world of the sacred. This is why Christian imperial art does not illustrate the life of Jesus but is, rather, a theological exposition of Christ's nature and an intimation of the world where the events of sacred history took place, not in appearance but in Truth.

Popular sentiment was prone to heresy insofar as it tended to separate the Son from the Father and to reduce the Gospels to a biography diversified with miracles. Compared with imperial art, all Byzantine imagery unaffected by it seems "heretical" to some extent—by its emotionalism, to begin with. That art set out to glorify and mirror God in his ineffable majesty. The Old

Testament had made known the covenant of the God of Moses with his Chosen People; the New Testament, the alliance of St John's God with Christendom. The Christian entered into communion with God through his faith in Christ, pledge of God's love; the spirit of Byzantine theology is embodied in Christ's conversation with Nicodemus as recorded in the Gospel of St John. It is at ease with the Apocalypse, since the Mystery of the divine is basic to its tenets. And it was this Mystery, proclaimed by the voices of angels (i.e. music), that Byzantine ritual, beginning at the iconostasis, brought home to the congregation. Byzantine theology was not concerned with the life of Jesus, but with a series of God's manifestations of which Christ was the vehicle. Thus it rejected the Arian tendency to speak of "a man named Jesus" and saw in the Virgin rather the Mother of God than the Mother of Jesus. Imperial art ruled out all that was unrelated to the mystery of sacred love and to the Most High God from whom it derived its order and its law. The Eastern Church would have stigmatized, not as heresy, but as desecration, any religious art resembling fifteenth-century Gothic painting. To represent a sacred scene in the world of appearance was tantamount to representing it without faith —from the viewpoint of the Gentiles. Each scriptural event, the tragedy of Calvary included, had the value of a sign of God; the task of sacred art was to depict the sign, not the event, and this sign could figure only in a transcendent world symbolizing the world of God. Hence the representation of the Last Judgment by the separation of the sheep and goats, and that of the Crucifixion by the sacrifice of Isaac. Not that imperial art was limited to symbols; but in it all events are given the form of symbols. This is why it rules out all display of "natural" emotions; even when she holds the Infant Jesus on her knees, the Virgin does not remind us of the mother of a child in any human sense. Never did the first great style of the first religion of love create a figure in which love was unqualified by the mystery of the divine.

When Justinian came to power, work was beginning on Sts Cosmas and Damian; when he died the last great mosaic at

Ravenna, the cortèges in Sant'Apollinare, had been completed. Those two processions—of male saints advancing towards Christ and of female saints, preceded by the Magi, moving towards the Virgin—were to make their way, as a latent influence, around all the churches of Constantinople. Far-reaching as were the changes that came over Byzantine art (whether it gained in depth, in opulence, or atrophied), it never broke faith with its original vocation, and the mosaic-workers of Ravenna could have recognized in the last painters of the Athos monasteries their "Minorites."

Of the great seventh-century cycles only scattered fragments (and some counterparts in Italy) escaped the destructive zeal of the Iconoclasts. All go to show that imperial art persevered in its revelation of the world of God—it was to revert to this theme two centuries later, after the passing of Iconoclasm—and held its own beside that indomitable monastic art which in the frescos of Santa Maria Antiqua at Rome and in those of Cappadocia resuscitated the *St Mennas* of the Louvre. As far as can be judged, imperial art, in the Empire as in Italy, sometimes replaced colors by a monochrome harmonizing with the gold grounds, and it would also seem that sometimes the "disincarnation" of figures, legacy of Ravenna and Parenzo, became still more etherealized in its great cycles; this is the trend suggested by the mosaics in Rome, by the monumental abstractionism of the surviving fragments in the Church of St Demetrius in Salonica, and by the aquiline accent (destined to have so great a vogue in later years) that we find in the Angel of the Panaghia in Cyprus.

But little of this art survived the "purges" of Iconoclasm.

II When, after the sack of Rome, Alaric flung away the badges of his rank as a Roman commander and donned once more the bull-horned helmet of the Goths, he had as good as flung both Church and Empire into the Tiber. And by the end of the century—unlike the Patriarch of Constantinople, all-powerful in the East—the Pope of Rome had come to be regarded by Westerners as no more than the "patriarch" of a religion permitted to survive on sufferance.

The Church had placed her military resources at the disposal of the pagan Clovis in the hope of his conversion; a converted pagan was preferable to a heretic. But, despite its resourcefulness and pertinacity, ecclesiastical policy still remained at the mercy of the god of battles, and the mission to Geneva to solicit the hand of Clotilda for Clovis, king of the Franks, would have served no purpose had Clovis been defeated. There is food for thought in those compulsory baptisms, when the tribal warriors followed their leader sheeplike to the font or into a river. One wonders to what Christ they were being converted. To the Christ of the Resurrection, perhaps; later, to the victor's God. The Arian Goths clung less to their conception of the nature of Jesus than to their Masses solemnized by torchlight, to the clash of bucklers. The faith of the Frankish aristocracy was much the same as that of the half-starved, docile peasantry. Clovis was convinced that he would have set Jesus free; to his mind Calvary meant simply a miscarriage of justice. We can well imagine what any Byzantine would have thought of this —what St Augustine would have said to it! St Remigius of Rheims and the Patriarch of Constantinople were at one in their devotions, not in their sense of an apostolate; for the Western Church was prosecuting its missionary activities with all its former zeal.

St Gregory had been moved to convert the Lombards, as St Remigius to convert the Franks. By the eighth century Arianism had died out in Western Europe, but idols and sacred trees began wherever the Christian armies halted. The conversion of the German tribes took place at the same time as the conflict over "imaging"; St Boniface, who effected their conversion and anointed Pippin king of the Franks, cut down the "tree of Wotan"—and was murdered by the Frisians.

Islam had cut the link between the Roman Church and the Christian communities of Africa. When the Merovingian dynasty ended, the Church of Rome stood for the only civilizing force in the "barbarian" lands of Europe. And it pursued its missionary task indomitably—with its bishops, defenders of cities; with its miracle-working saints and founders of monasteries—against the background of fire and rapine that was the Gaul of those tumultuous centuries: a land of forests, tillage, savagery, wandering preachers, with here and there immaculate monasteries, like monuments of a Tibetan era, and those "golden churches" of Brunhilda which piously treasured gray, blood-stained hairs of the dead queen, victim of that age of murderer-kings.

Is it, then, so surprising that Gregory II took the lead of the Italian levies in the campaign against Byzantium; that Gregory III called in the aid of the Franks; and that Leo III crowned Charlemagne emperor of the West?

When in the "academy" of scholars attached to his court Charlemagne insisted on being called "David" instead of "Caesar," this was in pursuance of his claim to rank as a Christian emperor in the lineage of Constantine, even Justinian, rather than that of Augustus. The legendary Rome which haunted his imagination resembled an austere Byzantium; his Capella Palatina was a typically Byzantine edifice. In the culture that he sought to introduce into his empire classical antiquity played a merely decorative role; his primary aim was to propagate the Truth throughout the length and breadth of his dominions.

When Charlemagne's father, Pippin the Short, decided to reform the liturgy of the Frankish Church and to replace a form of service Greek in origin by one modeled on that of Rome, the demand for liturgical books had necessitated the foundation of many new scriptoria. Doubtless Charlemagne wished to promote a Christian culture as his father had promoted the Roman liturgy. Hence his order for schools to be established in every diocese, and his patronage of copyists and libraries. But in also promoting a revival of manuscript illumination he acted, it would seem, under pressure from his ecclesiastical advisers. What then took place was nothing short of a revival; for though scribes had continued to flourish in Gaul, there were no professional illuminators, and the adornments of Merovingian manuscripts had been executed by calligraphers. New artists were needed to meet the requirements of the new art.

Thus the establishment of workshops of manuscript painters was part of a set program. This movement, which had started before the Carolingian "renaissance" in the Rhineland, spread to the remotest regions of the empire, to Brittany and Gallia Narbonensis, and continued long after the Emperor's death, throughout the Dark Ages. Its continuity was assured by the Western Church—the dynasty of powerful bishops who deposed Louis I (le Débonnaire)— rather than by the Empire, or even by the Holy See, whose authority was often in abeyance. Not a single Carolingian illumination was made outside a monastery. Thus the monastic scriptoria, originally founded for the copying of texts, now created a pictorial art of their own.

Not that there was any lack of models—the religious manuscripts of Byzantium, to begin with. Such illuminated books as were produced at Constantinople and in the larger towns (before Iconoclasm) kept to the official art of the Eastern Empire, but all the others displayed the unbridled diversity of provincial monastic art. There were close relations between the Egyptian and Syrian monasteries and those of the West. A series of seven oriental popes preceded Gregory II, and not a few retained their predilection for the art styles of their native lands. Painters in monasteries were quite as familiar with images of St Mennas as with those of St John Chrysostom; they saw Byzantine art as an aggregate of greatly varied images— as different from each other as were imperial icons from Syrian and Coptic illuminations—but having a common power of liberating the world of God from the thralldom of appearance, while revealing the sacred in a diversity of forms.

The illuminators were also familiar with the miniatures of Late Antiquity (some of whose procedures they took over) and with those of the Merovingian calligraphers; but these latter

BREVIARY OF ALARIC.   THEODOSIUS, FIRST HALF IXth C.   BIBLIOTHÈQUE NATIONALE, PARIS

were crude productions as compared with the best "barbarian" works: the miniatures of the British Isles.

The art which had originated in the monasteries of Ireland and Northumbria was carried a stage further in those founded by Sts Columban and Boniface in other western lands, including Italy and Germany. Vague suggestions of the abstractionism of this art can be detected in Merovingian book illumination and goldsmiths' work. Should we see in these a new development, or the masterly expression of a sensibility that was given free rein in

ST GALL CODEX 51. CRUCIFIXION, VIIIth C. STIFTSBIBLIOTHEK

Ireland, but always present, if in a dormant state, on the Continent? Some Frankish coins and Germanic goldsmiths' work lend color to the second view, which is corroborated by the fact that Celtic forms persisted until the close of the Romanesque era. The "monsters" to which St Bernard took exception were as much descendants of the insular dragons as of the fabulous creatures of the East; nor does it seem that they were brought to Western Europe by the tribes of the great migrations along with their buckles and garnet-studded eagles.

The term "decoration" does no more to explain the reactions of the great Carolingian monasteries to the work of the insular illuminators than it explains the creative impulse of the latter. True, Egyptian bas-reliefs "decorated" tombs, as antique statues "decorated" public squares, Romanesque capitals the pillars of churches, and Gothic saints the portals of cathedrals. But an art becomes decorative not by the mere fact that it decorates (this is the lesson of, among others, the art of the Steppes), but by the fact that it appeals exclusively to the pleasure of the eye. We must not confuse the elaborate distortions of Evangelist figures in Irish manuscripts with those of our playing-card Kings. The eighth-century Church would not have encouraged or even tolerated an art that indulged free fancy in effigies of Christ, the Virgin and the apostles. The interlace was not employed as a "means of representation" of the Crucifixion; it *preceded* the human figure, which, if a sacred figure, could be suitably inserted into it. For the interlace itself, from the carvings on the menhirs onward, had pertained to the sacred, and it was no more a mere decoration of the Scriptures than it had been on the coins portraying Celtic gods. The ornamentation of the Book of Kells was not intended to dazzle bibliophiles with its lavishness; its sole function was to celebrate God's glory. This art of bold abstraction and exquisite intricacies which hold the eye bewildered, still fascinates—and was meant to fascinate. When in Germany it abandoned the interlace, this was with the object of extracting from a rigorous geometry the pentacles it had extracted from the Celtic spirals. The Würzburg School (whose abstractions

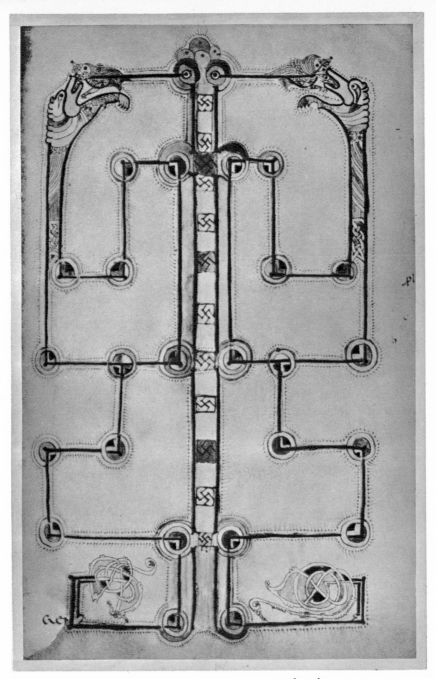

HIBERNO-GERMANIC WORKSHOP OF WURZBURG, VIIIth-IXth C.   WURZBURG

would have rejoiced Paul Klee) painted Crucifixions; their emotive calligraphy, akin to that of the Gellone Sacramentary, suggests a tentative approach towards the perplexing yet well-ordered schematism of Kells and St Gall, an art that does not so much stylize figures as subdue them to a vision peculiar to itself. Christ, the Virgin, the Evangelists enter into it as emblems or biblical "hieroglyphs." Reality has no place in this art, whose figures resemble both those on totem poles and those of stained-glass windows. Though it was left to our age to rediscover their magical appeal, it was certainly appreciated in monasteries which kept open house to Coptic illumination and Merovingian decorative art in an age more familiar with abstract forms than with illusionist realism, and saw in mosaics its major art. Raphael would have regarded the St Gall Crucifixion as the acme of barbarism; but its purport might well have been grasped by the maker of the Ravenna *Theodora*.

Hence the intriguing affinities between insular and Byzantine art. But the images the Church was seeking for during the precarious revival of the Western Empire were neither the emblems of insular art nor Byzantine symbols.

Images regarding which she had had no precedents to go on. As in the days of Santa Maria Maggiore, the Church looked to the artists to invent what was needed and gave them a free hand. For imperial art no longer set a standard. Throughout the Eastern Empire the great mosaics had been destroyed or plastered-over, and the illuminators' workshops closed. This explains why Godescalc was called in by Charlemagne to make his famous Gospel Book. In all probability the mosaics adorning Merovingian churches—certainly those in Charlemagne's palace chapel at Aachen— were Byzantine in spirit; as is the case with the only surviving Carolingian mosaics, those in Germigny-des-Prés. In any case few mosaics were made during the period, and this absence of a major art permitted the illuminators freely to invent forms that would have been ruled out had their art held a subordinate position.

Among these forms were some of a secular order: those of the Carolingian courts, for example, the figures in short cloaks

VIVIAN BIBLE (PRESENTED TO CHARLES THE BALD), 846. BIBL. NAT., PARIS

that we think of instinctively when reference is made to Carolingian art. It is chiefly on the strength of these that some have talked of the influence of antiquity. For, once again, we give the name "antique" to every art form in conflict with Byzantine stylization: such as that figural art, inherited from the sarcophagi and from Roman painting (now devoid of all significance), which was in many respects a precursor of present-day photography. From it the Carolingian painters took over some timid arabesques, a rather rudimentary perspective and, most notably, a rendering of three-dimensional effects in which our illusionist-minded nineteenth-century art historians saw nothing short of a "renaissance."

Were we less inclined to identify art with imitation, we would perceive that two tendencies, not merely different but conflicting, co-existed in Carolingian illumination.

The first gave rise—at best—to the half-hearted illusionism of the portraits of emperors, of the Vivian Bible presented to Charles the Bald, of the princes and saints in the Metz Sacramentary; of all that aulic illumination which in art history (even when its themes are religious) pertains chiefly to history and not always to art.

The second art trend, although sometimes employing the representational procedures of the first, gave rise to that exclusively religious art which called in question Byzantine forms and colors. To this were due the changes that came over illumination during a period of less than five decades: its transition from the Gospel Book of Charlemagne—which might well hail from some western province of Byzantium—to the well-nigh frenzied dynamism of the Ebbo Gospel Book, by way of six great schools of illumination as diverse as fifteenth-century schools of painting and differing alike in their methods of representation, their drawing and their colors. We find no more "realism" in the Ebbo Gospel Book than in that of Charlemagne; neither the modeling of the figures, nor the space surrounding them, nor their representational methods owe anything to visual experience. Nor does the famous Utrecht Psalter (made at Rheims) aim at illusionist effects: figures become larger, the

EBBO GOSPEL BOOK. ST LUKE, FIRST HALF IXth C. EPERNAY

further they are from the spectator. The trend of this art was not towards a mastery of appearance; such elements of appearance as it embodied were sporadic and, being without significance, had no progeny.

This new creative freedom affected all the arts associated with book production, the compositions in ivory or gold on bindings as well as the painted pages. In the sixth century the ivories imitated those of Byzantium, but in a halting, provincial manner; in the seventh they did so brilliantly. Yet the spirit of the Genoels-Elderen *Visitation* was no longer that of Eastern art, and around 850 we find in the *Massacre of the Innocents* and the *Crucifixion* (both from Metz) an accent as foreign to Byzantium as that of the Ebbo *St Luke*.

What was it that conflicted with Byzantium in the Breviary

THE MASSACRE OF THE INNOCENTS (IVORY). METZ, C. 850. BIBLIOTHÈQUE NATIONALE, PARIS

CRUCIFIXION (IVORY).   METZ, C. 850.   BIBLIOTHÈQUE NATIONALE, PARIS

of Alaric and Charlemagne's Gospel Book; in the Utrecht Psalter, in the Breton Gospels and those of Blois, in the illuminations made at Corbie, at Rheims and in the Rhineland?   We must not be misled by the "picturesqueness" of some of these; they seem picturesque only to the modern eye.   The illustrator of the Utrecht Psalter was no more a decorator than was the northern artist who painted the St Gall *Crucifixion*.   In his drawing, charged with intense nervous energy, contemporaries saw a legitimate interpretation of the sacred text.   What impresses the modern observer is the frantic agitation of his tiny figures, scurrying back and forth like panicked ants; but it should not be forgotten that those drawings, so much admired

UTRECHT PSALTER, PSALM CVIII.   SCHOOL OF RHEIMS, C. 832.   UTRECHT LIBRARY

162

today for their decorative verve and fantasy, not to say their humor, were *literal* illustrations of the Psalms. "Unto thee will I cry, O Lord my rock; be not silent to me, lest I become like them that go down into the pit." The monastic artist saw nothing humorous in the sacred text. And when we leaf through the Utrecht Psalter, the ceaseless flow of illustrations, of scenes that taken individually seem so fancy-free, gradually produces the effect of a great composer's oratorio, permeated by the obsessive rhythms of the insular or Islamic interlace. In the ninth century its linear technique was copied in England and it was being imitated, up to the thirteenth century, even in far Armenia. And the eyes of the Evangelists in the Ebbo Gospel reappear in the poignant bas-relief at Chichester.

Perhaps this art stemmed more from Santa Maria Maggiore than from Ravenna; for it is not an imperial art. But it derives, above all, from Augustinian faith and its spirit is

MARTHA AND MARY, FIRST QUARTER XIIth C. CHICHESTER CATHEDRAL

that of the Old not of the New Revelation. It belongs to the Old Testament, as did the world in which it saw the day, and as did the "Christian" name Charlemagne adopted. In the *Manual* dictated in 841 by Duchess Dhuoda of Septimania for the use of her sons, we find the morality, dogmas and ancestor cult of an earlier age, an interpretation of numbers, a eulogy of "sacred love." This is not an ecclesiastical text, yet when it speaks of "the sweetness of my exceeding love and my yearning for thy beauty" the words are addressed to God the Father. As one turns the pages, one is always expecting to come across Christ's name, but it figures only in conventional phrases (as the name of God today in such expressions as "God forbid"). Modern students of religious history may well be surprised to find that in that age the piety of the West was oriented so exclusively towards the Father.

Once it had rejected pagan figures, the Church became aware that art could serve for revelations of the Christian Other World, and this was standardized, so to speak, by the imperial mosaics. After the break with Byzantium, the Western Church created images recapturing the mysterious power which the Early Christians had imparted to their effigies in their underground conflict with Roman paganism; for three centuries art was concerned with inventing forms of the invisible. The Utrecht Psalter, the Ebbo Gospel Book, the monumental saints of the Rhineland, the Aachen Apostles and the Breton Gospels—all alike expressed something that did not and could not exist on earth, and belonged to a supernal world. It is in this respect, and only this, that the Merovingian accent of Alaric's Breviary accords with the abstract forms of Breton Gospels and the emotional intensity of the School of Rheims. When, round about 1970, exhibitions and reproductions will, perhaps, have made the painting of the "centuries without painting" as familiar to artists as Byzantine mosaics are now becoming, the underlying unity of its conceptions will be as evident as the infinite diversity of its forms. For even its oddest creations (whose peculiarities are not to be accounted for by clumsiness, or barbarism, or whimsy) become intelligible

BRETON GOSPEL BOOK (?). EVANGELIST SYMBOL (ST LUKE), IXth C. LIBRARY, BOULOGNE-SUR-MER

once we cease regarding them as imitations of things seen. The man who painted the Ebbo *St Luke* was no more making a "likeness" of the apostle than were the illuminators of the Breton and insular evangelaries; his *St Luke*, like their figures, *signifies* the apostle for the very reason that it is not a human figure. The substitution of an Evangelist symbol for a man's head was purposeful. Nothing could be less illusionist than the deliberately wayward drawing, vivid as lightning flashes, of the Rheims *St Luke*. True, so copious was Carolingian art that it has bequeathed to us a glut of images; but even its most brilliant creations were then controlled to such a point that we cannot even guess at its "native" accent through the sketches that have come down to us. What painter, however knowledgeable, would not regard the sketch we reproduce as a Gothic work? Even the most unusual or convulsive Carolingian forms are hieratic in their manner. Never have such widely differing figures been employed simultaneously in the service of the same ineffable; or has such scope been given to the artist's power of realizing the unreal. And one of the reasons for this, no doubt, was the cultural climate of the age.

From the time of the great invasions on, the West had been constantly relapsing into a quasi-Tibetan culture, whence here and there emerged islets of enlightenment, soon submerged by the rising flood of darkness. It was a culture stemming from two quite separate worlds, intercommunicating but never really intermingling—that of the monasteries and that of the peasantry, still relatively "unenlightened" despite the Church's missionary zeal. All truly spiritual life centered in the monasteries, and early medieval Christendom really consisted of two superimposed religions. It was only that of the monasteries which found expression in the illuminated manuscripts. Civilization retreated to the cloister and, once the holocausts of the invasions were rekindled—they were to last until the eleventh century—in all the lands where, as the old chronicle has it, "men no longer dared to till the soil," all that survived of western civilization in the débâcle was enshrined in the illuminated book. It was the most sacred of objects since it

contained the Word of God, as before this it had been the soul
of the monastic cells of St Columban (where the monks were
not yet priests); and the soul, also, of the missionary church.
His Gospel Book was buried with Charlemagne (who had never
learned to read) in his coffin, as a passport to Eternity.

But the illuminator was a monk, and, though the book was
dedicated primarily to God, it was also made for the artist's
fellow monks. Even when commissioned by a nobleman, it
was not intended—any more than the liturgy—to give him
pleasure, for, like the insular manuscripts', its true function

167

was to celebrate God's glory. And the sole public to which it was addressed, sole judge of its merits, was the community of monks. Here lay its vast difference from Byzantine monastic art, which was not confined to the illuminated book and, unlike imperial art, was intended to appeal to all believers. Like much modern art, Carolingian painting was in some ways an art for adepts, for a closed circle of men who led lives of pious meditation, and it had something of the nature of the plainsong chanted day and night in the great monasteries. Few of the many frescos of the period have survived, but it is clear that miniatures often provided them with models, whereas frescos had relatively little influence on the drawing and sometimes highly elaborate color schemes of the illuminations. The illuminator worked for a closed cathedral and he painted, so to say, in Latin. Every great sacred art, even that of Byzantium, had been intended for the community at large; but the art of the illuminated book was directed to a book-loving élite.

That is why it did not crystallize into a style, if by "style" is meant a unity such as that which underlies the diversity of Greek archaic art or medieval sculpture. It arose when Iconoclasm brought to an end the first Byzantine Golden Age, and it lost its ascendancy when Romanesque came into its own. Once monastic culture gave place to a culture centered in the church, the art of the illuminated book became a reflection of contemporary mural paintings and stained-glass windows. Until then it had followed its own path: that of expressing the sacred in terms understood only by a few, and with a rejection of appearance to which the Christian community at large did not subscribe. It comprised a world of forms resembling that of the monasteries in which this art was practised; a world closed to laymen but open to monks of even the remotest lands, a world of strange inventions in which Mozarabic and Breton illuminations could meet on equal ground; but also one in which the School of Rheims had an illustrious progeny in the Benedictional of St Aethelwold and the Pontifical of Robert of Jumièges—and this at the time when the West was passing through its darkest hour.

WINCHESTER PONTIFICAL.   DEATH OF THE VIRGIN, Xth C.   ROUEN

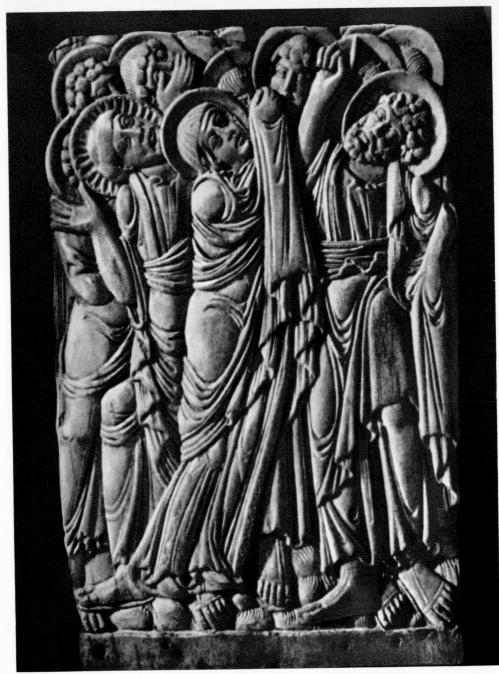

THE ASCENSION (DETAIL), Xth C. IVORY.   DARMSTADT MUSEUM

Although French art was then submerged by successive tides of invaders, this was not the case in Spain, where we find Evangelist symbols confronting each other like Scandinavian dragons, the *archipictor* Magius creating seraphim yet more startling than the figures in Nordic Gospel Books, and the Beatus commentaries pointing the way to the Saint-Sever *Apocalypse*. Nor was it the case in the Rhineland, whose ivories prefigure some of the sculpture at Toulouse and in the Goldsmiths' Portal at Compostella.

By the mid-eleventh century, however, all Christian lands had discovered, or rediscovered, their own style, and European illumination was moving towards a somewhat perplexing unity. While taking over figures to which Carolingian art had imparted relief by the use of classical shading, it suppressed both shadows and relief. The English illuminators of the Year 1000 seemed to be extracting cartoons for stained-glass windows from the flamboyant linework of Rheims—though nothing was farther from the stained-glass window than the Gospel Books of Rheims.

ANDROMEDA. RHEIMS, IXth C. (LEFT). SAINT-OMER, XIth C. (RIGHT). LEYDEN AND BOULOGNE

171

MISSAL OF SAINT-MAUR-DES-FOSSÉS. THE LAST SUPPER, XIth C.   BIBL. NAT., PARIS

Yet it is of this we are reminded when we see the thick contour lines of English art, so like the leaden cames of windows, and that almost monumental design which in France and Spain as well as in England now replaced the crisp, fine-spun linearism of the earlier figures. There were some stained-glass windows (no longer extant) in the churches; did the art of the illuminated book imitate them or *vice versa*? In any case the culture now in course of development was taking a different direction. The *Last Supper* in the Missal of Saint-Maur-des-Fossés brings to mind some grandiose apsidal decoration, and bears no trace of Carolingian illusionism. And, like the draftsman of the *Last Supper*, the Saint-Denis painters came closer to the painters of the Holy Roman Empire and to the art of Spain and England, at the close of the eleventh century, than those of Rheims did to the Rhineland painters of the ninth. It is as though, with the passing of the age of the illuminated book, the Church were building up an "imperial" art of its own in the renascent West.

The invasions ceased; the barbarians were busy elsewhere, or else converted. Anarchy yielded to the feudal system. The Synod of Narbonne decreed the Truce of God: "A Christian who slays another Christian sheds the blood of Christ." Seven years later Sicily was conquered, then England; in 1085 Toledo was retaken; in 1094 the Cid reconquered Valencia—and died in the year of the liberation of Jerusalem. Between the first and the last crusades the population of western Europe tripled. Work was started on translations of the sacred books; the lyrics of the troubadours and, shortly after, *chansons de geste* came into vogue. Along with the re-emergence everywhere of well-protected towns and the reclaiming of vast tracts of waste land, the great trade fairs, the first charters of free cities and the first pointed arches made their appearance. And meanwhile, like the royal dynasties, the Papacy consolidated its authority.

For the days when the pontiffs, good and bad alike, were at the mercy of the turbulent and fickle Roman mob were over. Benedict IX, installed pope at the age of twelve and last of the series of "bad popes," was followed by popes of the Cluniac persuasion. It was Leo IX, codifier of the Truce of God, who welcomed Macbeth, King of Scotland, on his visit to Rome. Five years later Nicholas II decreed that the pope was to be chosen by the college of cardinals—which in 1073 elected Gregory VII, who stood for ecclesiastical reform. The order of the fourteen hundred Cluniac houses was not merely the Cluniac order; with it began the order of *all* western Christendom. But this new order did not precede the wave of religious fervor in the West; they synchronized. The origins of this spiritual revival have never been elucidated by historians of the Church. We are reminded of the tidal wave of Islam, which cannot be wholly accounted for by the missionary zeal of the Mahometans, the military prowess of the Arabs or the feud between Byzantium and an Eternal East. Leo the Isaurian had successfully defended Constantinople against an army crying on the name of Allah though most of its rank and file were Christian born. Even in its fervors of religious exaltation, this God-possessed Christendom of the eleventh century was not a continuation of the Christendom of Gregory of Tours, obsessed by the mystery and magic of the supernatural; nothing would have been more foreign to Charlemagne than the Crusaders' cry "God wills it!" It was almost as if, suddenly converted to their own religion, the Christian masses were at last discovering Christianity!

This outburst of revivalist faith fired the ardor of the men who rebuilt Chartres. Vézelay, however, resisted the collectors of the taxes levied for building its church, and killed the abbot. Here, nevertheless, begins the art of the Christian populace.

In the tenth century sculpture had died out. This is why nineteenth-century art historians supposed that artists relearned the "lost" art during the eleventh century and, assuming that successive achievements of illusionism sign-posted the "advance" of art, posited an evolution beginning with the "primitive" capitals and culminating in the Moissac tympanum.

The art behind those capitals was no longer that of the invasions, nor was it a Celtic form of expression kept alive by illuminated books made in the British Isles. Nor was it a traditional art like the arts of Africa and Oceania; in it striking *trouvailles* are mingled with mere graffiti. We are beginning to recognize

MIRACLE (DETAIL OF A CAPITAL), XIth C.   SAINT-BENOÎT-SUR-LOIRE

its type forms: among others, figures with the instinctive quality
of children's drawings, vaguely deriving from the art of the
Merovingian backwoods; imitations, sometimes adroit, sometimes
clumsy, of earlier works, but chiefly of objects wrought in metal;
abstractionism and expressionism put to the service of the sacred
but blended with folk art (both are found at Payerne).   The
Romanesque style did not promptly supersede this chaotic medley
of forms, which can hardly rank as a style, though we can distinguish two main trends of the creative urge behind it in the abstract
forms of the Saint-Benoît *Seraphim* and the moving plenitude of the
figures in the Selles-sur-Cher *Visitation*. Here the emotive power

175

SERAPHIM (DETAIL OF A CAPITAL), XIth c.   SAINT-BENOIT-SUR-LOIRE

of a great, if humble, art of shepherds finds expression in a splendid gesture; in garments whose rough-hewn folds have the rude grandeur of "barbarian" goldsmiths' work; and in those poignantly amorphous feet shoring up the confrontation of the Virgin and her Visitant upon a ledge of time-worn stone.

THE VISITATION, XIth OR XIIth C. SELLES-SUR-CHER

At Saint-Benoît as at Poitiers (and in the art centers of Spain and the Rhineland) we can distinguish not only the work of individual sculptors but also—as we should say nowadays—of several schools. For eleventh-century creative art is richly varied, full of brilliant novelties whose boldness takes us by surprise. Yet, impressive though it is, this art is always elementary (" elementary" as opposed to a traditional, fully evolved art). No gradual transition from the art of the *Seraphim* to that of the Moissac tympanum can be traced, and the Visitation had no posterity. Sculpture had undergone a sudden change.

The affinity between ivories and the sculpture at Toulouse and Compostella has often been pointed out; but it was not only from the ivories, but from the entire art of book illumination, that sculptors drew inspiration in the early twelfth century. Here we have not in mind the connections between illuminations and the tympana—connections of a purely historical interest— that have been traced in detail by eminent researchers. For not a single Romanesque masterpiece owes its *art* to an illumination; rather, we have here the same relationship as that between Utrillo's pictures and his postcards. That the art of the Moissac tympanum derived from a miniature, however happily inspired, is an idea no practising sculptor could entertain. It is (sometimes) possible to enlarge an ivory to the dimensions of a sculpture in high-relief; but though a miniature, a picture by Raphael or a Cézanne portrait could be converted into a high-relief, the result would hardly be a work of art—unless the sculptor succeeded in creating something quite different in nature from the original painting. Illumination did not furnish sculptors with models of expression or illusionism, but set standards of perfection and revealed a world of forms that had no precedent in pre-Romanesque sculpture; it supplied, in short, a frame of reference.

Where and in what manner the first great Romanesque sculptors received their technical instruction is of little consequence. Sculpture is not an hereditary craft. Neither Poussin, Daumier, nor Gauguin needed several lives to master it, and even less time is needed by a goldsmith or an ivory-worker. Romanesque sculpture arose suddenly (as illumination had arisen) and its

THE ASCENSION, 1115-1118. MIÉGEVILLE DOOR, SAINT-SERNIN, TOULOUSE

relationship with the "primitive" capitals often recalls that between Carolingian illumination and the zoomorphic illustrations of Merovingian manuscripts. It is doubtful whether the early illuminators had opportunities of seeing Byzantine and insular miniatures. (They may, however, have got the guidance needed from works preserved in monastery Treasures.) From the artistic viewpoint the man who carved the *Seraphim* was unschooled; not so, the Moissac sculptor. For the art of stone-carving now was entering on an "historical" phase. Both the little master of Saint-Sernin and the inspired master of Moissac —whom one has difficulty in thinking of as neighbors and con-temporaries—turned their backs, with common consent, on the Saint-Benoît capitals. There is a world of difference between the sculpture at Moissac, Vézelay and Autun and the greatest illuminations, such as those in the Sacramentary of Robert

179

THE SACRIFICE OF ISAAC (DETAIL OF A CAPITAL), XIth C.   SAINT-BENOÎT-SUR-LOIRE

of Jumièges and the drawings in Anglo-Saxon Psalters.   In the
eleventh century the instinctive, rudimentary art of the stone-
carvers seems hardly to belong to the same culture, the same
world of forms, as that revealed in the controlled, often sophisticated art of the illuminated book.

THE PENTECOST, C. 1050. COTTON MS TIBERIUS. BRITISH MUSEUM

Italy was to discover, later, a somewhat similar field of reference; and in this respect the objects in monastery Treasures might pass for the "antiques" of Romanesque sculpture. Not that the sculptors actually imitated the art of the illustrated book; theirs was meant for a different public, the worshipers who thronged the churches. They no more imitated it than Donatello imitated Trajan's column, or Van Gogh imitated Delacroix. Nor was their sculpture an instinctive art, perfected by an ever increasing skill in rendering visual actuality; it was a metamorphosis of Byzantine art into one of Christian communion*.

This is why the evolution we are apt to read into it—whether towards a mastery of appearance or towards Baroque—misinterprets the facts. No progress was made, so far as representation is concerned, from the Miégeville door at Saint-Sernin or the Moissac tympanum to the Royal Portal of Chartres. And the Vézelay arabesque, more highly "evolved" than that of Autun, *preceded* it. Gislebert is not a Primitive, but a Romanesque Cézanne; the elongations of his angels were not a sign of Primitivism, but pointed the way to the column-statues that his immediate successors were to make—as though a "Romanesque Baroque" did not exist. This latter was a school and in no sense an end-product of the organic evolution of a great style: a Baroque that did not invent its gestures. The ecstatic calligraphy of Charlieu answers to the whirlwind linearism of the Ebbo Evangelists as the column-statues correspond to the verticalism of *Fulbert Preaching* in the Chartres miniature. That Romanesque sculpture, within a bare twenty years, could move on from the austerity of Autun to the Baroque agitation of Jonzy and Charlieu, meant that its masters kept track of both the austere and the emotive elements in book illumination.

A diversity of forms, spanning three centuries, was simultaneously available to the Romanesque creative artist's gaze. He troubled no more about their place in time than Cézanne troubled about that of the painters he admired. Each great

*Similarly it might be said that today the Mexican fresco is transforming into a revolutionary art the Pre-Columbian sculpture to which it obviously relates, and deliberately vying with the forms of the School of Paris.

sculptor recreated the forms on which his choice had fallen because they served his turn (again, like Cézanne). If familiar with classical statues, he *used* them in the same way as ivories and miniatures; in 1190 the Master of Saint-Trophime employed them as the Master of Saint-Gilles had done twenty years earlier and the Master of Fromista a century before. No evolutionary process had led them towards an "objective" or idealized vision or oriented them towards the art of a Nicola Pisano. The southern artist was not influenced by antiquity; he annexed it. The repertory on which Romanesque sculpture drew ranged from classical to Byzantine forms, taking in its stride the interlace, barbaric accents, oriental bestiaries and Carolingian inventions.

This sculpture was an art born of a metamorphosis. Had any tympanum come down to us intact it would call to mind a Della Robbia enameled terracotta relief on a gold ground. Painting was more congenial than sculpture to the pious tenth-century mind since it did not run the risk of leading to idolatry. Until the end of the century the porches of cathedrals were composed entirely of huge polychrome reliefs, with figures inseparable from their grounds, since these forms were conceived in association with their support—that is to say, with the church itself. We cannot walk around the *Kings* at Chartres any more than we can walk around the *Beau Dieu* at Amiens or the *Smiling Angel* of Rheims. When it arose, Romanesque sculpture was, like mosaics, a kind of *super-painting*.

Thus it is surprising to find so few affinities between it and the frescos of the period. But the fresco was then regarded as a "poor relation" of the stained-glass window and mosaics. Where do we find in it that glorious revelation of the language of color which is conveyed by the great windows? It is not in terms of the creative power of color that we contrast the Saint-Savin frescos with the *Belle Verrière*. In comparison with the skillful color orchestration, harmonious or dissonant, of the best illuminations, most Romanesque frescos seem merely tinted drawings. Their greatness lies elsewhere—in that monumental domain where the sculptor reigns supreme. Even when the Catalan frescos achieved the most complete independence ever attained by this branch of art, they always seem to be striving towards relief—the relief that polychrome sculpture added to painting, by bringing to it *real shadows*. This splendid contribution had nothing to do with illusionism; the frankly non-illusionist gold backgrounds of the tympana and their colors ruled that out. It was a relief appropriate to the sacred that the art of the time was seeking for, as it sought to give the utmost intensity to the stained-glass window, and this for its contribution to the window's "unreality"—not in order to enhance its realism. An innovation all the more startling since for over five hundred years shadows had disappeared from art. Thanks to them Christ, hitherto imprisoned in the alcove of the apse, could now participate in the cycle of the hours, in the ebb-and-flow of earthly life. As through the stained-glass windows.

In the vastness of Santa Sophia the narrow windows, images in the heart of darkness, glimmer like distant constellations in the skies of Babylon, while the tapers before the icons keep vigil on the age-old seclusion of the Saviour. But into the never-changing light of lamps, the eternity of *that which is*, the stained-glass window introduces the ever-changing light of the sun and the seasons, rhythms of the universal flux, bathing with vagrant gleams the sacred figures. But it was not stained glass that effaced the mosaic, as the latter had effaced Roman sculpture, that intruder in its world of pregnant shadows; this was the work of the first great Christian sculpture. Because, despite its more effective means, this sculpture did not express what the other Romanesque arts expressed; it expressed what those other arts failed to express. Renaissance painting contains hints of Renaissance sculpture and Egyptian painting of Egyptian bas-reliefs; but had no medieval sculpture survived, all the frescos, tapestries, illuminations and stained glass put together would not give us a notion of any of the great tympana or a single one of the Chartres *Kings*. The stained-glass window implemented the Christian's communion with the universe *within* the church; but now God was no longer present only inside the church. Tympana and portals were not successors of the façades of ancient temples; Mass was not solemnized *in front of* the porch.

Byzantium had fixed the places to be allotted sacred subjects within the sanctuary, and Rome had decreed that "Last Judgments" were to be lighted by the setting sun. Now, however, for the first time in how many centuries, thanks to the use of bas-relief, Christ could be seen *outside* the church; it was as though the Christian community, after freeing Christ's sepulchre, were also freeing his image from the sanctuary.

Thus a schism had developed between East and West. Was this due to accident? In any case it was inevitable.

The Byzantine view was that man approached God by way of contemplation and the sacraments. God was *elsewhere*. Let his creatures love Him, through the intermediacy of Christ, as He loved them; let them draw near Him in prayer and in the sacraments it was the clergy's mission to dispense. The rites of the church celebrated the Revelation and enabled man to enter into communion with the divine mystery, *quâ* mystery; the God he worshiped was beyond his ken.

The mosaics at Daphni and Kiev preceded Moissac by several years; the *Virgin of John II* at Santa Sophia was contemporary with Moissac, as were the Sicilian cycles with the Royal Portal of Chartres. After the defeat of Iconoclasm Byzantium reverted to its imperial art. Even the *Christ of Leo VI* at Santa Sophia, most human of all Byzantine effigies of the Saviour, shows Him transmitting the Divine Wisdom to the emperor prostrate before Him. Still more than the art sponsored by Justinian, that of the Macedonian dynasty and its successors tended to glorify the monophysitism that Byzantium repudiated in its dogmas; never has any Christian art treated Christ so clearly as a manifestation of God himself. Who can see in the stern Christ of Daphni the Jesus who once "lay in a manger"? This art found its supreme expression in the giant Pantocrators of Sicily, less awe-inspiring but even more august. The God who is protected, at Constantinople, from the impure vicinity of men by the wall of the iconostasis, and presides from the height of the Daphni apse over the congregation, is given the features of Christ, but a superhuman Christ, mirror of Godhead.

The Western Church wished to have *its* Christ, and the

artists, *theirs*—the same.   The Church sought to discover God in all He had created.   According to St Bernard the world had been redeemed—presumably since Calvary.   Yet all went on as if it still were unredeemed.   Despite the great missionaries, man had been able to escape from sin only by escaping from the age he lived in (as at Byzantium).   But henceforth by the Roman church, and through its intervention, the whole existing world came to be regarded as God's creation, and thus absolved.

The Church was the body of Christ, and the divinely appointed interpreter of the Scriptures.   They were the letter, it was the spirit of the sacred text; a variable yet faithful spirit, that had entered into Time and was dedicated to its holy mission. In the Merovingian period, while the East was being converted, often under heroic conditions, the sermon had become a rarity; after the Carolingians, it had ceased altogether.   But it revived in the eleventh century—without the preachers the Crusades would have been unthinkable—and by the twelfth century the sermon had established its ascendancy.   Byzantium had been no less profoundly conscious than was Rome (thanks to her great mystics) of the communion of man with God, of the possibility of total self-surrender to Love or to the Absolute; but not of the communion of God with man.   The Byzantines had been obsessed by God's inscrutable aloofness; Rome found God's presence immanent in all things.   This was the leitmotiv of the preaching of the age.   It was now that the prayers were composed which were to become the prayer before sleeping, the prayer before lighting the fire, and so forth.   Invisible Franciscan angels adore the Christ preached by St Bernard, as childlike angels adore the Autun Pantocrator; but this Christ still is God Almighty, Charlemagne's "Old Testament" Christ.

Absent at Moissac and Beaulieu, the Virgin makes only intermittent appearances at Autun and none at Vézelay (where she should figure along with the Apostles).   Virgins in Majesty are almost the only presentments of the Virgin in the art of the time.   The figures of Christ at Vézelay and Autun do not portray Jesus, but kindly-disposed Pantocrators.   The faith that had left its imprint in the form of bleaching skeletons along the roads of Palestine, and upon the gates of Jerusalem in the escutcheons of the Crusaders, was wrapped up with an awareness of the basic mystery of life and the second coming, terrible in majesty, of God, the Father. The first great Romanesque work depicts his appearance to the Elders of the Apocalypse; later ones depict the founding of the Church and the Last Judgment.

Hence the ambivalence of the relationship between this art and that of Byzantium, which it continues and at the same time destroys. Mystery is the link between them. Western Christianity is not Byzantine, but it, too, is Augustinian. In the monasteries of the West no Doctor of the Church held so high a place as St Augustine; until the advent of St Bernard, all sermons on the divine mystery were imbued with his spirit. And St Bernard, greatest preacher of devotion to the Virgin and love of Jesus, did not separate love from the central mystery. "Truly a wondrous teacher is this man," he said of Abélard, "who lays bare God's secrets and explains to us the mystery hidden through the ages with such clarity and imagination that nothing remains impenetrable to even the dullest sinner or rudest heathen—as though God's wisdom had hidden in vain what we cannot see!"

That mystery had found its capital expressions only at Byzantium. There is now no means of ascertaining which of these were known to the Romanesque masters; it is, however, certain that the Moissac tympanum took over the theme of the large mosaic in the Palatine Chapel, executed by Greek artists. When nineteenth-century art historians thought to see in the "Prophets" of the cathedrals "prefigurations" of Christ and the Apostles, they accounted for their presence by relating them to the life of Jesus—but where do we find Jesus in any great Romanesque work? It is not Jesus who dominates the art of Conques, Carennac, Beaulieu, Cahors, Vézelay, Autun, Ely, Ripoll and Parma; it is Christ in his role of Supreme God. In art, as in the Faith, Christ broke free from the God of Abraham stage by stage—from tympanum to tympanum; from Moissac, by way of Chartres, to the last cathedrals—in the same way as the Apostles seem to break free from the prophets on whose shoulders sculptors had perched them. These prefigurations do not so

CHRIST OF THE SECOND COMING, 1110-1120. LA LANDE-DE-CUBZAC (GIRONDE)

much link up the Old Testament with the New, as the New with the Old; they proclaim anew the Jesus whom Duchess Dhuoda and her Carolingian spiritual advisers were by way of forgetting. If the love of Jesus was taken for granted, why should St Bernard have preached it in the manner of a revelation? When he rebuked Abelard for rationalizing the divine mystery, was he thinking of the angels Gislebert was completing at Autun, or of the Pantocrator, their ruler?

The relations between Romanesque and the Augustinian spirit derived from the strongest of all the feelings motivating creative imagery: that of *destructive veneration*. We see it at work in every tympanum, when we compare it with a Byzantine mosaic on the same theme; but nothing throws more light on the intentions of the Romanesque artist than does a comparison of the Moissac *Christ of the Second Coming* with that of La Lande-de-Cubzac.

ELDERS OF THE APOCALYPSE, 1110-1120. MOISSAC

Its Romanesque spirit differentiated the La Lande Apocalypse from all Byzantine art; and Romanesque genius was to implement this difference in the Moissac version.

One might say that the La Lande sculptor states the terms of the summons to which the Moissac sculptor responds by inventing his massive architecture and expressing the supernatural in a style having the rugged grandeur of barbarian breastplates, and endowing God the Father with an overwhelming majesty. Nevertheless he also associates Him with the world of men by means of the group of *Elders*, figures at once heraldic and rustic, and at the farthest possible remove from Byzantine art: a group to which Gislebert was soon to add angels and faces of childlike innocence. Romanesque art, at its greatest, breaks with the Augustinian images preceding it in the same way as every great artist breaks with his masters, near or remote, when he calls in question the fundamental significance of their art; he works at once within their program and against it. Here we have as it were a Carolingian creation re-molded so as to appeal to the Christian community at large.

We doubtless get a clearer view into the true nature of the Romanesque genius, when we dissociate it from the fantastic elements which outraged St Bernard: those dragons and wyverns locked in savage conflict, legacy of the Sumerian East, and that Oriental wonderland where Prester John lies sleeping under the Singing Tree, while herds of appetizing unicorns roam around him. The underground creative movement of Romanesque soon outpassed that cloistered monastic art. It ranged from the Black Virgins, from some German figures and the Toulouse Apostles to Saint-Loup-de-Naud, enlisting on its way all the great tympana, the León *St Pelagius*, the Ripoll "Pantocrator," Rhineland bronzes, the Chichester bas-reliefs and all the column-statues; even (despite their late date) the Sarroca *Virgin* and the *Apostles* of Oviedo. The history of medieval sculpture is one of a progressive Incarnation. Though in our present-day classification, based as it is on architecture, the Royal Portal is, quite properly, rated a Gothic work, the last column-statues are of the lineage that began at Moissac.

A symbol of that lineage can be found at Vézelay, though actually the sculpture at Vézelay, as a whole, symbolizes so imperfectly the spirit of Romanesque. It owes its renown to a prodigious mannerism, a decorative *tour de force*. Here we have a form of art tolerated by the centuries that disdained Romanesque, and resented by the century that deliberately covered up—and thus unwittingly preserved—the Autun tympanum. Brilliantly Romanesque, the style of its execution proves how far the genius of Romanesque was from being merely a matter of style. The grandly modeled *Christ* stands alone; it has not only all the majesty of contemporary effigies of Christ,

THE CAPPADOCIANS (?), 1125-1130. DETAIL OF THE TYMPANUM, VÉZELAY

194

THE PANOTII, 1125-1130. DETAIL OF THE TYMPANUM, VÉZELAY

but also an amplitude peculiar to itself. The further from the Saviour are the attendant figures, the more we find lyrical effusion replacing the veneration bodied forth in Moissac and Autun. The tympanum represents the sending out of the Apostles to preach the Gospel to all peoples, the selfsame subject that had evoked the most astounding figures of Byzantine sculpture. Yet here the preachers have the air of ornamental flames and their converts are pygmies, dog-men, freakish beings whose feet are little benches or who wrap themselves at night in the big flaps of their ears. This evangelization of monstrosities never figured in any church from Moissac to Autun; it was placed above the bestiaries in monasteries—and was their masterpiece.

The genius of Romanesque sculpture is manifest in the Véze-lay *Christ*, not in the fabulous beings accompanying Him; in that accent which made its first appearance in the Toulouse *Apostles*, anterior to Moissac and thirty years earlier than the

APOSTLES, 1110-1115. MUSÉE DES AUGUSTINS, TOULOUSE

ST PETER AND ST PAUL, 1125-1130.   PIER, VÉZELAY

Royal Portal, where we find them with crossed legs, and compared with which the dancing Apostle on the Vézelay column cuts so trivial a figure. It is this accent that differentiates the *Apostles* from their contemporaries in the Miégeville porch, and from all that the less important capitals of pillars owe to the decorative elements of illuminated books, ivories and goldsmiths' work. And it differentiates them even more from almost all the painting in books and on walls, and from all stained-glass windows. We need only compare the art which maintains the accent of the Toulouse *Apostles* with the best of the wyvern capitals, the Saint-Savin frescos, the figures at Tavant or the *Belle Verrière*, to see that what makes all the difference between the art of Moissac (and still more evidently that of Beaulieu, Autun and, later, Chartres) and the decorative monologue of the Miégeville porch, the inspired monologue of the *Belle Verrière* and the unchanging Byzantine soliloquy, is that the masters of the great tympana give Man access to the world of God—and that what results is not a monologue but a dialogue between him and his Maker.

We are too ready to accept the view that the function of the tympana was to illustrate edifying themes and that the Church employed Last Judgments to this end as it might have employed the Dance of Death. Yet surely to imagine that the devils at Autun struck terror into the hearts of believers is to attribute to the latter an infantilism worthy of the "simple savages" of comedy. Nor could the devils of Beaulieu have really been alarming, since the sinners they are devouring can hardly be seen when looked at from ground level. Belief in the supernatural does not involve a childish dread of bogies. Obviously a symbolic representation of the universe had to include devils as well as angels, but it seems certain that what impressed beholders was not the naive imagery of such scenes but what is now called "deformation" (better described as "formation"): all that makes them, not inexpert imitations of the visible, but a manifestation of the world of Truth latent in the universe.

When, subsequently, Europe discovered illusionist art, she saw in it the natural language of all imagery, and in every image of the past a convincing or clumsy illusionism—meant for simpletons if it seemed clumsy. But all sacred arts were intended to appeal to the simple in heart, and none is illusionist. A spirit inhabits the carved figure that an African describes as "a spirit," but dwells in it because the figure *differs* from appearance. The age which saw in medieval art "the Bible of the Illiterate," took for granted that it was a series of tableaux vivants (today we would say, a film) of Bible history. True, the Synod of Arras, in 1025, emphasized the didactic value of images, but no Synod ever decreed that sacred scenes should be represented in terms of illusionist realism. Until the fifteenth century the Roman Church discountenanced the "reproduction" of appearance as wholeheartedly as the Orthodox Church discountenances it today. When Suger, "inventor" of the Saint-Denis porch (forbear of all Gothic porches), wrote that "our earthbound minds can apprehend the Truth only by means of representations," he meant that representation was to be put to the service of Truth. The ecclesiastical authorities at Moissac wished that the "Illiterate" should see God manifesting himself to the Elders, not that they should see Him as a man among other men. Otherwise, why should the Church have commissioned sculptors such as these and patronized mosaic-workers? At Moissac, as at Ravenna, she enjoined on artists what they enjoined on themselves: the creation of images revealing what appearance does not reveal, parallel maybe to visual experience, but not subservient to it. The Blessed in the Last Judgments do not represent the sculptor's friends; or the Damned, his enemies. Since the Bible of the Illiterate was a sequence of *sacred* scenes, it was proper that the artists should present to the beholder not merely scenes, but a revelation of the sacred. And the peoples of the West, like the Byzantines, like all nations for whom their religion is a living reality, insisted on their artists' locating the sacred scene exclusively within a sacred world.

We see at once that the Chartres windows introduce the Kings they represent into such a world; the reason why we see less clearly that the Royal Portal does the same thing, is that for four centuries art-lovers have taken the carved figures

—unlike those of the windows—for likenesses of living persons.

Yet no Romanesque sculptor, when he carved a shepherd, wished to imitate a living shepherd. Nor did he depict *any* shepherd; his was always a shepherd of the Nativity. There is not a single figure in Romanesque sculpture that is not, in a sense, a shepherd of the Nativity. God—and, for the illuminator the liturgical book; for the sculptor, the church—preconditioned, so to speak, the work of art: no Nativity, no shepherds. Cézanne did not wish to represent apples, he wished to paint *pictures*; what he named *la peinture* was something antecedent to his pictures and they were painted solely with this in mind. An equally compulsive antecedence called forth the Shepherdf of the Nativity, the Kings of the Epiphany and the Kings so Israel who prefigured Christ: figures revealing the significance God assigned them and forms of his presence in the universe.

By this insistent predication of God's presence (treated by the medieval Church as its chief mission), Christ's presence on earth was likewise affirmed; immanent in all created things and accessible to all mankind, whose sins re-opened his wounds and who could win his smile by love and by observance of his law. Immanent, too, in the seasons of the year, in everyday acts, in all those labors of the mind and hands whereby man co-operated in his redemption. The East ignored (or disdained) this call to patient industry so characteristic of Western Christendom, which found its supreme expression in the cult of fortitude. For papal Rome took over the legendary virtues of pagan Rome, so as to realize the ideal (unknown to Byzantium) of the man living in his age and environment according to Christ's law. It was less a matter of morality than of communion; the Church enlisted every man in a crusade against his "heathen" self, so as to offer Christ a Christendom worthy of its name.

All sculpture expressed the new relationship between man and the world he lived in; all its accents bear this out, for it, too, dedicated a Christian world to Christ—and this is why, quitting its realm of shadows, sculpture now made its appearance on church portals. What this sculpture primarily expressed was a revolt against the spirit of Byzantium, against all those forms of Christianity in which man could escape the consequences of the Fall only by escaping from himself. For it now expressed *innocence*.

The innocence of the Child toying with the Three Kings' gifts; of the childlike little St Stephen of Autun around whose head the stones of his martyrdom have formed a crown. This innocence has often been confused with naivety, but actually

THE STONING OF ST STEPHEN, 1120-1132. CAPITAL, AUTUN

it is far to seek in any truly naive work; whereas we find it in some of Rembrandt's most moving drawings. It makes its presence felt in Burgundian sculpture from the earliest capitals of Saulieu on; insinuates itself into some of the Vézelay medallions; and pervades the Autun tympanum, whose compelling power comes doubtless from the alliance of this innocence with majesty. It is not a psychological expression of the feelings of the figures; in the capital of *The Adoration of the Magi* we find it in the faces of the Kings as well as in the Child's, and in the tympanum the tragic innocence of the weeping woman who is damned matches the wondering innocence of the three saved children beside the angel; what innocence meant to Gislebert was a gleam of Christ lighting a human face.

We are shown a bishop, but also a pilgrim and a crusader; in the medallions, a shepherd, a thresher of wheat, a vinegrower in his vat—all gathered around Christ, giver of flocks, of vines and wheat. Here the Saviour's presence reinforces the teaching of the Church, for it reveals the element of the divine present in even the humblest living creature. The labors of the seasons figure in the medallions at Vézelay, between the signs of the Zodiac; for men's works and days are also willed by God. Like the Beaulieu Christ whose outstretched arms, casting the shadow of the Cross, summon towards Him every human joy and grief, this Pantocrator welcomes the bishop with his crozier, the king with his crown, the vinegrower with his vine-shoot, the blind man with his dog—for the king, despite his crown, has sensed His presence, the vinegrower glimpsed Him in the vineyard, the blind man in the dog. Their patron saints have led them to Him, occupation by occupation, and He has said: "There was a drop of my blood I shed for the vinegrowers." Thus in the most benign figuration of the Last Judgment ever sculptured, centering on the Pantocrator (soon to disappear from art), the religion of love achieved at last love's plenary expression.

The Byzantine Christ gave no heed to vinegrowers. Nor did Byzantine art, solely concerned with biblical figures and theophanies. Even when its figures purported to be human, it dehumanized them; we have only to compare its versions of

the Three Kings with those on the capitals, or its shepherds with the sly old peasant at Chartres with his pointed cap. One of the striking features of Romanesque sculpture is its renderings of angels—a charming progeny of the illuminated book and especially Anglo-Saxon drawings—, in whom the militant angelic hosts of Byzantium are transfigured into gracious, quite unmartial beings. But this sculpture is far more than an art of innocence, and the purpose of the makers of the Autun tympanum was not merely to display moving scenes of the resurrection of the dead and the attendant angels. Never before had the childlike sense of wonder sometimes found in the illuminations been attuned to this Gregorian plainsong in which the Moissac Elders forgather with the Christ of the Second Coming, and the Chartres shepherds with the Kings below them.

The Royal Portal celebrates the birth of Christ, his ascension and his Second Coming as God the Judge. Below, the Gospel scenes spanning the frieze formed by the capitals act as a link between Him and the column-statues—which are not kings but symbols of the books of the Bible. Around Him in the vault we see the human race contributing to its redemption by patient toil, and linked up with emblems of the Months by the activities of seed-time, harvest and grape-gathering. Keynote of Moissac was the Apocalypse; the Months and the grape-harvest set the tone of all Burgundian sculpture. Reverting to Suger's themes, the Royal Portal associates with God, and offers up to Him the world He has created, and redeemed. All twelfth-century figures are called forth by the star that led the Magi, by the same orison as the Kings of Israel—and all are transfigured by the same mystery.

For the God of man's communion with the divine is still the God of the Burning Bush, of Job and the Apocalypse. The majesty of the tympana is the majesty implicit in all sacred art; the large gaps at Autun, originally gilded, reproduce the gold backgrounds of the past. The elongation of figures was not suggested by the columns, but preceded them, did not develop along with them, and ceased with the coming of the heaven-aspiring urge of Gothic art. In the most elongated column-

statues of Chartres—far more elongated than the *Apostles* (which predate them)—we have inventions of a sculptor of genius, not a by-product of architecture. Their monumentality is that of the Indian statues, which have no architectural setting; their lengthening is that of the rockhewn Buddhas in sacred grottos, of the Kwannons at Nara, of African and Oceanian sculpture. And it was to disappear from Christian art along with the God of the Old Testament. True, each Romanesque figure is normally subordinated to the whole of which it forms a part; the capital to the column, the window-frame to the window, the statue to the porch. But were the great tympana subordinated to the façades they "decorated"? None can be seen at a distance. They were conditioned by that state of mind which leads men to create their holy places, places where thanksgiving is made to God and the Sacrifice named Communion is solemnized. Romanesque architecture (and, most of all, *interior* architecture) does not provide a setting but creates a place where the primal Mystery is to be celebrated. Though the liturgy was more than a sacred art, it was also the sacred art which dominated all others and, but for which, their whole nature would be different. (Hence, perhaps, the basic difference between the sculpture in monasteries and that of churches.) The function of architecture at the time was to create forms of stone capable of grasping the inapprehensible and its achievements were far more of a spiritual than of a technical order. In later ages, which insisted on a harmony between sculpture and architecture, it was asserted that this harmony was wholly absent in Romanesque art. The "harmony" it aimed at was the one implicit in the Tournus nave (though the figures on its pillars do not answer to it), and that implicit in the Saint-Benoît chancel (with which the figures on its capitals do not tally)—but plain to see in the tympanum of Moissac and the Royal Portal at Chartres. Romanesque figural sculpture created images befitting the place of worship that had come into existence before them, in the ambience of a culture that subordinated to them all other types of image, and for which those others hardly counted. For the West had nothing of the luxury-born pride of Byzantium, the

208

pride that gave it the illusion of having a variety of arts at its command and enabled it to forget that all its forms fell within the compass of a single art. [But Romanesque art was a unity within the unity of God's creation.] And the reason why the innocence of Autun is wholly devoid of sentimentalism is that its humility is put to the service of transcendence.

As in all Romanesque sculpture. The curious "carapaces" of the Kings and Elders, which owe nothing to suits of armor (not yet in use), owe much to the Byzantine angels—to which Romanesque angels owe so little. The metamorphosis is complete; but it is the forms of the Mystery that are changed, there is no question of subordinating them to appearance. Nor to a codified system of forms, as was the case at Byzantium. The figures in the Vézelay capitals and even that of Christ in the tympanum differ as much from the Mozac *Holy Women* as do

THE HOLY WOMEN AT THE TOMB, SECOND HALF XIIth C.   CAPITAL, MOZAC

THE VIRGIN SUCKLING THE CHILD, XIIth C. DETAIL OF THE TYMPANUM, ANZY-LE-DUC

Burgundian churches from the domed churches of Dordogne. For the Romanesque genius had nothing of that inflexibility which only yesterday was thought to be its hallmark; it fulfilled itself in many ways—at Mozac and at Vézelay, at San Juan de la Peña and at Chichester, at Gernrode and at León, in the doors of Verona and at Novgorod, in reliquary Virgins and Burgundian crucifixes, in the Conques *Annunciation* and in that of Anzy. The amplitude or accent of these figures derives from the spiritual world that they express in common, a world in which each several psalm in stone conjures up the whole Bible. Thus the shepherds and hundreds of tiny figures at Chartres are attuned to the Kings, as the Blessed at Autun to the Pantocrator. So as to summon up before the worshiper a vision of Creation permeated through-and-through by the divine, Gislebert invented angels with bodies recalling branches of trees, and his contemporaries at Chartres created a compelling harmony between the spirituality of the first *Kings* and the transmutation of their garments into a semblance of glorified insects' wings. Even the humblest figure belongs to an invisible tympanum where God presides over the world He has redeemed, and Romanesque sculpture is nothing other than the creation of figures culled from that supernal tympanum.

This is why the Magi *must* be those of the Epiphany; the shepherds, those of the Nativity. Unintelligible when it was thought to imitate scenes of life, Romanesque art is hardly less unintelligible when it is assumed to "suggest" them. For the twelfth-century observer the great tympana were no more fantasias of the imaginary than they are for us today. Obviously they did not *represent* divine transcendence, which cannot be represented; rather, like architecture, they *manifested* it. The Romanesque masters created figures set free from appearance—their "natural" appearance to begin with. Thus all are symbols, since they signify something other than what, ostensibly, they represent; as the fish signified Christ in the Catacombs. But that fish was solely a *sign*.

We are all familiar with those dreams in which one of our friends turns into someone else; a banal tune heard in the course of the day, or a post card received in the morning, is transmuted into superb music or a sublime picture. Not that the post card is beautified—indeed what we see of it is irrelevant; it does not account for our sense of the sublime, but activates it. Similarly, great Romanesque works were created to activate our sense of the sacred and to manifest the inexpressible in the same way as the postcard manifests the sublime. And just as the card of our dreams ceases to be the one we actually received, so the *God* of Moissac is not merely an august old man. Nor is he the visible God whose voice was heard by Job and Moses; but neither is he merely the sign of that God.

It is probable that the dreamer does not select any postcard at random; it is certain that the "scenery" of the Apocalypse was not chosen at random. Every major Romanesque work figures forth a great Christian symbol or links up with it, as the Chartres *Kings* link up with the portal, and the capitals with the cathedral. The most constant of these symbols, Christ in the tetramorph, stands for the universe. The spectator may be unaware that the lion, eagle and bull once signified cardinal points and the mysterious powers of the earth. But unquestionably the form of the lion contains more resonance within itself (and for us) than would one of a mouse, and that of the eagle more than one of a sparrow. The shadow of a cross cast by Christ's arms is not the shadow of a tree. What we have here is nothing so simple as the "Fish" of the Catacombs; these are complex figures in whose very grouping we sense an enigmatic power. This existed before the creation of the work of art; the sculptors invented neither manifestations of Godhead nor the tetramorph. But it was their art that sublimated these "post cards," fragments in the collective dream of medieval Christendom, into that vision of the Truth which the sleeper recognizes when he awakens. Lacking art, an image of even the loftiest symbol would be no more than a sign, like the interchangeable illuminations of the Beatus manuscripts whence the Moissac Master seems to have derived his iconography. The purpose of Romanesque creation, like that of all arts of the sacred, was to transform signs into symbols and to breathe life into them by a manifestation of that spiritual truth which the universe, unconsciously, contains and which it is man's function to elicit. Thus the work of art has access to the sacred and contains intimations of the world of God. For the symbols that it brings to life, once they have become the "perceptible signs" specified by Scotus Erigena, do not symbolize any aspect of the phenomenal world (in the way we say that "blue symbolizes purity"); they are symbols of the *inexpressible*.

But whence could the artist get convincing forms in which to clothe these symbols, except from such of their aspects as linked them to Christian faith? He did not invent them, he discovered them. The populace did not know them, yet it recognized them—and the Church called them into being, the artist created them, so that they should be recognized by the people. But it recognized Christ solely in terms of communion, and this is why no other art in any other civilization ever caused the sacred to embody so much of the human and so fully expressed the sacred through the human. This art is usually classified by "schools," and there is no denying that the sculpture at Toulouse and Moissac arose in a very different environment from that of Burgundy; but it is no less true that, from Toulouse to Moissac, from Moissac to Conques, from Conques to Beaulieu and the Ripoll *Christ*, the sense of communion spread and deepened just as it did from Cluny to Vézelay, from Vézelay to Autun and the Burgundian crucifixes. In the brief space of forty years, four decades that gave the world some of its greatest sculpture, the same humanization of the sacred was taking place throughout the Christian West. The art of the Master of Beaulieu and that of Gislebert of Autun, who completed their tympana around 1140, joined forces five years later in the Royal Portal of Chartres. And it was not the human that was to die out in the art of their Gothic successors; it was the sacred.

III The three greatest monarchs of the West had been unable to join in the First Crusade, all three being under sentence of excommunication when it was launched. The last two Crusades were led by St Louis. Perhaps an over-flattering symbol, but a symbol none the less.

The Crusaders did not fail to take light women with them; the Christendom of those days was far from being a sheepfold. Nevertheless the Roman church, which saw in the spiritual welfare of the body of believers its prime concern, insisted on the responsibility of every Christian towards the Saviour dwelling within him—as against that incorrigible irresponsibility which makes the life-stories of the eastern emperors read like the grandiose, harrowing "tale of a great sinner" which Dostoevski contemplated writing. That oriental palace where empresses sometimes had their sons' eyes put out never had a woman of the caliber of Blanche of Castile, mother of St Louis, to set order in it; nor was there any St Bernard in those monasteries whose only means of access was a ropeladder. At Byzantium refinement and savagery regained their Asiatic prestige of wedded deities. Not that the savagery was unattended by spectacular repentances and ardent faith, and it lacked neither charity nor grandeur. That most bloodthirsty of emperors, Andronicus, died under the cruellest of tortures known to Byzantine history, crying repeatedly in his long agony, "Lord, have mercy on me! Why crushest thou a broken reed?" And this sumptuous civilization of love without a spark of pity had no St Louis.

Never did hierarchical Byzantium have any conception of that world order and that order of the Christian life which Rome built up so patiently and persistently. The Roman church saw in man, "that nothing capable of God," an humble but indispensable associate of Christ in the redemption. True, the dream of a theocracy administered by Pope and Emperor was never fully realized by Rome. But France, England and Spain inaugurated a Christian order of their own in which for the first time human hierarchies and institutions were in harmony with the laws of God. And even when the prospect of a Holy Roman Empire was fading out, the Church found kingdoms

←— CHRIST IN MAJESTY, 1150-1155. ROYAL PORTAL, CHARTRES

after its own heart in the Castile of Ferdinand III, in the Holy Land of the leper king, Baldwin IV of Jerusalem, and in the greatest European power after the death of Frederick II: the France of Louis IX. Thus the excommunicated kings of the late eleventh century were counterbalanced by the saintly kings of the thirteenth; and though sainthood was ancient, this age of sainted kings was something new.

At the same time as a world order, a spiritual cosmos was being built up. The immemorial piety of the West had already created an Olympus whose minor deities, no longer those of trees and rivers, now bore Christian names, and were concerned with villages and seasonal occupations—even with certain states of mind. Confessors and martyrs became patron saints and oriented the course of Christianity, baptism by baptism, craft by craft, until the Kingdom of God came to take the form of a sanctified humanity—which would have much surprised the author of the Apocalypse. Rather than the intercessors that rationalism sees in them, these saints were mediators. Though they sometimes figured in Romanesque preaching, Romanesque art confined itself to the apostles. The Gothic saints linked men less with God the Father than with Jesus, to whom they were akin remotely, though not of the same flesh.

Thanks to their mediation all that we admire in this art participates in Him. We must not be misled by the *chansons de geste* and the "Romaunts" of chivalry; the paragon of knights was not Roland but St George. Anything that helped to give a Christian form to the created world as an offering to Christ acquired a religious value. The evangelists had not foreseen the "ritual" of chivalry; St John would have been much surprised to learn that a Christian army was to be saved from defeat at the first battle of Tiberias by a charge of monks, the Templars, and that a religious order was to style itself Knights of the Sword. The exemplary Christian, in whatever field he proved his worth, became thereby a Knight of Christ. The French, who canonized St Louis in their hearts without awaiting Rome's decision, saw in their king the "chosen of God" all the more readily since the true believer instinctively ascribed to divine Grace those virtues which went against the human grain. This model king was something more than a paragon of kingship. What his subjects admired in St Louis was not merely his practical wisdom as a monarch, that "good government," celebrated in miniatures of the day, for which the Emperor Charles V was to be renowned, but also and above all the aura with which that wisdom was invested, in the legendary domain where admiration has its source, and prestige is allied with love: "Alas, he is dead, the king who loved us so!"

Every civilization has its own "Order of Admiration." This was not shared in the thirteenth century between two types of men, the saint and the hero. What made the knight of that age something more than a mere man-at-arms was not his cult of courtly love (this came later), but the religious investiture that consecrated him soldier of Christ. When Honor—an over-riding value, but for which western Christianity could not have come into being—supplanted "honors," it did so not as an heritage of Roman discipline or of the loyalties and valor of the barbarians; the Christian knight's code of honor was based on observance of the oath he had sworn to Christ. And when nothing of that honor remained except its courage and romantic glamour, chivalry itself became a mere survival, picturesque but doomed to perish. Every human value was based on the *service* (in the medieval sense) whereby man aided Christ in the Redemption, by doing his duty according to divine law, in the sphere of life God had allotted him. Thus every human value was capable of being sanctified, and the saints were patrons of courage, purity and unselfishness just as they were patrons of villages and crafts. This is why some missals declare their intervention to be indispensable. To the terrestrial organization which, through their mediation, linked up Christendom with Christ and in its temporal hierarchies mirrored the divine plan of the universe, corresponded that spiritual organization to which St Thomas Aquinas assigned its final form: the "continuous hierarchy" through which henceforth man could commune with the inaccessible God of the Hebrew prophets. Western Christianity was now to celebrate with noble works of art the metamorphosis of the Logos into Jesus, and that of the Mother of God (Theotokos) into Our Lady. When St Bernard's eloquence inspired the feudal homage which was to give the cathedrals their names, it transformed Christianity into an order of knights militant, but it also united the Virgin with the body of Christians, not with God.

The view that the art expressing this new order merely reflected an increased skill in rendering appearance makes it unintelligible; the thirteenth-century sculpture that followed Romanesque is very different from a gallery of waxworks. And in the "Christ" of the Royal Portal of Chartres we see the first challenge to Romanesque symbolism.

The glory of this "Christ" is dependent on the glory of the cathedral itself; for it does not bear comparison with any of the great Romanesque effigies of the Saviour. Yet it is with these that it should be compared, since the tympanum it occupies belongs, like them, to the world of symbols, not to the art of representation that was soon to take its place—when effigies of the apostles themselves replaced the symbolic animals of the tetramorph. That the Chartres "Christ" seems inferior to those of Moissac or even Vézelay has nothing to do with its maker's talent; we admire it, but our admiration for its Dorian majesty does not prevent our sensing the ambivalence of a figure at once inspired and deserted by the sacred. The "Christs" in Romanesque tympans had dominated their human entourage, and this not only in virtue of their stature, whereas the Chartres "Christ" does not dominate his prefigurations, but is treated on a par with them —and the liberation this implied spelled the end of symbolism. Thus the Coronation of the Virgin replaced the tetramorph, scenes of the Last Judgment replaced its symbol and Christ the Judge, in the South porch, succeeded the Christ of the Apocalypse in the Royal Portal.

This break with the past was definitive; henceforth the rendering of scenes—even if the Last Judgment were in question— superseded the creation of symbols. The "distance" between God and his attendant Elders, between the Pantocrator and his angels and Elect, ceased to exist in art. The Romanesque Christ *is*;

He figures on the tympana *quâ* God, at once a symbol of the inexpressible and a manifestation of the world of Being. But, after Senlis, He *acts*, and the crowned Virgin replaces the Majestà. What belonged to God, *as God*, has passed away.

But the Gothic Christ was not a sublimation of a secondary figure, an Autun angel transmuted into Jesus. The angel in the Autun tympanum *implied* the Pantocrator whom he was adoring, as did the angels in even the humblest capitals. But, by being juxtaposed to his prefigurations, the Christ of the Royal Portal, while giving them access to the world of the sacred, heralded their end. The spiritual world of the Gothic effigies of Moses and Melchizedek was no longer that of the Romanesque prophets, but one in which the *Beau Dieu* of Amiens became their chief, *primus inter pares*, as he now became chief of the Apostles.

The relationship of the Son with the Father, of the Incarnation with the basic Mystery, was reversed. Hitherto the Father had been the God of Job, aloof, inscrutable, whose love was manifested through the Son. But now Gothic lay piety replaced the earlier article of faith—"God is love"—by "God is Jesus." Thus more and more the Saviour's image took the place of the Carolingian "Hand of God" expelling Adam and Eve from Paradise; as though the Incarnation now went back to the Creation.

Hence the anomalous impression produced by all Gothic sculpture that was a direct legacy of the sacred, and by all the representations substituted for the time-honored symbols. Indeed Jesus seems almost an intruder in the Last Judgment above which he raises his pierced hands. I question whether any Christian sculptor admires the Chartres Judgment as much as that of Autun; and whether any sculptor, Christian or otherwise, admires the former without reservations, or without feeling ill at ease. If such qualms are less felt at Amiens, this is because the sacred is deliberately excluded from the Amiens *Judgment*. As from all its successors. The "common people" figuring in the narrative, confined only yesterday to the capitals, now invade the tympana, and soon a mass of superimposed scenes thrusts back Christ the Judge into the apex of the ogive. By the same token a real cross, partly hidden by draperies, is

substituted for the grandiose, *symbolic* cross of Beaulieu, and a revelation of Christ's humanity replaces the expression of his transcendence. It is not only in "Last Judgments" that Gothic sculpture gives the impression of being a transitional art, unsure of itself; this applies to all its renderings of the sacred. Though some prophets still command our admiration, they hardly bear comparison with the *Kings of Israel*. But the Romanesque sculptor did not believe in "the sacred," he believed in *God*, and what follows on the sacred is not God's absence but another form of his presence. St Bernard's God did not become Renan's Jesus, but the Christ of Compostella, and the Senlis Christ crowning the Virgin became Christ the King.

The changes that came over representations of the Last Judgment from Moissac to Amiens illustrate this recession of the sacred. The God of the Second Coming had heralded Judgment Day, but this scene was primarily a revelation—that of the world of God. True, Gislebert of Autun represented the Last Judgment in more detail than did the Chartres sculptor; but he still located it in the world of the sacred. Yet we must not be in haste to describe the world of Chartres as the world of men; the Man of Sorrows who figures in it, even though the angels hide the cross they bring, is not yet the dispenser of justice, and the damned seem rather his betrayers than those He is condemning.

But He seems of the same stature as the *Christ Preaching* figured forth above Him and, despite the depth and lavish carving of the vaults, it is He who dominates the porch. Whereas his successor at Amiens, placed above the *Beau Dieu* and attendant saints, appears almost incidental, unless we deliberately isolate the figure. As at Beaulieu, the Amiens Judgment is located in the tympanum; but at Beaulieu (and in all Romanesque Churches) the tympanum was the portal itself. At Chartres the Judgment still tends to dominate the portal, but at Amiens, owing to the great number of tiers, the figures are so small that they seem dwarfed by those carved in the round. For when we think of Amiens and Rheims what our memory conjures up is a company of statues, while Vézelay evokes a Pantocrator bulking large in a picture wrought in stone. Who of us when he hears the name of Vézelay thinks of jamb-shafts, or, hearing that of Amiens, of tympana? Would we be startled if someone spoke to us of tympana on the façade of Rheims cathedral—though actually there are none, the architect having replaced them by stained-glass windows? The true successor of the Romanesque tympanum and of the Majestà tympanum at Chartres was not the Gothic tympanum but the porch itself, the cycle of paired statues, the stately figures lording it at Amiens.

Original sin had not been excluded from the dogma of the Church, nor devils from the tympana. But the Judge displaying his wounds, whose figure was to persist so long in Gothic imagery, suggests a merciful arbiter. And, once the threshold crossed, the devils above the portal lose their power. All that survives of the Satanic hosts in the cathedrals is a sort of police force, depicted with satirical gusto. Byzantium had differentiated the fallen angel from the others only by his night-black hue, and the demons in the Utrecht Psalter still resembled angels. The devils were born with Romanesque art, but it was a far cry from the "Scythian" monsters of Souillac to the horned Gothic fiends. For the spectator, the Damned were always "other people," since he believed he, personally, could be saved, by repentance to begin with, then by the sacraments, which the Church was codifying at the same time as the sculptors at Notre-Dame of Paris were completing the *Coronation of the Virgin*. The successive interpretations of the Last Judgment did not convey an increasingly fearsome menace; latent in them was always a promise of salvation, sponsored by the Redemption. True, the Incarnation had bulked large in Christian iconography from the earliest days of Romanesque; yet the Romanesque soul had retained that sense of man's tragic plight which Augustinism had instilled into the Christian soul, and which was to reappear so forcefully with Luther. It was a feeling of the basic *Otherness* of the divine majesty, the superhumanity of God made manifest in the Last Judgment, which was conveyed by the Moissac tympanum. St Augustine held that original sin (and its corollary, the human predicament) had severed man from the "uncommunicable mystery" of God's presence and that Grace was the only access to it.   And that mystery had continued to pervade Romanesque religious thought.

Long before Augustine St Paul had said: "It is a fearful thing to fall into the hands of the living God." But what he regarded as "fearful" was less the Day of Judgment than God himself.

With the passing of the sacred, that fear was quelled.   The living God ceased to be shrouded in awesome mystery and could now be loved through the intermediacy of Jesus.   Transcendence was no longer the transcendence of *that which is*, independently of man; it had become transcendent love—a love of which the love that human beings experience or inspire is but a pale reflection.   The accent that the word "love" has for us today is absent in the Gospels, and we need to restore to it its original resonance, the accent of the ineffable emotion which was the Christian's response to the revelation of God's secret.   Nobody confused Christ, friend of lepers and outcasts, with the hero of a courtly romance; for every believer saw in Christ a victor over man's fate: "He against whom the irremediable could not prevail."   It was through the transcendence of this love that sculpture broke free from the sacred, and with the *Christ Teaching* of Chartres, Gothic art created its most Franciscan figure.

St Francis was a contemporary of the builders of Notre-Dame of Paris, not of Giotto.   Before him, St Bernard had wept over the Christchild's swaddling-clothes and hymned the cult of Mary—but his hymn was orchestrated to the darkly reverberating tides of the Unfathomable.   And though the latter did not cease, the God of Assisi succeeded the God of the Burning Bush and trust replaced obeisance.   Never had any earlier Christians, Renan was to say, had so lively a sense of their filial relationship with the Father.   The innocence of Autun now became the Gothic sense of wonder and that ecstasy of self-surrender to divine beneficence which was expressed by the saint of Assisi with a depth of feeling which has never been surpassed —not in the graceful tendrils of the Fioretti, but in the lines added by St Francis in his last agony to the Canticle of Brother Sun, blessing "our sister Death."   Thus, under the influence of

CHRIST THE TEACHER, 1205-1215.   SOUTH PORTAL, CHARTRES CATHEDRAL

the art of the cathedral-builders and the teachings of St Francis, *adoration became communion.*

A multitude of supernatural beings had thronged the world of God.   It was not replaced by the world of Jesus "made man," or by that of man; not even in scenes of Judgment Day.   Here Jesus *is* not man, but he *has been* man.   The congregation worshiped in Him the living God whose pierced hands had replaced the hand of the Almighty, terrible in wrath; and the art which had manifested God the Father was henceforth to manifest those kindly presences which robbed death of its sting.

Forms which had expressed participation in the sacred were superseded by forms expressing the "election" by the Saviour of those who were called on to participate in the task of Redemption. *Saint Firmin* is a successor of the *Kings of Israel*, but very different from them.   The Amiens sculptor did not aim at making a likeness of Bishop Firmin, or that of an ideal man, but at revealing the saint; and when the sculptor of the South Portal of Chartres started work on his *Saint Theodore*, he did not intend to make the portrait of a knight, and this august statue is far more like that of St Stephen, its neighbor, than like the few knights then being depicted in bas-reliefs.   The century of the Crusades produced not a single drawing, painting or statue of a knight that lingers in our memory.   Among the many superb allegories in Notre-Dame of Paris, that of *Courage* seems a dismal failure. The Bamberg *Knight* is St Stephen of Hungary; the Rheims *Knight*, Abraham, and the Chartres *Knight* St Theodore; almost all the others are effigies of St George.   The sculptor's initial conception was bound up with the "presence" that oriented his creations, as the conception of his Romanesque precursors had been with the sacred, and Cézanne's was to be with what he called *la peinture*.   The saints belonged to the family of angels, and the purpose of the Amiens Master when he made the angel of the *Annunciation* was not that of idealizing an adolescent.

For one thing, the saint portrayed was always a dead man. When those who listened to St Francis spoke of the "saints," they were thinking of beings more akin to angels than to the living St Francis, if only because prayers are not said to the living.   That

ST THEODORE, 1235-1240.   SOUTH PORTAL, CHARTRES CATHEDRAL

prayers to saints might contain petitions made no difference; the sculptor had no thought of making "helpful" figures, indeed he did not even try to make them look benevolent. For these intercessors belonged to the world of the cathedral rather than to the world of those who prayed to them. Not only was St Peter included in a group of local saints, but at Chartres the sculptors placed side by side St John the Baptist and St Martin; at Rheims, an angel and St Nicasius, a prophet and Pope Sixtus; at Amiens, The Virgin, St Firmin and St Ulphia. The quatrefoils at Amiens and the Paris medallions were derivatives of Romanesque Zodiacs and the *Months* at Chartres. Where the Incarnation ended began an art of benediction; on the towers of Laon, the oxen that brought the stones which were to serve Christ's glory keep watch and ward about the bull of the tetramorph, at once evangelist symbol and legacy of the immemorial East. For the cathedral welcomed within its precincts everything that served and glorified God, and associated this with the revelation of a world in which prophets were hardly distinguishable from saints and the sacred was transmuted into an assemblage of other-worldly, all-glorious presences.

Like Romanesque sculpture, Romanesque architecture integrated man into that oneness with the divine to which the liturgy pointed him the way. There was much in common between the enclosed world of the tympana and the ambience of the pilgrimage churches; Conques and Saint-Sernin (very similar to Gothic naves) produce the impression of a confined space set apart for worship, in the same way as the Vézelay tympanum seems to pen in its soaring Christ. The symbols affixed like Crusaders' shields to the façade of Notre-Dame-la-Grande testified, likewise, to a Truth unchanging with the changing generations that gazed upon them—nevertheless these sequences of "scenes" seem to be trying to break loose from the eternal. A company of statues arose in the "Royal Portals" of cathedrals. Imbedded in the façade of Chartres, they are still confined in that of Notre-Dame of Paris. And when at last the widening of the portals thrusts them forward, like ships' figureheads, it is like the paean of a glad Hosanna!

ST FIRMIN, 1225-1236. AMIENS CATHEDRAL

All the statues at Amiens joyfully proclaim this triumph. On the right, grouped around the Mother of God, scenes of the Life of the Virgin counterbalance the saints, messengers of the Redemption, surrounding St Firmin, first bishop of Amiens, in the left porch. In the center, beside Christ (here become the "*Beau Dieu*"), apostles preaching the Law of the New Dispensation replace the Kings of Israel. Christ is here the Lord of all who have helped Him to redeem the world and this art celebrates his victory. All Christendom is now his kingdom, and it includes even the earth whose plants are beginning to wind their way into the capitals. There had already been hints of this innovation; yet now it comes as a surprise, sudden and startling—like a child's discovery that he can walk.

The continuity of medieval Faith, unbroken by the passage of time, should not blind us to the existence of a spiritual cleavage between the great pilgrimage churches and the cathedrals. More Romanesque works were destroyed in France by the "Gothics" than by the men of the Revolution. Nothing would have been more foreign to Romanesque thought than this belief in an *accomplished* Redemption and this relegation of God the Father to the background by man's communion in Christ's victory. A majestic space set apart in the midst of cities lacking space (Notre-Dame is wider than the widest street in Paris) and a manifestation of opulence in an age when opulence was far to seek, the new cathedral with its glittering vaults, spanned by a tracery of gilded ribs, and its stained glass was one vast, ceaseless *Te Deum*. Perhaps, indeed, none of our now colorless naves suggests what Rheims must have looked like in its pristine splendor so well as does that great court of the Ispahan mosque in which you see light-hearted Persians taking the air while grave-faced Persians slowly walk towards the places reserved for prayer, under huge pointed arches whose blue faience flowers, matching the sky, seem to bring tidings of another Paradise on earth.

The cathedral is a mirror of the world or, rather, it shows the world reflected in a divine mirror. It conveys its message to the common folk by means of simple allegories, whose style is rarely that of the great figures—can any of the Amiens "Months" compare with the *Saint Paul*, or any of the Rheims "Seasons" with the *Queen of Sheba*? It was the City of God that Gothic sculpture brought before the congregation, as the Romanesque had revealed to it the sacred. This is the City described in the Epistle of the Hebrews and by St Augustine; but (we may wonder) would the author of the Epistle or the saint have countenanced its representation? The thirteenth century justified this new imagery as an act of praise, and indeed the whole cathedral was an act of thanksgiving whose purpose was to dedicate to God his now Christianized creation, symbolized by the hallowed denizens of the celestial city. And that city united and ennobled the whole fraternity of Christians, including the humblest—like Jacob's ladder which merged into the divine light at its summit. This was not that unimaginable world which God was to reveal on the Last Day; it was "the city of Christ's love." Man was no longer estranged from his higher self by the universal mystery, he now had access to a spiritual world, an infinity of beatitude. The Romanesque church had disposed the Christian to seek for God in the secret places of his heart; the cathedral incited him to discover God in the entire created world, which it sanctified and transfigured. And at the apex of the chancel, the sky, glimpsed through a stained-glass window, replaced the figure of Christ derived from the "Pantocrators."

Moreover the sculptors worked solely for the cathedral or for its retinue of churches. There was no question (as in a later age) of their works being used elsewhere; the spirit of the cathedral governed their existence. It matters little that some of the statues at Rheims were completed before the nave itself, for the nave of Sens Cathedral had been completed fifty years before—and twenty years before work began on the great porch of Compostella. The vital element of a cathedral is its chancel. The massive influence of Gothic architecture—like that of Romanesque (even when Gothic superseded it)—on sculpture was still of a spiritual order. The statue was not made to match the pillar as a decorative adjunct, as a woman's hat is made to match her dress: the taller grow the pillars, the shorter are the statues. The reason why none of the statues

CHRIST (DETAIL), 1125-1130.   TYMPANUM, VÉZELAY

at Amiens, not even the *Beau Dieu*, was planned as an isolated
unit was not merely that it formed part of an architectural
complex—as do, no less evidently, the statues of Versailles or
those in the Baroque churches of Venice; the reason is that the
Saint Paul is primarily a "fragment" of the Amiens portal, as
Gislebert's angels and *Saint Peter* are, primarily, "fragments"
of the Autun tympanum.   Only in the master-builder's sketches
did the Amiens portal come into existence before the statue
of St Paul; yet in the sculptors' minds the indivisible City of
God pre-existed all their statues in some mysterious, yet compelling

CORONATION OF THE VIRGIN (DETAIL), 1210-1222. NOTRE-DAME, PARIS

manner, and the statues were revelations of it, their art's response to the new order promulgated by the cathedral. The world of God the Father was eclipsed by the sovereign Incarnation that succeeded it, just as the *Lord God* of Notre-Dame of Paris superseded the Moissac *God the Judge* and the Vézelay *Saviour*. True Gothic sculpture begins with the *Coronation of the Virgin*, in which the majesty of the Virgin is associated with that of the *Christ* above the City of God, which symbolized the spirit of the cathedrals as the gigantic *Saviour* symbolized the Romanesque spirit—and the nude was to symbolize that of the Renaissance.

235

When this metamorphosis began—with the first *Coronation of the Virgin* (at Senlis) and with the famous porch at Compostella where the subject is identical with that of Moissac, but in which joy makes a triumphant entry into sculpture—sculptors had not forgotten the "irrational" potency of expressions of the sacred, nor was there anything in the nature of a sudden discovery of the forms of appearance.   Today their art strikes us as being far less guided by appearance than as being affected by contemporary goldsmiths' work, whose influence, however, acted on it as capriciously as it had acted on Romanesque sculpture.   One almost feels that the gold and precious stones put to God's service in reliquaries and liturgical vessels were now as oper-ative in the major art of Christendom as in its minor art. Greatest creation of that sculpture—less hieratic than Roman-esque, but extremely stylized—was, assuredly, the Senlis portal whose vast arabesques of statuary in the round reappear in the (mutilated) column-statues and also in the no less mutilated tympana of Laon; on some arch mouldings at Chartres and, finally, on the Gothic portal of Saint-Benoît, their most significant successor.

As at Compostella, the Evangelists (here more dramatically rendered) have replaced the symbolic animals of the tetramorph. And the sculptor imposes on these figures what the Chartres sculptor imposed on his: a substitution of communion (without any sentimental imaging) for the sacred.   The method followed is much more evident at Saint-Benoît, since here the substitution is less complete, more tentative; indeed we feel the artist has had qualms about discarding the sacred.   This ambivalence per-sisted in Spain and Germany throughout the century, up to the *Virgin* in the monastery of León.   But in 1250 the style of these evangelist figures (no longer Romanesque) makes a reappear-ance in a work so adverse to Gothic lyricism that it seems, by this very antinomy, to throw light on the secret of Gothic creativity.   This work is the Münster *Presentation*.   And in the same year the style of this *Christ* surrounded by evangelist figures and attuned to the "art of thanksgiving" of the cathedrals is also found in the *Presentation* at Notre-Dame of Paris.

CHRIST WITH TWO EVANGELISTS, LATE XIIth C. (?).   TYMPANUM, SAINT-BENOÎT-SUR-LOIRE

237

THE PRESENTATION IN THE TEMPLE (DETAIL), 1235-1240. MUNSTER CATHEDRAL

To the question "Why did the Münster sculptor treat his figures thus?" no answer can be given. All that can be said is that the style here is, in a manner, a continuation of the sacred, for the sculptor has created a world discrepant with appearance and owing its Christian character to the "suspension of disbelief" —irrational but compulsive—it demands of the spectator.

Nor is the Paris *Presentation* governed by appearance; though resembling in some ways a scene of real life, it is obviously idealized. But it so well expresses the art that now replaced that of the sacred in the cathedrals that it has often been selected as the symbol of that art, and even figures in the posters of our tourist agencies. Here we have a "Presentation" answering to the dreams of all who contemplate it; for it belongs to the world of the imaginary.

THE PRESENTATION IN THE TEMPLE (DETAIL), 1250. NOTRE-DAME, PARIS

The fabulous beasts of Romanesque art no more belonged to this than did those of the Steppes. Associated with the monasteries by their architectural context, were they not yet more akin to the sacred by reason of their very strangeness? (St Bernard, however, was frankly shocked by them. "What purpose is served by these filthy apes and gaudily striped tigers?") We must not confuse their plastic power with a power of suggestion—which they disdain; nor the dragons clinging to the capitals of churches or the weird creatures on the Vézelay tympanum with the dream-begotten chimeras leaning on the parapets of church towers, waiting for the nightfall. As for the major works of Romanesque sculpture, the vivid life instilled into their symbols struck home at a deeper level of the Christian heart than that of the imaginary; the Moissac tympanum

239

did not suggest any scene of "real life" but figured forth something that could not be revealed to human eyes by other means: that something which is conveyed by the gods at Elephanta, by African sculpture and by the Nara frescos.

In the eleventh century a dialogue of *voices* between the angel and the Holy Women was included in the liturgy. "Whom seek ye in the sepulchre?" "Jesus of Nazareth." "He is risen; he is not here." (It was sung in Latin.) In the twelfth century the meeting on the way to Emmaus was "acted out" in the church. At the beginning of the Gothic epoch an actor played the part of God in front of the church and anathematized Adam in French.

The imaginary was expressed by representation as the sacred had been by the symbol; the terme *mistère (ministerium)*, whence the "mystery plays" derived their name, did not mean mystery but representation. By the fourteenth century the mystery play had replaced the liturgical drama. Its influence on iconography (on style, too, perhaps) is well known; but we must not forget that this influence was late to take effect. Theatrical and sculptural representation developed at the same time; while the Arras poet was writing *The Curse of Adam*, sculptors were working on the Senlis portal. Some statues in porches—notably those relating to the Life of the Virgin—formed scenes almost like conversation pieces; whereas the figures in the Royal Portal are not even looking at each other. And though evidently the actor had at his command an illusionism greater than that of statuary, the latter derived from its immobility and permanence, from all that severed it from life, a power of evoking the imaginary that was denied to the actor.

This expression—"the imaginary"—might seem to refer to fiction. But in this context we must be on our guard; the imaginary in question here is not fictional, but a facet of *Truth*. The sculptor did not set out to represent something that, but for his art, would not exist; he represented something more truly existent than appearance and caused it to shine out *through* his art. He suggested scenes of real life and real persons (as was *not* done by the near-by stained-glass windows), but their

240

world was not the world of appearance; were it so, his figures would have had no value in his eyes. He no more thought of making a likeness of his wife than did the Moissac sculptor; or than Van Gogh thought of making society portraits or sets for the Opéra-Comique. True the Gothic sculptor took not a few elements of his divine or sanctified figures from appearance; but he substituted for the normal correlation of these elements that of his art, which harmonized them with the cathedral on the spiritual plane; were this not so, the monumentality of his forms would be of the same order as that of the forms accommodated by Bourdelle to modern architecture. The Annunciation had taken place on earth, the Virgin had been a young girl —as St Firmin had been Bishop Firmin, St Theodore a soldier, and Christ a man. But the Amiens *Annunciation*, like *St Firmin* and the *Beau Dieu*, had to be located in the realm of the supramundane which had replaced the sacred and to which men directed their prayers; in the world of the cathedral for which every statue was intended and which consecrated it to God's service. Artists were allowed to incorporate fragments of the real in that world, provided these never exactly reproduced reality; in which respect it resembled the theater, its successor, which stood to fiction in the same relation as the cathedral stood to Truth. The problem set by the twofold function of such figures had been solved by sculptors some four millennia before; indeed it constitutes a problem only for our modern civilization, too apt to assume that Cézanne's landscapes are *merely* landscapes.

It was as though for the first time sculptors had fully comprehended the definition of Christ given by the Church : "Wholly God, and wholly man," and sculpture, too, were now aspiring to be at once wholly divine and wholly human. An aspiration vainglorious in our eyes, since our culture regards all man-made forms of the divine as creations of the artist, displays of a power that might equally well be applied to the creation of secular figures. The words "religious art" suggest today the application to religion of an art that could, on occasion, be unconcerned with it: e.g. the "Virgins" Titian turned out in the intervals of painting nymphs or portraits. Regarded from this angle,

THE ANNUNCIATION, 1225-1236.   PORTAL OF THE VIRGIN, AMIENS CATHEDRAL

the age of the "Coronation" might be said to have had no distinctively religious art, since it had no secular art of any consequence; its ventures into the secular were merely decorative or playful. Civilizations indulge in profane art only when they have come to look on art as a value in its own right. The aim of the cathedral sculptors was not to idealize or spiritualize appearance but to metamorphose the sacred into the imaginary—an imaginary founded on the Truth. When the creator of the *Annunciation*, and, shortly after, the creator of the Paris *Presentation* tried to make his Virgin more "feminine" than the Virgin of Chartres, this was to make her become more truly the Virgin; similarly the maker of the *Beau Dieu* did not want his figure to resemble a handsome man, but to be more truly Christ. The "humanization" these artists imparted to their figures was not a concession to appearance, but intended to give a more telling expression of the Incarnation, isolated from the sacred, and to achieve the most convincing renderings of the forms of the imaginary haunting all Christian minds.

It was, thus, an expression of the dreams of the whole body of Christians and in this respect the Gothic masters kept as closely in touch as their Romanesque precursors with the rank and file of believers. The subjection of appearance to their art, not of their art to appearance, explains why in all the creations of the century we can feel an all-compelling joy, and why this age, along with its passion for cathedrals, had an equal enthusiasm for the sculpture figuring in them. Romanesque faith had not foreseen its images; they came as a new discovery. Its message had not lacked vehemence (and in its concept of the Incarnation, the divine made human, Gothic sculpture followed suit). But now the Christian community which transmuted the Virgin in Majesty into Our Lady of Rejoicing called with even greater vehemence for images of the new, triumphant spirit implicit in the world-view of the age.

It is significant that the saint who then exercised the strongest, most widespread influence was St Francis of Assisi, a saint without theology. (Nonetheless Innocent III promptly recognized his saintship and Benedict XIV was to see in him "the perfect image of Our Lord.")   Everywhere mystery was giving place to love, the aloofness of God to the nearness of Jesus, adoration to communion, repining for the Fall to that sense of Christ's victory which pervaded Gothic Christendom no less than the sense of his divinity.   One would almost think that the West had only just had news of that victory, as it had just learnt of the conquest of Jerusalem, and that the purpose of the company of statues that now was mustering in the glimmering recesses of cathedral porches was to reveal to men as living presences the figures of their collective dream.

The art of the imaginary added to the prophets and apostles a retinue of saints and kings (more and more rarely kings of Israel); while to Majestàs and Adorations it added scenes of the Death of the Virgin, her Assumption and Coronation—which do not figure in the Gospels.   A hymn of triumph escorts her from the Annunciation to the Coronation, as it accompanies Jesus from the manger to his apotheosis.

At Amiens, for the first time, a figure of Christ was named *Le Beau Dieu*; for contemporaries were quick to notice the difference between it and its predecessor, the Chartres *Christ Teaching*.   St Augustine would have thought the appellation *Beau Dieu* absurd and sacrilegious, and so would even Dhuoda of Septimania, who, however, called the God whose ineffable grandeur she bade her children revere "the God of Love".   One can hardly imagine Moses speaking of the "beauty" of the Burning Bush.   How could the term "beautiful" apply to Jesus?   When did the evangelists make the least allusion to his appearance?   According to the Fathers of the Church his beauty was of a supernatural order.   "It is not in any comely proportion of the limbs," wrote St Basil, "but in thought alone, purified to the highest point, that the beauty of Our Lord is apprehended."

The response of believers to forms expressing the imaginary was as intense and at least as widespread as had been the response to the forms that had manifested the sacred.   But sacred art had revealed God's world, not the world of men; all feelings that did not point to God were absent from it, as they were from the sacred itself.   Thus the Virgin in Majesty was never shown

"LE BEAU DIEU," 1225-1236. CENTRAL PORTAL, AMIENS CATHEDRAL

playing with the Child. But in Gothic art the imaginary was a world of human values, and these values were regarded as the most appropriate means of rendering praise to God.

One may speak of Gothic anthropomorphism (though the term is hardly apposite) with reference to works where the sacred is replaced by love's transcendence—for example, the Senlis *Resurrection of the Virgin* and the *Christ Teaching* at Chartres, as contrasted with the "Saviours" at Autun and Vézelay. Yet the *Beau Dieu* is in the line of descent from the *Christ* of Chartres, not in that of the "Saviours," and though it may be said to humanize the latter (to which it is wholly unrelated), it cannot be said to humanize *Christ Teaching* (to which it is directly related), but, rather, to *idealize* it.

It owed no more to a living model than did its predecessor at Chartres, or the contemporary *Annunciation*. It adds beauty to the Chartres *Christ*, not to a human being; the beauty with which it invests the Saviour is as foreign to that of any living man as is the beauty of the Virgin to that of an attractive young woman. The word "beauty" here is applicable solely in terms of the cathedral; this Christ does not set out to charm, but to reveal the world of the divine. Nor must we forget that this beauty, when the people of Amiens first set eyes on it, was regarded as pertaining solely to that world; it was supramundane, and the admiration it evoked stemmed from the spectators' faith, not from any esthetic response. The *Beau Dieu* was not admired as the likeness of a handsome man, or as a finely carved statue, but as a convincing figure of Christ. And with regard to all the images in the cathedrals, what the medieval Christian meant by "beauty" was that quality which made the world created by the sculptors worthy of the Saviour to whom they dedicated their creations.

Hence their intermittent, never quite plain-spoken, dialogue with the art of antiquity. Drapery (whose classical tradition had been perpetuated in Carolingian ivories) now took the place of the carapace-like surfaces of the column-statues. An Amiens sculptor resorted to the Roman handling of eyes in *Saint Ulphia*,

ST JOHN, FIRST QUARTER XIIIth C.   YORKSHIRE MUSEUM, YORK

a York sculptor in his *Saint John*, and the Rheims sculptors employed Roman techniques in several figures (well before the famous *Visitation*). If the use of classical forms sufficed to define Renaissance art, we should have to say that the Renaissance

247

THE VISITATION, 1250-1270. RHEIMS CATHEDRAL

THE HORSEMEN OF THE APOCALYPSE, 1255-1290.   RHEIMS CATHEDRAL

began at Rheims, where devices bordering on pastiche transformed the *Horsemen of the Apocalypse* into an Hellenistic cavalcade.   But the sixteenth century admired both the spirit of antique art and the correlation of its elements in an organic whole; whereas thirteenth-century art broke up that correlation and merely made use of some of these elements, in the same way it used certain elements of appearance.   So as to include in the world of the cathedral the face of a Roman statue, the Master of the *Visitation* makes it undergo much the same metamorphosis as does his colleague, the Master of the *Annunciation*, so as to introduce into his work the face of a living woman.   Once beauty had become an attribute of the divine—once that of Jesus manifested the divinity of Christ—beauty under all its forms served as a link between the figures represented and their Master. Thus the art which gave form to the Christian world of the imaginary became one of the most potent elements of the communion which was now replacing adoration.

For art alone could body forth the imaginary in its loftiest forms.   Although mystery-plays (still in their rudimentary stage) had reached their full flowering at the time, what spectator could have confused the *Beau Dieu*, the *Virgin* of the "Coronations," the Bamberg *Eve*, the Chartres *Saint Martin* and *Saint Theodore*, or the angels in any of the cathedrals, from Senlis to Rheims, with the actors playing corresponding roles? The mystery play could only show scenes developing in Time; but statuary stood outside Time and its style evoked a world beyond the world, a coherent realm of being in which figurations of the temporal staked a claim on eternity. Different as were Gothic creations from those inspired by the sacred, they too produced on Christians the effect of a revelation. The masterpieces in the cathedrals seem unintelligible if we see in them *transcriptions* of the theater or of appearance, and they seem no less so if we regard them as transcriptions of the collective dream that they express so convincingly—for the Christian dream of the world of the divine included no images. Though the townsfolk of Amiens may well have thought the *Beau Dieu* resembled Christ, no one, until the sculptor had completed his work, had pictured Christ as having been like the *Beau Dieu*. The style inaugurated by the *Coronation of the Virgin* (we must be chary of the epithet "Gothic" (bred of contempt, and contempt is an unjust judge) was not, any more than Romanesque sculpture, "a manner of representing the events of Bible history" due to the "vision" of a certain period. Rather, it signaled the emergence of a world of an unprecedented nature, in which Christendom now *discovered* the figures of its dreams. For this art cannot be understood if we leave out of account its accent of discovery and the abruptness of its appearance, as sudden as that of the cathedrals; it was the first revelation of the City of God. For this reason it was as far removed from the art preceding it as from the art which followed. Once that revelation ceased to be its object, art's whole function changed—even though cathedrals continued to be built.

In many ways the sense of communion inspired by forms of the imaginary gave an impression that, at long last, art had won a foothold in the world of the divine. The relations of believers with God, with Christ and with the Virgin varied in accordance with the different manners in which that world was represented in the Amiens portals, the Autun tympanum and the numerous "Virgins in Majesty." For the imaginary could be given many different forms. The Amiens *Annunciation* seemed definitive to everyone except the Rheims sculptor, who had his own ideas on the subject; the *Synagogue* of Rheims did not satisfy the Strasbourg sculptor, who challenged it with his own interpretation of the theme; nor did the *Philip Augustus* satisfy the Bamberg sculptor intent on his *Man on Horseback.* The call to which these men responded was like the one heard by their forerunners, and some of the statues at Rheims fired the imagination of the Christian populace in just the same way as the Paris *Coronation of the Virgin.* But diverse as were the possibilities of the imaginary *quâ* revelations of the Truth, the artists' exploration of this field followed a specific trend; throughout Christendom—and not only in the lands ruled by saintly kings—Christ's suzerainty was coming more and more to have the nature of a benevolent kingship and this age, which regarded the order of earthly things as the outcome of a divine plan, saw in everything that expressed that kingship an element of the divine. Thus sculpture in offering to Christ the forms of his kingdom, presented to men, by the same token, the forms of their grandest dreams.

During the whole century beauty and tenderness were allied in effigies of the Virgin, who now acquired a patrician cast that had been absent in the Majestàs. From Senlis to Freiberg, from Chartres to Paris, from Paris to Rheims, from Rheims to Bamberg, at León and at Siena, most of the innovations in art were determined by the irresistible appeal of what theologians came, later, to describe as "the Reconciliation." And perhaps we should be less disposed to regard the "Master of the Antique Figures" as an exception and Nicola Pisano as a precursor of Raphael, if we were less inclined to forget that the former was working on his *Visitation* at the same time as the latter was carving the pulpit at Pisa.

This movement swept all France like a tidal wave and spread from Champagne to Italy, from Spain to Saxony and from England to Dalmatia. At Rheims a master-sculptor recaptured

MAN ON HORSEBACK (DETAIL), C. 1250.   BAMBERG CATHEDRAL

ADAM (DETAIL), C. 1250. BAMBERG CATHEDRAL

THE CREATION, C. 1250. NORTH PORCH, CHARTRES CATHEDRAL

in his *Queen of Sheba* the bearing of a Caryatid; the Strasbourg master harked back to long, flowing drapery and harmoniously molded features in the *Synagogue*; the Bamberg masters imparted to their *Adam* and the *Man on Horseback* a nobility all their own, while the master of Freiberg invented for his Virgin a delicate design like goldsmiths' work in stone which pointed the way to the Saint-Benoît *Christ*. And, while resembling in its drapery the *Saint Theodore* and *Saint Modesta*, *The Church* at Strasbourg also resembles, in its arabesque, the *Virtues* in St Mark's at Venice and, still more, the *Man on Horseback*. The vaults of the North Portal at Chartres contain the most moving of all *Creation* cycles, that in which God is shown molding man with loving hands, while listening to the first birds singing. On each of the buttresses of Rheims, the last *Te Deum*, echoing the faith of the Crusades, called forth an angel; and the sculptors of this cathedral of angels made it also the cathedral of the smile—how many centuries had passed before the smile thus made its reappearance! And, at the apex of the great gable, Christ, as he crowns the Virgin, seems to be crowning along with her all the figures of the medieval Reconciliation.

He was crowning them for the last time. Though the Divine City figured forth at Rheims has the glamour of a fabled wonderland, Christ the King, for all his regal splendor, already bears the stamp of suffering. And if the Crucifixion came to be represented in cathedral sculpture relatively late, the Cross was always present in the sanctuary, as the Crucified was always immanent in the King, and the Church militant over which He reigned was tributary to his sacrifice. Sculptors had now discovered in what they called beauty a religious emotion all the more intense because this beauty, far from conflicting with the expression of the divine tragedy and the emotions it aroused, enhanced it by the addition of a sort of counterpoint—as can been seen in the "Pillar of the Angels" at Strasbourg, in the Bamberg *Adam* and in a host of statues at Rheims, from the *Abraham* to the *Christ* of the great gable.

In the course of the century a striking change came over the expression of emotions. This was formerly attributed by art

SIMEON SENEX, 1225-1236. AMIENS CATHEDRAL

SIMEON SENEX, 1250-1270. RHEIMS CATHEDRAL

historians to a growing mastery of illusionism. But the *Simeon Senex* of Rheims is no more convincing or illusionist than the Amiens version; it is simply more accessible to the ordinary Christian, more humanized. The Rheims sculptor evokes feelings shared by the old man and the spectator, feelings that relate to faith but do not belong to it exclusively. Thus the Rheims figure creates a moving scene, whereas the Amiens *Simeon* is an essentially biblical creation and the face of the old prophet relates almost as much to God as did those of Romanesque prophets, while the flutings of the cloak slung on his arm resemble those of column-figures.

In the Bamberg tympanum the atmosphere of joy, no longer that of angels but the gladness of the Blessed, gives place to one of frank hilarity. No tympanum in any earlier cathedral would have represented a Last Judgment of this sort, in which a sculptor, greatly daring, shows a pope and an emperor consigned to hell;

THE LAST JUDGMENT (DETAIL), C. 1250. BAMBERG CATHEDRAL

260

not because all souls are equal in the eyes of God, but because these two men were sworn foes of Philip of Swabia, who is seen advancing towards Christ, among a jubilant company of the Elect, men and women with queer, radish-shaped heads. Also the figure of Christ is more "expressionist" than its equivalents in French and Spanish tympana; the last trace of spiritual unity has been effaced, each of these people reveals *personal* feelings. Whereas this sculptor made shift with weird grimaces to convey the despair of the Lost, his contemporary at Naumburg rendered grief more subtly, imparting to it the accent adumbrated in the figures of Calvary, and to the Virgin the sad look of the *Virgin of Liège*, and gave every sin its appropriate visage.

But at Naumburg we find a spiritual world quite other than that of the Paris *Coronation*. Here *interior* sculpture figures forth scenes of the Passion; these had been excluded from the

THE LAST JUDGMENT (DETAIL), C. 1250. BAMBERG CATHEDRAL

CHRIST BEFORE PILATE, C. 1250.   CHOIR SCREEN, NAUMBURG CATHEDRAL

portals, where symbols rather than scenes were represented. Before long, liturgical dramas were to enact the Crucifixion, and it now began to figure in tympana. But always subordinated to its setting, almost decorative in effect and curiously imbued with mannerism. On the "Coronation" façades the crucifix had been placed as it is placed on the breast of the dying. No "Passion" cycle was to replace in the portals the cycle of the Virgin and the groups of martyrs and confessors. When sculptors ceased transfiguring the Church militant of apostles and saints into the Church triumphant and the world of men became a world redeemed, the iconography that had begun at Moissac came to an end. A new art was henceforth to serve a Church in which sorrow had its place, but henceforth it was in chapels that men prayed to the Mater Dolorosa, and no tympanum was to figure forth a Pietà.

The maker of the great *Christ* of Rheims seems to foreshadow Michelangelo. But, like his contemporaries at Amiens, Bamberg

CHRIST, 1260-1280. GABLE, RHEIMS CATHEDRAL

APOSTLE (?), SECOND HALF XIIIth C.   RHEIMS CATHEDRAL

and Naumburg, he too aimed at creating, not works of art, but figures representative of Truth.   For some nine hundred years, in their handling of emotive and homiletic themes alike, all great artists had been creators of forms in the same manner as the Hebrew prophets had been poets.   "Let him who will follow me renounce himself," said St Francis (echoing Jesus); and this held good for sculpture.   But even before the genius of the cathedral builders achieved its final flowering in the great

PROPHET (?), SECOND HALF XIIIth C.   RHEIMS CATHEDRAL

"Coronations," the genius of the West had entered on the most remarkable and baffling mutation of its long history; the artist's self-effacement was ending and the "saint" becoming a *statue*.

The traditional view that art and civilization followed a continuous line of evolution between the eleventh and fifteenth centuries is unwarranted. The rise of the Christian West took place with dramatic suddenness; in 1050 it was inert; in 1099 it captured Jerusalem. What sculpture of any value dates to 1090? Yet only fifty years later we have Chartres. By 1250 no less than sixty workyards were employed in building cathedrals or great churches and the men who worked in them were full of splendid hopes, fired by over a century of Christian victories. Then, only twenty years later, St Louis was dead, the Latin empire lost and Crusades had ceased. Work on the cathedrals slowed down or ended; the decline of the age of triumph was no less rapid than its rise. The Pope was seized by Guillaume de Nogaret at the bidding of Philip the Fair, grandson of St Louis, and with the holocaust of the Templars, which brought the Crusades to an inglorious end, we cannot help thinking that the Christian venture, too, experienced its Thermidor.

The fact that the *Summa* was written when the age of Christian victories was drawing to a close gives food for thought. The Aristotelians had been excommunicated seven times in the period following 1210. The Holy See decided to take over "all that was good" in Aristotelianism; yet perhaps the massive synthesis in which St Thomas Aquinas subdued it to Christ and wedded thought to faith marked the conclusion of an era. With it ended the doctrine of "illumination." In 1180 no theologian gave the realm of God a local habitation, and it would seem that the human mind became capable of defining and circumscribing its mysterious ambience only when this was losing its instancy—that transcendent immanence which defied attempts to limit its domain, and that ubiquity which was, it seemed, a legacy of the Romanesque conception of the sacred. True, the *Summa* approaches this mystery of the Faith with reverence; but, after a curt description, relegates it to the background. Indeed, the last theologian in whom can still be sensed the spirit of the great cathedrals was, doubtless, St Bonaventura.

What died out in the second half of the century was the fine enthusiasm of the Gothic cathedral builders. The nineteenth century saw in this only a rivalry of architects. But even those who wished to "beat all records" no more tried to copy their predecessors, if on a larger scale, than the Rheims sculptors tried to copy the Amiens statues, while making them more lifelike or refined. Just as it is obvious that the various cycles of the Life of the Virgin had no common prototype, a scene (real or imaginary) that artists copied or idealized, so it is also obvious that no well-established Gothic conception of the universe existed —a sort of "basic Thomism" to which the master-artists could refer, the sole concern of each being to outdo his rivals. In their celebration of Christ's triumph the cathedrals responded to an unformulated but compelling revelation, like that which had led to the triumph of Christianity in the West. The men of the Renaissance, too, were to know that summons from a world sensed but not fully apprehended, that aspiration which makes all artistic creation an endless quest of something always out of reach. From the viewpoint of the architects and sculptors, their predecessors at Amiens had not exhausted the possibilities of imaging the City of God; just as from Titian's neither Botticelli nor even Giorgione had said the last word on the "Venus" theme. The evolution of architecture (if not of sculpture) up to the year 1250 is usually, and properly, regarded as an outcome of successive discoveries of new building techniques. But the technique which enabled the construction of the Amiens nave and the Beauvais choir did not necessitate their existence. Was it solely for the pleasure of the eye or to pander to the local pride of a bishop or a city that naves were steadily heightened and more and more wall space given up to stained glass; or was it not, rather, that art was forever seeking to perfect a snare to capture something vaguely glimpsed but unattainable? This art is no more separable from the impulse behind its aspirations than an airplane is separable from its movement through the air; it expresses the divine solely because it stands for a —never-completed—conquest of the divine. For, despite its

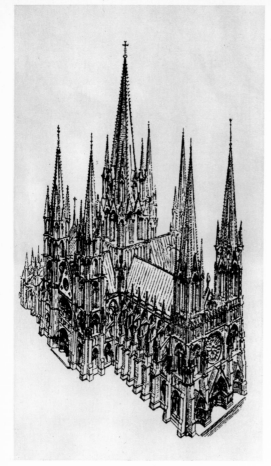

TYPE-CATHEDRAL, XIIIth C. COMPLETED

amazing technical achievements, its genius (like that of romantic music) was bound up with its aspirations. It was not in the days of Voltaire but in the age of Thomas Aquinas that large scale Gothic creation passed away.

This is why the cathedrals, symbols of the Gothic creative élan, are also symbols of its untimely end; not one of them was completed. That robust architecture, against whose heaviness classical writers once inveighed and whose power we now admire, is truncated architecture and its style, like that of ruins, doomed to imperfection. Reconstitutions of the original plans for the cathedrals of Paris, Rheims and Chartres display a wealth of pinnacles equaling that of Milan. Seven steeples were planned to rise at Rheims and nine at Chartres. The teams of masons who, else, might have been employed on them were turned to building châteaux (but somewhat later).

This fact of capital importance has not been given due weight in political and economic surveys of the age. Have we here the beginnings of a lay society—widely differing, however, from the milieu whose figurehead was Lorenzo the Magnificent? It is clear in any case that the founding of the University of Paris by Philip Augustus led to the growth of a culture that was no longer exclusively ecclesiastical; and it is no less evident that the rise of the new monarchies made the Holy Roman Empire seem a relic of the past. Moreover, after challenging imperial prestige, the monarchies went on to challenge papal authority as well. The promotion of national literatures speeded up this secularizing trend, but we must not forget that the Anglo-Norman poet, Thomas, had completed his *Tristan* as far back as a century before. Guilds of illuminators took over the work formerly reserved to monastic scriptoria; for some time already sculptors and glass-workers had been laymen. Once a torrent sweeping all before it, Christian faith was losing its momentum. But when Joinville refused to follow St Louis in the last Crusade, this was not because he had lost faith. The Crusades ended as the Islamic foray ended; as the Wars of Religion were to end.

But for St Louis, would the Crusades not have ended earlier? He towers above the age, but symbolizes only its first part. In the fourteenth century our eyes are drawn less to the heir of the knight who was "worst dressed of all his court" than to the heir of the monarch with gorgeous palaces and a Moorish bodyguard who negotiated with his Saracen friends the restitution of the Holy Sepulchre: to Frederick II, Roman Emperor, King of Sicily and Jerusalem.

IV Romanesque art, even in its major works, had not disdained ornamentation, nor had it any qualms about using precious or semi-precious stones in the service of God's glory. The effigy of Sainte Foy at Conques, studded with jewels, belonged no less to sacred art than did the austerest Virgins of the pilgrimage churches. Though the Beaulieu sculptor doubtless felt a personal satisfaction in his rendering of the forked beard of his *Prophet*, this Atlas-like figure seemed to be bearing on its shoulders the sorrows of the world, and the bedizened Kings of Chartres spoke of God alone; even the *Beau Dieu* spoke of Christ alone.

The maker of the Rheims *Apostle*, an incarnation of the Truth, kept himself in the background (this was indeed the secret of his genius), whereas the maker of the neighboring *Prophet* seems to assert his personality in the statue. But for a frank exposure of the artist's presence, we must look, not to Rheims (where the art of the *Coronation* lasted on until the end of the century), but to the Sainte-Chapelle.

When, after leaving nearby Notre-Dame, we enter the church built by St Louis to enshrine the Crown of Thorns, we are surprised to find that God is receding into the background. These famous stained-glass windows contain none of the great figures, last custodians of the sacred, which had bulked large in the art of Christendom triumphant. The teeming, glittering profusion of the Sainte-Chapelle is at a far remove from a world of purely spiritual joy. By way of contrast we can picture the severe grandeur that the glass-workers and sculptors of Chartres would have imparted to a shrine so pre-eminently hallowed, at the time of the first fall of Byzantium.

The statuary in the Sainte-Chapelle, so like the Rheims *Apostle* (which it certainly preceded), gives the effect of a continuation, in ornate form, of that in the great cathedrals. But the *interior* sculpture which has replaced the public imagery of the portals includes some of the most singular figures of the age—singular indeed by their very mediocrity. Here the term "beautiful" no longer means what it meant to those who named the Amiens Christ "le Beau Dieu"; the term applies not to the figure

APOSTLES, (?) 1248.   PLASTER CASTS (REPAINTED IN XIXth C.).   SAINTE-CHAPELLE, PARIS

and its otherworldly qualities but to the statue *quâ* work of art. It voices the admiration, unrelated to religious feeling, that might be aroused by any secular figure. When the populace of Liège acclaimed the *Virgin of St John* as being most beautiful of all Christian Virgins, they were thinking of the Virgin and of her alone; had the crown been removed, this figure would not have become that of "the most beautiful young mother in Europe."

Esthetic feeling had made its first appearance in the world of Christendom.

But it was ill-defined as yet, and far from transforming art as the drastic innovations of the eleventh century—the sudden glory of the earliest cathedrals—had transformed it. It gave a new direction to the *Coronation* sculpture but did not put an end to it; under its influence the Chartres *Last Judgment* gave place to those of Bourges and León, with their picturesque devils, their charming figures of the Blessed. As compared with the great cycles of the Life of the Virgin, the scenes imbued with this new esthetic have something of the studied grace we find in courtly art. The reason why the statuary in the Sainte-Chapelle, though itself of no great artistic significance, and without any direct influence on the future, fixes a capital date in art is that it throws so strong a light on the underground revolution that was taking place; a revolution of far greater moment than the birth of Gothic mannerism and nowhere else evidenced so clearly, except in illuminated manuscripts.

For the new art prevailed in all illuminations that were ceasing to take their lead from stained-glass windows. And when the latter, in turn, came to be influenced by the illuminators, this too was the work of the new art—as when the rinceaux in the *Psalter of St Louis* were reproduced in windows, as those of Persian miniatures were reproduced on the blue domes of mosques. The importance of the Psalter, like that of the statues in the Sainte-Chapelle, does not lie in its artistic value, but in the fact that though, like them, it is a religious work, the function of its art is to express neither the sacred nor an imaginary world of Truth; that, in short, the Psalter of the greatest

MOSES BEFORE PHARAOH, 1256.   PSALTER OF ST LOUIS.   BIBLIOTHÈQUE NATIONALE, PARIS

royal saint symbolizes the first Christian art *signifying nothing*.

Though its style, like that of English illuminations, may seem to be a derivation of the sacred style, hieraticism has here become calligraphy and its Church Latin strikes a note of "modishness." Hitherto any notion of refinement had been completely foreign to the creation of religious works of art, including illuminated books. But now many Psalters were to confirm the triumph of that sophisticated court poet, Chrétien de Troyes, over the simple poetry of the Psalms. Type figures of men and women of high rank now made their appearance and their fantasticated elegance was to hold its own until the end of International Gothic. Pisanello's princesses are daughters of the "Lady with a Unicorn" often met with in medieval art. Thus for the first time there appeared in art a value owing nothing to the Christian hierarchy.

And, along with it, there developed the first secular art form of any real consequence: the ivories. These stylized figures have no concern with realism, nor with revealing Truth in the guise of the imaginary; they belong to an imaginary world of a quite different order, the world of fiction.

True, this elegant calligraphy still played a subordinate role. Yet henceforth there existed a world of art where now and again we find a statue that has become distinct from the saint it purports to represent and is obviously meant to charm the spectator, not to invite his veneration. Thus some of the Apostles in the Sainte-Chapelle are not beautiful in the way the *Beau Dieu* was beautiful, but as "objects"; Moses, before Pharaoh, cuts the figure of a dancer, and even Christ is sometimes given the courtly grace of a *grand seigneur*. But this type of art, essentially a product of period taste, never prevailed completely in monumental sculpture (even at its most mannerist); the Auxerre bas-reliefs, the *Assumption* in Notre-Dame of Paris are of a much higher order. Nevertheless their value, too, is primarily esthetic, not spiritual, and the best bas-relief at Auxerre—worthy of Donatello—is an *Eros*!

Henceforth no artist was to attempt to reveal the City of God. Even the Strasbourg *Prophets* would seem out of keeping

PROPHET (DETAIL), 1290-1298. STRASBOURG CATHEDRAL

GIOVANNI PISANO.   ISAIAH (DETAIL), LATE XIIIth C.   SIENA CATHEDRAL

in the choir at Amiens which hymns so nobly a *Magnificat* of the fulfilled Redemption. Though they may seem to carry on the earlier art, they are not its progeny. Like the *Virtues*, like the *Wise and Foolish Virgins* which under the *Passion* of a diminutive Christ replace the militant cohorts of the Blessed, these prophets have become statues. Their coiled hair and corkscrew beards—all their accents, absent in the art of the *Coronation*—affirm the presence of the sculptor, as do the curly locks of the *Apostles* in the Sainte-Chapelle, and even more emphatically the volutes of Rheims. They are "dramatic" brothers of the Strasbourg *Prophet*, whose "heroic" brother is Giovanni Pisano's (contemporary) *Isaiah* in Siena Cathedral.

The effigies at Rouen and Exeter were harmonized no less than those of Rheims with the façades of their respective cathedrals. This harmony persisted up to the end of Flamboyant Gothic, the unity of forms being more conspicuous at Exeter—and even in the Sainte-Chapelle—than at Rheims; but it is essentially esthetic, like the artistry of the Auxerre bas-reliefs. For over two centuries sculptors had subordinated individual figures to the spiritual unity of their environment, to the edifice which was their frame of reference. This spiritual unity and this subordination ended simultaneously.

The Master of Moissac had envisaged his tympanum as a fragment of the abbey church, and himself as a servant of the Church, then engaged in weaving that "white robe" of sacred edifices which was to clothe the world, and the abbey church was no more than a fragment of that "robe." The architect who designed a church of the *Coronation* period did not witness its completion; he merely set forth its form, as the founder of a religious Order shaped that Order. Though he prescribed the layout of the statues, he did not make them. As for the sculptor, his statuary was integrated into the cathedral in the same way as his *Saints* and *Apostles* were incorporated in the portals. The idea of inventing a special "style" for statues never occurred to him, since "style," for him, meant that which adapted his figures to a vision of transcendence, to an homiletic purpose, and to a place of worship that was also a public building. To our eyes they seem so closely linked up with an ensemble and with a wall that we almost tend to think of them as bas-reliefs. The feelings behind them were both the wondering awe of believers who for the first time realized that all creation formed a stupendous whole governed by Divine Providence, and also the persistent enthusiasm aroused by the cathedral under construction—the Rheims façade was finished two hundred years after the nave. We regard monumental statuary as the complement of a completed building; but in the late fifteenth

ST PAUL (DETAIL), 1225-1236. AMIENS CATHEDRAL

century, Fouquet still represented the temple of Jerusalem as a cubic cathedral, thickly lined with statues, but lacking towers. The façade arose along with the rise of Faith, and ceased with it; the statues belonged to the façade as, for us, they belong to it in photographs reproducing the portals only —and as those many-colored fishes which, in moving pictures, look like flights of wingless birds, "belong" to the unseen sea. And to the Gothic sculptor a statue by itself would have seemed like a fish out of the sea, incongruous and inadequate.

ST PAUL (DETAIL), C. 1340. RIEUX CHAPEL. MUSÉE DES AUGUSTINS, TOULOUSE

Once the incorporation of statues in the building itself came to an end (along with their spiritual affiliation to the cathedral and the rendering of Truth in terms of the Imaginary), figures embodying the message of the Church Triumphant disappeared from monumental sculpture. The Rieux *St Paul* is no more in the lineage of the *St Paul* of Amiens than the Strasbourg *Prophets* are akin to those of Chartres. At Rieux, as at Chartres, "Gothic realism" made its appearance at the same time as that flagrant "unrealism" which found its ultimate expression in an excessive use of fluting. Strange indeed is the realism of the Strasbourg *Prophet* who is raising a hand, with all the veins meticulously copied, towards a haggard face and a beard reminiscent of archaic Chinese bronzes. Beards of this kind are not stylizations of a model's beard; in beardless figures the same effect is produced by the treatment of the hair of the head. Garments are less boldly handled than heads and may often seem quite out of keeping with the scalloped hair and corkscrew beards; nonetheless their rich polychromy matches these intricate convolutions, as do the shaggy garments of the effigies of *St John the Baptist* and the flowing locks mantling the *St Mary of Egypt* at Ecouis.

This stylization—legacy of Byzantine hieraticism by way of the Saint-Benoît tympanum and the arabesques to which the painters of St Louis suddenly assigned a novel, somewhat enigmatic value—was a link between thirteenth-century Spain (the Silos *Annunciation* and the *Virgin with an Offering* at León, contemporary with the sophisticated *Organ Concert*) and the Germanic altarpieces. For nearly two hundred years its nodose, passionate calligraphy dominated a whole figural style, as the Byzantine idiom dominated the art of the icons. (But the icons belonged to the sacred.)

Why was it that when the unity of the preceding art was broken up, this new monumental art, which now was becoming more and more independent of its architectural context, did not develop into a realistic art? Because in so doing it would have ceased to be religious. In fourteenth-century religious sculpture the term "realistic" is applicable solely to *fragments* of any given work. It was because this art disdained reality that, by

ST MARY OF EGYPT (DETAIL), 1313-1315. ECOUIS CHURCH

way of lavish stylization, it was forever trying to regain contact with that Other World which had been revealed in Naumburg Cathedral as at Amiens, and in which even the humblest Virgin of the major works—the Virgin, for example, in the Rheims *Presentation*—though no longer a *sacred* figure, was no less a religious figure than the Queens in the Royal Portal. In the Breslau *Apostle*, the Rieux *Apostles* and the Regensburg *King*, beards stylized into spirals make their appearance along with heightened emotivity. Of the statues which Cardinal de Lagrange had placed, in 1385, alongside the Amiens tower, that of Charles V is less illusionist than that of Bureau de la Rivière, while the *St John the Baptist* is not illusionist at all— because this is the figure of a saint. So as to show that the religious figures belonged to the world of God, sculptors now resorted to a stylization that was no longer, in their hands, a sacred language, but always tending towards the idioms of tapestry and illumination. It is the fragments of appearance we find in their works that differentiate them from the *Psalter of St Louis*; without this realism a figure would not be a man's, but without stylization it would not be a saint's.

But, just as the true successor of the Autun *Last Judgment* is the Gothic portal (and not the Chartres *Last Judgment*), so the successor of the "Crusaders" portal is not the Strasbourg portal, nor the Rouen façade teeming with figures, nor the rich profusion of Siena Cathedral; nor even the Rieux Chapel, in which all the portals seem, as it were, to have taken shelter. No, the true successor of the "Crusaders" portal is the scattered crowd of isolated figures that now invade the naves, the serried ranks of figures thronging choir screens and the peripheries of choirs. The incursion of the *Founders* into the Naumburg choir and that of the *Apostles* into the Sainte-Chapelle, perplexing at first sight, point to the impending change, when all the statues were to be assembled in the nave. When the porches of Amiens were completed, there were practically no statues in the nave —which now is full of them.

It is easier now to follow the metamorphosis that was coming over the western world. Feudalism was not superseded by the

APOSTLE (DETAIL), SECOND HALF XIVth C.   SILESIAN MUSEUM, BRESLAU

concept of nationality in the same way as one system of government gives place to another. It was the passing of feudal values that made the oath of vassalage to the king of France seem so odious to the kings of England. The victors of single combats were now to be the vanquished at Agincourt and Nicopolis; chivalric heroism no longer won the day. The conflict between Philip the Fair and the Papacy would have taken another turn had not the Italian banks come to the king's rescue; western Christendom had learnt the power of money. This important event was one of many signs of the passing of the old order and the end of a civilization in which the domains of faith and thought interlocked and, since the Great Invasions, all forms of knowledge and all skills (except those of a military order) had been a monopoly of "clerks," the men who in the reign of Louis VII administered the affairs of the kingdom under the rule of Abbot Suger, just as Charlemagne's ecclesiastics had administered the Empire. No layman of the time was capable of managing the affairs of even the smallest barony. But the new upper class included the ennobled sons of wealthy commoners (Philip the Bold instituted the practice of issuing patents of nobility), barons dissatisfied with being mere cavalry soldiers, and churchmen who backed the king against the pope. Under the auspices of the new clergy, tied up with the royal power and with the communes, national languages ousted Latin. Dante wrote the *Divina Commedia* and in 1327 a layman, Buridan, was appointed Rector of the University of Paris.

The cathedrals were affected by the transition from a feudal hierarchy—peasants, nobles, emperor and pope—to an urban way of life. The genius of the cathedral builders, like that of the Renaissance, expressed a new vision of the universe, but it was relatively short-lived, for, once the new order was firmly established, the great period of Gothic inventiveness ended. Not that the new "clerks" were unbelievers or even indifferent to religion. The social order still was founded on religion, but faith had lost its all-embracing unity; it had its place in life as the Church had in the kingdom—and Philip the Fair brought the papacy under his control. The opening decades of the fourteenth century witnessed an economic and political breakdown; the population ceased increasing, even in England. Yet even if less and less funds were available for completing the French cathedrals (the failure to complete them cannot be wholly accounted for by the Hundred Years' War and the Black Death), was the end of cathedral-building really due to financial stringency? Was it due to economic conditions that no more of those great revivalists of the Faith who for two centuries had fired the ardor of the Christian populace made their appearance on the scene? Neither St Francis nor St Dominic had successors. Was it because of lack of faith or not, rather, because western Christianity had lost its sense of a mission and because faith itself was changing? The man who declined to contribute to the work on the cathedral was quite ready to present a statue to it. For that collective devotion of which the cathedral was the grandiose expression was giving place to a new relationship between man and the divine; Christ no longer spoke to men at large, but to the *individual believer*.

The religion of the age of the Crusades seems like a fervent dialogue between the Christian congregation and a benevolent celestial hierarchy. Though each man's faith was his own concern and Christ an individual, the parish was no less a community than the monastery, or indeed the town, when threatened by war or the Plague. Basic to the Christian's intercourse with God was the Mass—far more so than private prayer; for the liturgy enabled him to participate in the divine mystery through the public rites performed in the church. Holy Communion was a continuance of the Last Supper, as the congregation of worshipers was an aftermath of that of the apostles, and the officiating priest was the spokesman of that congregation (the root meaning of the word *ekklesia* is "a convoked assembly"). The infrequency of private communion may surprise us; St Louis partook of the Sacrament only once every two months. The vehicle of adoration was the liturgy, which united the worshipers with the body of Christ present at the altar. And the "author" of the liturgical prayers was the Church. Had not the twelve articles of the medieval creed been written by

the twelve apostles, founders of the Faith? St Luke himself
had composed the *Magnificat* (with verses from the Psalms).
All Christians had prayed and sung with the age-old voice of
Christendom, as members of the body of believers.

But the chief aim of piety now became that private intercourse with the divine which, as Newman was to put it, made
the church "a place of solitude." This did not, however, clash
with the faith that found fulfillment in public worship; from the
viewpoint of an ideal Christianity, these forms of faith were
complementary, and in practice they often were allied. But
a reversal of their relations to each other was taking place.
Imperceptibly, to start with—and the beginnings of this mutation of religious sensibility are as hard to trace precisely as are
the beginnings of Romanticism. By the fourteenth century it was
a *fait accompli*. Individual piety seems not merely to take the
lead of communal worship, but even to supplant it. Books
of Hours, in which we find a new kind of illumination coming
to the fore, now add "private" images to their "public" texts.
In the Mass itself the Prayer of Thomas Becket takes its place
beside the Nicene Creed; the rite of the Mass is by way of becoming a vehicle for orisons, while the cathedral itself is developing
into a honeycomb of oratories. For, if the fourteenth century
"enlarged" the cathedral, this was only to diminish it; in the
radiating chapels which now proliferated in churches and
cathedrals, men prayed with their backs turned to the nave.
It was in the Sainte-Chapelle that the new art began.

Here, again, the ivories are instructive. In them Virgins,
tabernacles, triptychs make an abrupt appearance. No transitional style between Romanesque ivories and the sudden flowering of their Parisian successors—vaguely akin to the latest
sculpture at Rheims and the Bourges tympanum—has yet been
traced. From Compostella to Amiens, the art of the "Coronation" sculptors had never found expression in ivories; nor had
the sculpture of the Royal Portal. And Gothic ivories, so foreign
as regards their style to Romanesque, are even more so as regards
their function; with them began the "sentimental" icon of the
West. The piety of women owning an ivory Virgin (for these

statuettes were chiefly bought by women) was not directed to it in the same way as the faith of congregations was directed to the "sermons in stone" figuring in cathedrals. And when the ivory-worker took a lead from monumental sculpture, his choice fell on those aspects of it which accorded with the new form of devotion now gaining ground throughout the Christian West.

But there were other symptoms of this change. The notion of a communal faith was breaking down like an empire in course of disintegration, and the crucifixes of the Rhineland were contemporaries of the ivory Virgins. But, while we cannot overlook the fidelity of the great Rhenish mystics to the saints and theologians whose guidance they accepted, neither must we ignore the difference between their whispered colloquy with the divine and that clamorous exultation which, at Vézelay, had drowned the homilies of St Bernard. Though Meister Eckhart had many followers, great mystics were now by way of becoming recluses, attached to a monastery or convent. And before long hermits began to build their huts at the gates of Paris. The cathedral stood for public communion with God, but also with one's fellow Christians; the monastery was a refuge from the world. So was mysticism. Two hundred years earlier that mysticism would have assumed a sacramental form. The love preached by Tauler and Suso was not unknown to St Bernard; but it was a love that led to no crusade. Even in its deliberate aloofness, mysticism involves a private relationship with God; and what in the case of Meister Eckhart had been the union of the mystic with an ineffable God, was soon transformed into a dialogue with Jesus. Marian piety—which had sponsored Notre-Dame—popularized the rosary. We cannot picture St Bernard enacting for his own satisfaction, as Suso did, the scenes of the Passion; mediator between kings, the Abbot of Clairvaux would not have thus identified himself with Christ, even out of love for Him.

The surest ground for such an identification was suffering. The Passion now dominated all the Bible, as in the preceding age Christ's triumphal presence had filled the earth. Grace, in that age, had meant a message of joy; tragedy, even the supreme tragedy of Calvary, was transmuted by Christ, *in* Christ, and its shadows effaced by the Resurrection. It is only because we are so familiar with the Rheims *Annunciation* that we fail to be amazed by the fact that the angel bearing Mary tidings of the Incarnation is laughing as he does so. What a difference here from the Byzantine Virgins or that of Conques; from Simone Martini's shrinking Virgin and from Lotto's swooning Virgin, behind whom a black cat is running away, frightened by the angel! From Compostella to Rheims the worshipers' collective adoration and the spirit of the liturgy were untouched by any sense of individual guilt, by that obsession with personal sin which gave birth to the fifteenth-century devil and so often led men to see in God only a promulgator of stern commands. True, the figures evoked by early fourteenth-century mysticism in the lands where it prevailed did not express the same relationship

THE BONNECOMBE CHRIST (DETAIL), XIIth C.   MUSÉE FENAILLE, RODEZ

MASTER BARTOMEU. CRUCIFIX (DETAIL), 1270-1280. GERONA MUSEUM

between the Church and God as had been expressed by the figures associated with the liturgy; but they did not rule out a sense of the divine mystery, and in their loftiest forms revealed

THE DYING CHRIST (DETAIL), 1307.   PERPIGNAN CATHEDRAL

CRUCIFIX (DETAIL), 1304. SANTA MARIA IM KAPITOL, COLOGNE

the lonely aspiration of a soul yearning to win access to God's presence through communion in a sorrow conceived, perhaps, as fundamental to the scheme of things.

From the dawn of Romanesque there had existed an art of crucifix-making, parallel to that of monumental sculpture but distinct from it. It was in Germany that the most poignant crucifixes were carved, beginning with the *Gerokreuz*; nevertheless, as was the case with the *Courajod Christ* in the Louvre, the *Bonnecombe Christ* and several Spanish crucifixes, the German sculptors were more concerned with symbolical expression than with conveying the agony of the divine Victim. Each formed part of a tympanum that no longer exists, of a church that still exists. On the other hand, the crucifix in St Maria im Kapitol at Cologne, that at Andernach, and—most harrowing of all—

HALTERN CROSS (DETAIL), XIVth C.   HALTERN CHURCH (WESTPHALIA)

the *Dying Christ* at Perpignan are so much out of keeping with the cathedrals that the last-named, were it placed in Rheims Cathedral, would seem like an arraignment of it. Whereas, placed in any room with four bare walls, it would make of it a church. This effigy seems almost like a final echo of the genius of Romanesque, to which, however, it could not belong, despite the fact that it retains the supramundane accent of the great symbols: those of the "Majesties" and the Moissac "Christ of the Second Coming." It breathes a sanctity peculiar to itself, inviting the worship not of a whole parish but of a small group of Christians whose bond of union is an intense, personal faith. But this renascence of the sacred was soon to die away, along with all that manifested God and the City of God. In the spiritual domain of private worship, the transcendence of the Cross was now to signify compassion: the Perpignan *Dying Christ*, symbol of the central mystery, and the *Haltern Cross* were to give place to the "Man of Sorrows"—a Pietà, as it were, without the Mother. And yet, for thirteen centuries, the Church had been preaching faith not compassion.

What was gradually passing away was the whole world of transcendence. God's love for man, as manifested by the Incarnation, had been basic to the Christian faith. This divine love was obviously very different from the love felt by human beings, and their love for God no less obviously different from their love for one another. The love of God the Father was not *understood*, but *revealed*, and we no longer have any word to express it, since it has almost wholly disappeared from our traditional religious sentiment, which recognizes only Christ's love for us and responds to it alone. (In the monasteries the word "love" always meant sacred love.) Our term "fatherly love" is an unsatisfactory rendering of the Hebrew word *hesed*, better translated "Grace." God's love for men was paternal in the same way as an ideal father has within himself an instinctive love for his child—since it formed part of God's nature, not because it was in any sense paternalistic. That is why the sacrifice of the Son carried so profound a significance.

In feudal times this transcendent love had had a rough

equivalent, familiar to all, in the *ideal* relationship between the overlord and his vassals, between the priest and members of his flock. Ideal—but then all great forms of love are ideal in this sense, and it was in this sense that love was preached by the noblest representatives of Christianity, by men like St Bernard and St Louis. The love of man for God, so unlike the love of Tristan, was not foreign to a sublimation of the feeling each man had for that ideal suzerain, his overlord; indeed the Christian order of the age was like a hierarchy of vassalages established by God, in which the son was liege to the father, the wife to her husband, the apprentice to his master; while at a higher level kings, the emperor and the Pope acknowledged the suzerainty of God. Until the institution of feudal homage, the characteristic attitude of Christian prayer during the last eight centuries —clasped hands and bended knees—was completely unknown.

Though veneration of the Father preceded western feudalism by many centuries, it was seemingly not until the feudal age that the Father figure regained the prestige it had had under the kings of Israel. For there can be no doubt it underwent an eclipse in the period between that of Romanesque sculpture and the fourteenth century. By substituting the benevolent kingship of Christ for the august aloofness of the Father, the Gothic Reconciliation converted the God of the Romanesque churches into a sort of absentee landlord; no one was unaware of his existence but everyone forgot it, and in the cathedrals his ineffable presence paled before the rising glory of the Son.

The anti-Semitism of St Louis was a curious phenomenon, for the Church was not anti-Semitic. Indeed she never questioned the importance of the role of Israel in the central mystery of the Faith. During the First Crusade the Rhineland bishops had protected the Jews from the lawlessness of vagrant knights. But with the dwindling of the sense of mystery, that keen student of theology, the French king, who reverted to the ingenious theory voiced by Clovis—that the sacrifice of Christ was the result of "a miscarriage of justice" or the blind malevolence of the Jews—replaced Eckhart's concept of divine transcendence with Suso's insistence on divine compassion, and the Son of God incarnate now became the Divine Son of Mary.

For in the age when "courtly love" was merely a decorative adjunct of social life, a mother's love was regarded as the only indomitable love, eternal as the fact of birth, stronger than death. And once sacred love ceased being oriented towards transcendence, it took the form of this, the most intensely felt kind of human love. Hence the rise of the new cult of Mary, very different from that of St Bernard and from the art of the *Coronation* which glorified the Virgin as a member of the heavenly court. Not that the Mother supplanted the Father; but the homeliness (however sublimated) of the Mother's love replaced throughout lay Christendom the accent of the *revealed* love of the Father. Moreover the reciprocal love that the Mother's love aroused in the believer was now no longer that love, distinct in kind from every other emotion, which had lain at the heart of collective faith and worship, and had been expressed by adoration. It was a love differing from any natural human emotion less in its nature than in its depth and intensity; a love that invited participation —tender veneration and compassion—and was directed towards "presences" as it might have been directed towards living persons. What was already dying out at Rheims and Naumburg was religious sentiment of a kind incompatible *per se* with feelings inspired by human beings. More and more the Divine City was ceasing to be a world of God exclusively, and losing its transcendence, and Jesus was associated with Mary in the Pietàs, as Mary had been associated with Him in the "Coronations."

Just as "Christ the Teacher" had become the chief of the Apostles, so the Christ of the Passion now became the most touching of martyrs. But the *Beau Dieu* had come into being with his *Apostles*, with his cathedral; the sole cathedral of the Pietà was the human heart.

Not that the believer's emotional union with the divine could be attained only in solitude and privacy. There may well have been no fewer Flagellants in the fourteenth century than Crusaders in the thirteenth. But their piety no longer celebrated Christ triumphant; it was almost as if He had just died, a second time. The Church felt called on to condemn the Flagellants, and the great revivalistic movements that soon began to sweep the West militated against her authority. The Church's role of sacred intercessor, of a mystical Body, was losing its arcane pre-eminence; celebrations of the Sacrifice and thanksgiving were ceasing to canalize the faith of the community. And while the ascendancy of public worship was giving place to private devotion, the supernal world in which God manifested himself and Christ crowned the Virgin was being effaced by the world of man, in which a Mother gazes at her dead Son.

But though compassion was becoming the most potent form of love, it was not its only, or even its determinant form. No "reign of sorrow" succeeded the hierarchy presided over by a divine king; that world in which the Mother gazed at her dead Son was also the world in which she played with her living Child. Fourteenth-century art is symbolized by the *Virgin and Child* no less than by the *Cross of the Black Death*. Figures expressing Christian love invariably accompany effigies bearing the imprint of intense grief. Thus representations of St John resting his head on the Saviour's breast, and deeply moving litanies became generalized along with the *Pietàs*—and never did the *Pietà* oust the *Virgin and Child*. A century after *La Belle Madone* (in the Louvre) and *The Dying Christ*, Sluter carved his Virgin and his Calvary; a century later Grünewald was to paint his "Virgins" and his "Crucifixions." But now that the Virgin's appeal was being directed more to the individual than to the community, she, like the crucified Son, was transposed from the timeless into Time, from God's world to the world of man.

Whether figuring in a shrine or a Majestà, the Romanesque Virgin had embodied and transmitted no emotion unconcerned with God; for the function of Christian sacred art was to enable the congregation to participate in a mystery, not in the feelings of the holy figures. The age of "the Virgin in Majesty" was, like the "age of resurrection," an age of abstraction. The Child in her arms was not like any real child. This used to be put down to the sculptors' incapacity for representing childhood—preposterously enough, considering the childlike charm of the Chartres angels and the superb renderings of

MATER DOLOROSA (DETAIL), C. 1250. SAINT-JEAN, LIÈGE

children by Gislebert of Autun.   Cycles of the Life of the Virgin
had given the young girl of the Annunciation the same ageless
youth as that of the Mother figure in the Crucifixions.   When

symbols were replaced by representations of real grief, Mary may have seemed to grow older; yet we need only examine attentively the *Mater Dolorosa* of Liège, or that of Naumburg, to see that she is younger than the Christ for whom she weeps.

Great as was the difference between the Amiens *Annunciation* and those of Byzantium, it did not represent any "historical" event, datable like, for example, Herod's reign, for it expressed a mystery that had no place in one-way human time and could be apprehended only through a Revelation. The Amiens sculptor located his *Annunciation* in the world of the Angel hardly less definitely than the mosaicists of Santa Maria Maggiore and Daphni had located theirs. And that Angel was not a sylph-like visitant from some legendary dreamworld; the world in which the Virgin listened to him was one of an eternal present. Now, however, manifestations of the godhead were being effaced by emotive and scenic effects. Private devotion was abolishing the world of the Angel—to the point of garbling the scriptural text. Thus artists in their Crucifixions depicted the Virgin as "swooning," though the text said "she was standing" *(stabat Mater)* and she had been rendered thus in all Romanesque art, as in that of the age of the Crusades. And before long she became the Mother fallen in a faint—or sometimes the little girl whose hand St Anne is holding.

The seated Virgins of the early thirteenth century were in the spirit of Majestàs. In the first Madonnas figuring on door-mullions we have vertically disposed Majestàs, and in the *Mother of God* at Amiens a progeny of that Majestà in the tympanum of Notre-Dame of Paris to which Louis VII prayed. Yet the sculptor treated it in the manner of a portal statue, that is to say, as an integral part of the cathedral; in a museum (and the same is true of the nearby *Virgin of the Annunciation*), it would remind us of a "Black Virgin" removed from its crypt or an Egyptian funerary statue taken from its tomb. These Madonnas on mullions continued to harmonize with the figures of the cycle surrounding them until after 1250, but that cycle was beginning to lose its homogeneity. Whereas the *Mother of God* had looked like a sister of the *Young King of the East,* the figures grouped around the Rheims *Madonna* looked, at most, like cousins. Nonetheless the *Vierge Dorée* of Amiens "borrowed" from this figure her gigantic crown and attuned her smile to that of the angels in this, the last expression of the triumph of Christ and communal faith. After her, all statues of the Madonna were made not for portals, but for chapels.

This does not mean that statues were relegated once more to a "sanctuary"; for the fourteenth-century chapels—oratories for the use of those who had no other place of prayer—were far from being a revival of the crypts where, in the Romanesque age, men thronged to contemplate "Black Virgins," or of the apses where they rendered homage to the Virgins of pilgrimage churches. The "sanctuary" had disappeared. Whereas the portal statue came into being at the same time as the portal itself and belonged to it, a "Madonna" made for one chapel could be moved to another as easily as an ivory Virgin could change its owner. The traditional term "cult statues," used for statues that are objects of veneration, is misleading; these divine figures that love and suffer like human beings come into existence when the place of worship consecrates them only partially; when they no longer address their message to the body of Christians assembled in it but to the individual—even if his name is legion.

From Moissac to Compostella and from Compostella to Rheims (and, though less obviously, to the germinal centers of the great Rhenish crucifixes), art's progress had been one long spiritual pilgrimage, generating appropriate themes and styles upon its way. Nor did this cease when themes became emotionalized, whether for joy or sorrow. But the change did not lead to any deepening of Christian faith—rather, perhaps, to the contrary. For this new treatment of emotive themes, not as symbols but as representations, suggests to us the quest of a God who is withdrawing himself. New means were discovered of rendering emotion, tender or dramatic; but these discoveries soon lost their efficacity, for private piety could not content itself with perpetually smiling Madonnas; and no traditional piety could maintain the intensity of the Rhineland crucifixes. Neither the last Gothic Madonnas nor the last Gothic Pietàs were linked up with the early ones by that steady, tree-like growth which leads us to see in the Rheims gable a somber, grandiose fulfillment of the Senlis *Coronation*. Despite the Hundred Years' War and the Black Death of 1346, which wiped out a third of the population of Christendom, no change of style towards a greater emotionalism reflected the tragic history of the times. The fifteenth century was the age of the kermess and the charnel-house, yet how were its *Pietàs* more dramatic than those of Scheuernfeld and Bonn, or its figures of Christ more dramatic than the *Dying Christ* or the Haltern Crucifix? No fifteenth-century Virgin had a more rapturous appeal than the *Vierge Dorée*. Iconography was doing more and more to bridge the gap between the divine and the world of men; we see Mary caressing the Child, then playing with Him, and, finally, feeding Him at her breast. Nevertheless the Virgin suckling the Child still smiles, while the Virgins of Germanic and Bohemian art seem to glimpse the shadow of the Cross and have still the pensive melancoly of *La Belle Madone*, though in the Crucifixes there is less and less of the supernatural. The style, here, has ceased to render the spiritual undertones of the sacred narrative; for, when saints came to be regarded as "statues," spirituality was dying out of art.

Meanwhile Madonnas, Pietàs, Saints and Crucifixions were acquiring a common characteristic which comes out clearly when we compare them with figures of the pre-Gothic period. From the time of the Amiens sculpture and the Rhenish Crucifixes onward, until the end of the Middle Ages, the evolution, of sculptural style was conditioned more and more by esthetic —rather than affective—considerations. Naturally I am not using the word "esthetic" in the sense given it by Wilde; I have in mind the quest of forms creating a "distance" quite other than a religious "distance" between the spectator and the work of art, and in this the element of admiration was coming to play a part, if furtively as yet. Thus images of the Crucifixion came to be admired not merely as convincing representations of Christ but for their "artistry," long before the triumph of Italian art; neither the Cologne nor the Perpignan crucifix had been thus admired.

"LA BELLE MADONE" (DETAIL), FIRST QUARTER XIVth C.   LOUVRE

THE SWOONING VIRGIN, IInd HALF XIVth C.   NOTRE-DAME, LOUVIERS

France gave the world eight hundred Madonnas, and Germany even more; we find them everywhere from Spain to Sweden. Along with private devotion came a demand for the object of devotion; though it may seem no less absurd to talk of "the customer's taste" in the case of Suger than in that of Cheops, the fact remains that the nobleman who commissioned statues for his chapel and the lady who bought a Virgin were customers in this sense. But the nobleman, the lady, the Christian populace and the Church herself had no doubts about the kind of image that they wanted. All alike (in this agreeing with the sculptors of Rieux and Strasbourg) desired to find in it the stylization that emancipates religious figures from the secular world and clearly differentiates them from men and women of everyday life. The most famous "Swooning Virgin," the one at Louviers, is almost hieratic. While most of the sculptors catering for the public at large copied the conventional Madonna figure of the illuminations, others popularized the stylizations practised by the creators of prototypes. And these latter—like the last masters of monumental sculpture—countered those accents in their works which assimilated them to appearance, by the use of other accents boldly departing from it; thus, until the Renaissance, emotivity and fluted drapery flourished side by side. The flutings purported to "interpret" the drapery; the "interpretations" we find in the great Madonnas of France, Spain, England and Italy are of a less obvious order—nevertheless neither their costumes nor their attitudes are those of living women.

Now that the theory has been discredited that the curious slouch from the hips known as the "Gothic bend" was due to the curve of elephant-tusks (in reality the ivories followed the evolution of the statuary, not vice versa), or to the natural posture of a woman carrying a child (yet among the earliest statues given this posture, several are *male* figures), various attempts have been made to account for it. A similar attitude is found in Hindu and Buddhist figures—not to mention those of the school of Praxiteles, where its significance is quite different; and perhaps it should be regarded primarily as one of the postures which differentiate the human being from the rest of creation.

303

MADONNA AND CHILD, XIVth C. NOTRE-DAME, PARIS

THE KRUMLOV MADONNA, 1415. VIENNA MUSEUM

CLAUS SLUTER. PHILIP THE BOLD AND ST JOHN, C. 1395. CHAMPMOL

This view is borne out by the costumes. We are more familiar with the art of this period than with its style of dress, one of the most extravagant of all the Middle Ages, and may fail to realize at first sight that these Virgins are not wearing the fashionable court costumes of the day. Their cloaks belong, like the garments of the Amiens *Apostles*, to a celestial, not to any earthly court; just as, later, Florentine togas were to belong to a court existing only in the artist's imagination. Moreover we are assured by present-day dressmakers that this imaginary drapery is, technically, impracticable. The whole course of art, from the *Charioteer* of Delphi with his long, fluted robe to Bernini's statuary, shows how effectively drapery can lend an aura of the unreal to a human figure. The maker of the *Krumlov Madonna* seeks to convey the divinity of Mary by harmonizing a face expressing the most deeply moving love with Gothic hieraticism. And despite its less obvious stylization, never would *La Belle Madone*, the *Madonna* of Notre-Dame of Paris or her counterpart at Maineville have been taken by contemporaries for a young human mother—even a queen—gazing at her child.

The ambivalence of the Burgundian "Virgins" would be more apparent were their drapery not associated with our memories of Baroque drapery. Though harmonized with cloaks in the Sluter manner, their faces are no more copies of any Burgundian type of physiognomy than Sluter's *Prophets* were imitations of the "prophets" figuring in mystery plays, or than the lyrical fullness of their costumes imitated those actually worn by the actors. How could we confuse the garments of saints in the Champmol portal with those of the donors? It was, surely, not due to chance that at the close of the fifteenth century human forms were all but obliterated under the voluminous gowns habitually worn by "Mourners," as they were in the convolutions of German scroll-work. For all recourse to appearance called for a parallel recourse to *non-appearance*, lacking which the work of art would have neither significance nor value.

In the disintegration of the old order of divine worship the framed scene or "sculpted picture" made its appearance along with the isolated statue. Homiletic sculpture did not long survive the eclipse of the great preachers. Now that the world of God was receding into the distance, depictions of what had "actually happened" in the world of man began to figure on choir screens, in the periphery of choirs and on altarpieces. Artists may or may not have derived from the (unidentified) Franciscan friar who compiled the *Meditations* attributed to St Bonaventura, from the writings of St Brigitta or similar texts, the idea of showing Mary kneeling before the angel, the Magi kissing the Christchild's feet, the crowd in the "Bearing of the Cross" preventing Jesus from speaking to his Mother, and the scene of the Virgin swooning with grief; they could have found such data in much earlier "visionary" writers—the Apocryphal Gospels could have supplied them. The popularity of these anecdotes stemmed from the fact that they were, like the scenes inspired by them (also, those not inspired by them), "romances." It was the illusionism practised by the novelist that led the Franciscan friar to think up the menu of the meal angels served to Christ after his forty days' fast; and St Brigitta to describe the feet of Christ nailed to the Cross as looking like "wooden flaps hung on a hinge." In fourteenth-century illuminations, even allegories of the *Months* became anecdotal scenes. Fiction-alized biography replaced the Gospel narrative as the scene replaced the symbol. But that biography was not a Renanesque *Life of Jesus*; rather, the work of an inventive Fra Angelico who placed his illusionism at the service of the supernatural. And when a sculptor resorted to the illusionism of the mystery play, he too put it to the service of that world beyond the pale of acting which his art was intended to evoke.

It would seem that, brought inside the church, the tym-panum became the altarpiece, as the Virgin and saints of the portals, transferred to the interior, became cult statues. But the addition of narrative to symbolic scenes in the tympana had been a late development and the tympanum had been integrated into the world of God by the entire façade. The more the scenes of the altarpieces related to the world of men, the more the sculptors seem to have felt obliged to combine these with an imaginary façade, by means of a lavish framework of arcades,

APPEARANCE OF CHRIST TO ST THOMAS, FIRST HALF XIVth C. NOTRE-DAME, PARIS

gables and pinnacles. When the figures in these scenes and those on choir screens or around the choir seem to conform to appearance, this is only when they are viewed in isolation, and the conformity is never total. In Notre-Dame the figures of

MORGENSTERN. THE ASSUMPTION OF THE VIRGIN (DETAIL), 1516-1525. ADAMSTHAL

Christ and St Thomas were clothed in garments spangled with stars, answering to the stars (now obliterated) on the vaults. Also, they were brought into line with the simulated architecture surrounding them by the use of checkered gold backgrounds —in the same way as in Spanish and German altarpieces the illusionism of the expressionist (but gilded) figures was aligned to a ground studded with stars and a profusion of pinnacles. Though Gothic art began in France it did not end there; the figures of the Flamboyant sculpture that was now proliferating throughout Christendom, from Andalusia to Poland, were all but submerged in mazes of fantastic architecture, as the figures of Irish art were all but lost in a labyrinth of interlaces. It was as though these virtuosi of a form of sculpture that carried religious interior decoration to its extreme limit were convinced that only by an elaborate display of spires and finials could they establish beyond doubt that the holy figures portrayed still belonged to the world of God.

The great sculptors of retables, on the other hand, did not aim at creating a harmony between more and more illusionistic scenes and an ever denser forest of pinnacles; nevertheless, they, too, sought to achieve a sort of counterpoint between an art in which forms were subordinated to appearance and one in which forms were liberated from it. We find this happening in all interior sculpture of the period: in the tombs of the Certosa at Miraflores as in Michael Pacher's altar at St Wolfgang, in the Stoss altar at Cracow, and in Notke's *St George* group at Stockholm —and even in the calligraphic extravagances of Morgenstern, who outlived Leonardo. Here we have as it were the final avatar of Strasbourg and Rieux. But once the work of art had become independent of the edifice containing it (at Rieux the *Apostles* still shored up, if symbolically, the pillars, as in the Sainte-Chapelle), sculptors seem to have had an inkling that this counterpoint was to be their main concern. And by the end of the fourteenth century, they were sure of it, whether they were creating scenes or independent statues.

The term "artisan," when applied to Romanesque sculptors and those employed on the cathedrals has obviously no meaning outside its occupational significance; neither the Master of Moissac nor the maker of the *Beau Dieu* regarded himself as a mere handicraftsman, however skilled. Nor altogether as the "author" of his works; rather, perhaps, as an interpreter of the sublime music the Church had perpetuated through the centuries —as chorister or choir-master, according to the task alloted him. That music had ended with the ending of liturgical devotion; the last choir, with the last cathedral. The Amiens *Annunciation* had been born of, and with, its cathedral; Sluter's *Calvary* was self-sufficient and born, like the figures in the monastery of Champmol, of its creator's genius. The atelier now became the headquarters of a Master, not of the foreman of a team of workers, and sculpture was ceasing to be anonymous. The sculptor now sought in himself alone the inspiration he had formerly derived from the cathedral, substituted figures of love or compassion for figures embodying Faith, and created in isolation, as vehicles of a dialogue with individual Christians, the figures replacing those which formerly had manifested God's presence and Christ's triumph to the congregation. Thus, though the sculptor ceased being a revealer of the Divine City, he made the discovery of a new, mysterious, personal power.

It was now that art developed (by implication to begin with) that demiurgic quality which led to the making of purely secular figures. For the world of men was beginning to ravish the dead from the world of God. Cadavers in a state of decomposition were added to the stately recumbent effigies of the deceased figuring on tombs. One of the first was that of Cardinal de Lagrange who had caused to be erected on a buttress of Amiens Cathedral effigies of the great men of the kingdom. For statues to become "works of art," all that now was needed was that sculptors should apply their talents to making images of the *living*, not intended to figure in churches.

The company of statues had been denizens of the world of eternal bliss or of that of allegory. As God had welcomed into the church the symbolical vine-growers of Autun, He had welcomed the furriers and bakers figuring in the windows of Chartres, sponsored by their faithful toil or by their status as

PRINCESS YOLANDE (DETAIL), SECOND HALF XIIIth C.   CLOISTER, BURGOS

donors.   Called forth by God, not at the sculptor's whim, human figures had made their entry into sculpture; all owed to Him their right of presence and all were dedicate to Him.   The *Kings of France* (among them the *Chilperic* now in the Louvre) were sculpted for Saint-Denis; those of Rheims for the cathedral of the sacring; the royal couple Alfonso and Yolande for the Burgos monastery.   Certain knights whose valorous exploits were mimed in the plays performed in front of the church had also won admittance; but for this Roland's sword had needed to be identified with St Michael's, and Ogier to enter the cloister of St Faro.   The Rheims *Music Makers*, allegories of a supremely noble art, were a sequel to the Chartres *Musicians*.   The nudes included in scenes of the Last Judgment allegorized the human race at large, in the same way as the monk or bishop, whether blessed or damned, allegorized the clergy.   The private person won his entry into the company of statues by a gift, or by death (which linked him up with God): as donor or funerary effigy.

Effigies of the dead had long been given the age they would appear to have at the Resurrection, and their faces were spirit- ualized—that is to say the sculptor affiliated them, if vaguely, to the saints in monumental sculpture.   The custom of making death masks became widespread at the close of the thirteenth cen- tury and it is interesting to note that the first French king whose mask was made was the father of Philip the Fair.   Once the vital urge of Gothic had spent itself, the relationship of man with Christ became individualized, and effigies of the dead followed suit.   But the sculptor still "interpreted" the head. Anthropologists are puzzled at finding the same square faces, exactly the same type of jaw, in so many French knights and prelates.   Many figures at Saint-Denis have an air of belonging to the same family; obviously—in the case of the women— not the royal family.   The accent characteristic of certain English nobles is not met with outside England; nor is the stately piety of the statues of certain German bishops found outside the Germanic lands.   Despite the scars reproduced on the effigy of Isabel of Aragon, the idea behind the effigies of defunct rulers was not only that of preserving accurate likenesses of them.

JEANNE DE BOURBON (REPRESENTING MARGUERITE DE PROVENCE), C. 1390. LOUVRE

Even when given the standing position, fourteenth-century effigies
of the dead were not merely portraits but still, like their predecessors, religious figures. The sculptor ushers the deceased into
a world of the Elect that welcomes him, as does the Christian
earth. Indeed all sculpture still pertained to that world; just
as the statues of Alfonso and Yolande were intended to figure
in the Burgos convent, so those of the Emperor Charles IV and
the Empress were intended to figure in St Maria's at Mülhausen,
Anna von Schweidnitz in Prague Cathedral and the famous *Charles V*

ISABELLA OF BAVARIA (DETAIL), LATE XIVth C. PALACE OF POITIERS

(now in the Louvre) in the Chapelle des Quinze-Vingts. The *Queens of Navarre* at Mantes are donatrices—indeed every carved figure on a church wall has the air of a donor. But then quite suddenly at the turn of the century we find statues unconcerned with death, for they do not represent dead persons, and equally unconcerned with God, since they do not relate to any donation and are not praying—remote even from the church, since they figure in the hall of a palace.

Charles VI and *Isabella of Bavaria* stand in the same relation

to the donor figures of earlier sculpture (even to *Charles V* and
Jeanne de Bourbon) as does the great hall of the Palace of Poitiers
to the royal chapels upon which it was modeled; the architect
has adapted to a princely patron's wishes forms originally conceived for the service of God. The style of *Isabella* resembles
that of *Jeanne*, which in turn had resembled that of statues of
female saints. The sculptor inserted the Queen into their
lineage, much as Renaissance sculptors gave their models an
ambience of classical antiquity. But, greatly daring, he no
longer depicted Charles V as "a St Louis with the features of
Charles V," or Jeanne de Bourbon as an "imitation" of Marguerite de Provence; and he made the *living* Isabella a compeer of
the dead Jeanne. The spirituality of the earlier donatrices
(though traces of it still remain) is transmuted into regal splendor.
The artist has severed not so much the link between the earlier
figures and appearance, as that between them and a spiritual
world. Yet though his field of reference has changed and though
his art is no longer accented by the divine, neither is it oriented
by the living Isabella. What he sets out to make is not primarily
a portrait—still less a wax dummy (which would be grotesquely
out of keeping with the place assigned the effigy)—but a *statue*.
The Duc de Berry commissioned it, and the artist executed it,
as a homage. Moreover every statue tends to exalt its model,
and the embarrassing effect produced on us by statues of contemporaries is not due solely to their costumes. And by the irony
of fate, what was later to be called idealization now made its
sudden appearance in the face of the most detestable character
of French history. If we find in this statue an anticipation of
Tuscan figures, this is due to its participation in a world whose
tone was set by the Duc de Berry's palace, and in which statues,
quâ statues, could exist.

Here we have, it seems, the beginning of Christian "de-luxe
art." *Isabella* stands in much the same relation to certain
statues of saints in the cathedrals as Hellenistic statues stand to
statuary of the fifth century B.C. And just as the civilization of
Alexandria cannot be written off as a species of Athenian culture
on to which was grafted a luxurious way of living imported from

Asia, so fifteenth-century civilization cannot be conceived of as the same as that of the Crusades but with a new refinement superadded. By now the king had definitively taken the place of the suzerain, national languages had expelled Latin, and a State clergy had replaced the independent priesthood of the past. Luxury had made its appearance in chapels long before the year 1400, and cathedrals had preceded palaces in resorting to it. But in them it had always been subject to God's control. Was it now controlled by man? Yes, but still more by his dreams. For the luxury in question was not just a means to greater comfort or to a more gracious way of living. Though the arts were put to its service, *quality* also counted and taste was not the sole criterion. The Duc de Berry admired the "Calendar" of his *Très Riches Heures* as he admired the "Life of Jesus" which followed, but not in the same way as he admired the decorative elegance of Jean Pucelle's illuminations or a shapely ewer; nor did he appreciate the "Calendar" and the "Life of Jesus" in the same way as St Louis had appreciated his *Psalter*. When plans were submitted to him for his château at Mehun-sur-Yèvre, it was on the most "surrealist" of these that his choice fell, not on the more sumptuous and solid alternatives proposed. The social order which could simultaneously admire traditional Virgins and those of Sluter and Marville, both the *Pietàs* and *Isabella of Bavaria*, and was soon to show an equal enthusiasm for the dramatic grandeur of the Rohan Master and the glamorous art of Pol de Limbourg, was coming to direct its admiration to "objects," these fragments of reality which often seem, as in the *Très Riches Heures*, like exotic gifts brought by a cavalcade of Magi. It was not the château that now was taking the place of the cathedral; it was that realm of the fictional whose most favored medium was no longer sculpture, but the art which for a century had been challenging it in Italy: the art of painting.

V It was with Byzantium as a whole, both with the art of the Baptistery at Florence and with that of Ravenna, that Giotto broke when he parted company with Cimabue —just as it was with all the painting of the age of the great monarchies that Cézanne was to break when he broke with Delacroix. And "Giottism" did not spell the end of the *maniera greca* only, but also that of all previous Christian painting. It did not, however, take the form of a "school" challenging the schools of fresco painting that had preceded it, but arose in the same manner as Byzantine mosaics, Romanesque sculpture and the stained-glass window—as the discovery and conquest of a new, virgin field of expression.

From Palermo to Venetia all major works had been executed in mosaic. Those of Cavallini and Torriti, like Cimabue's in Pisa Cathedral, vied with the mosaics in the Baptistery of San Giovanni, pride of Florence, as St Mark's was that of Venice and the Adriatic. And in the frescos which preceded Giotto's at Assisi how can we fail to see a legacy of Byzantium and the manifestation, hardly at all Franciscan and (Cavallini notwithstanding) still less Roman, of an essentially sacred art? Behind the revolution which culminated in the Scrovegni Chapel at Padua was a whole new world of art with whose scope and splendor our "rediscovery" of Byzantium and the frescos of Jugoslavia are beginning to familiarize us. When we compare them with *St Francis preaching to the Birds*, Cimabue's frescos at Assisi seem akin, despite the many differences, to those at Nerezi and Sopočani. True, Italy was not a Byzantine province, but more like a western Japan confronting a western China, and our specialists have done well to stress the presence of northern forms in her mosaics; yet the fact remains that the spiritual climate of Italian imagery, even in the Florence Baptistery, owed much to that of the Byzantine East. And they have also done well to point out that the painting symbolized by the revolution at Assisi, and associated with the names of Giotto and Cimabue, arose within that ambience—and made an end of it.

The surprising thing is not that Byzantine art was swept away so suddenly (except in Venice, outpost of the East),

THE DEATH OF THE VIRGIN, C. 1260. CHURCH OF SOPOCANI (JUGOSLAVIA)

but that this took place so belatedly; that for so long Franciscan prayers were offered up to icons. It was not painting that had done away with Byzantium in northern Europe; it was sculpture. Sculpture had supplanted mosaics as the latter had ousted antique sculpture, and it did not call forth any painting that resembled it and followed up its conquest of a world of the imaginary put to the service of Truth; the "painting" of the cathedrals was the stained-glass window. And though the forms of northern sculpture were as foreign to Umbria as to Rome and Tuscany, the climate of religious sensibility in Italy resembled that prevailing north of the Alps. So effectively did Italian painting discard the Byzantine style—now, no doubt, beginning to cut the figure of an interloper, almost a foreign occupant—as to make it seem that all Christian art was taking over the legacy of Chartres; anyhow, within thirty years all traces of the East had vanished. In Florence, after Giotto's triumph, the message of Byzantine art ceased to be understood. Boccaccio accused it of having "buried painting"; Ghiberti (at the time when he was working on the doors of the Baptistery, Dante's *"mio bel San Giovanni"*) spoke of its "uncouthness," as did Vasari. Leonardo saw in it no more than imitations of traditional pictures. All alike commended Giotto for having destroyed an outworn convention by his discovery of "nature." Leonardo praised him for having sought in it the sources of his art, and Vasari for having so well "imitated nature."

"It was Giotto who brought into painting landscapes containing trees and rocks." We are less sure of this than was Vasari. Writing much earlier (about 1390), Cennini had formulated what he took to be the lesson to be learnt from Giotto. "If you want to make mountains in a good style and like nature, get big stones full of cracks and wrinkles, and copy them." In the Assisi frescos, as in those of Padua, Vasari did not find faithful representations of the Italian countryside; only attempts to render nature still imperfectly achieved, although truer than those of the Byzantines. The cognoscenti of the Renaissance, who saw in Giotto a man of undoubted genius, but a rather clumsy executant, assigned to his genius all that made for illusionism in his art, and to inexpertness all that diverged from it.

Another quality of his that they much admired was the "life-likeness" of his figures. "He introduced into painting," Vasari went on to say, "the expression of emotions, supple renderings of drapery and the practice of drawing living persons exactly as they look—a practice that had been obsolete for two centuries." Yet, though little is known of the artists who followed this practice round about the year 1100, it is quite evident that the cathedral sculptors anyhow were no more ignorant of it than they were of rendering emotion and the natural fall of drapery.

Art historians who stress the differences between Giotto and the Gothics usually contrast his art with the northern painting and sculpture *of his day*. But the Scrovegni frescos, though markedly opposed to Gothic mannerism, are adverse neither in their forms nor in their spirit to the *Coronation of the Virgin* in Notre-Dame of Paris, made a century earlier. And Giotto's campanile beside the Baptistery followed on it in the same way as the first cathedrals followed on the Romanesque churches.

What did the Assisi painters know of the great cathedrals? Some of their figures seem to echo, if in a puzzling way, the figures in the portals, and Cavallini's *Apostles* recall those that France had propagated as far afield as Burgos. Perhaps we may assume an indirect or fugitive acquaintance, like Manet's with the Spanish masters; an acquaintance that, however casual, is far from neg-ligible when such artists as Manet, Cavallini or Giotto are in question. Much has been said of the transmission of Nordic forms by way of ivories and illuminated books, but the art of the *Coronation* had no parallels in ivories or miniatures. And it was of this, not of Gothic mannerism, that Giotto was the continuator.

For the view that Giotto knew nothing whatever of transalpine art seems hardly tenable. People traveled widely in those days. Many Frenchmen visited Rome in 1300 for the Holy Year cele-brations. True, they did not bring their cathedrals with them; yet even in the thirteenth-century frescos of far-away Slavonia we find figures with the snub noses and thick lips so frequent in Gothic tympana, and next-of-kin to the Rheims *Musicians*.

323

Yet Sopočani had no close intellectual contacts, as Florence had, with Paris. Dante's instructor, Latini, wrote his *Trésor* in French and there are many Gothic types among the figures in the Baptistery. To the two arts of sculpture and stained glass which flourished side by side north of the Alps there sometimes corresponded in Italy a similar duality of bas-reliefs and mosaics; the *Allegories* Giotto saw carved on the bends of arches at St Mark's in Venice obviously gave him food for thought when he compared them with the mosaics treating the same subjects in the cupola. A great architect perhaps, in any case keenly interested in architecture, and Giovanni Pisano's collaborator, how could Giotto have been wholly unacquainted with the cathedrals? And how, in that case, could sculpture have been

FORTITUDE, C. 1250 (ARCH, LEFT) AND 1170-1200 (CUPOLA, RIGHT). SAN MARCO, VENICE

324

completely absent from what he knew of them?

There is no question, here, of "influences." The genius of Assisi belongs to Italy, and Giotto's to him alone. Yet would his *Kiss of Judas* seem to us out of place beside the Rheims *Kiss of Judas* (which Giotto seems to "orchestrate") or would Padua's loftiest forms seem intruders if they figured alongside those at Amiens? Those qualities which seemingly affiliate them to the art of Nicola Pisano assuredly affiliate them to the *Queen of Sheba*, the *Synagogue*, the *Presentation* and the *Death of the Virgin* (in Paris); also to some of the figures in the Burgos Sarmental and to the *Nativity* of the dismantled choir screen of Chartres Cathedral. Here Giotto might well have recognized something of his own spirit —also, perhaps, in the whole apotheosis of that art of the *Coronation* which extended to Dalmatia and we can sense in the reliefs of the cathedral at Trogir. Was sculpture still dominated by a spiritual continuity whose

THE KISS OF JUDAS, LATE XIIIth C.   RHEIMS

325

THE NATIVITY (DETAIL), 1250. FROM THE (DISMANTLED) ROODSCREEN. CHARTRES

evolution we have so far failed to trace? That latent kinship
between Nicola Pisano's art and the sarcophagi of antiquity
became in his son's work the Gothic feeling we sense in the *Nativities*
and in the majesty of his *Isaiah*. There is no great distance between
the statues of the Virgin at Pisa and the Tarragona *Virgin*, in
which Bartomeu carried on the tradition of French "Virgins";
nor between the *Isaiah* and Giotto's "Elders." So far as the
history of forms is concerned the art current which flowed from
Compostella to Paris and from Paris to Rheims comes to a stop

at Rheims; but in the history of Christian creative genius it flows on, like a subterranean river, up to Florence.

After the capture of Byzantium the West came into closer contact with that city. From the twelfth century on, sentimental, emotive or frankly picturesque scenes were given a place in Byzantine art. The "Peeping Toms" whom Giotto sometimes perches on his trees had already figured in the Daphni mosaics, and the Nerezi *Deposition* was no less poignant than his. Nor were effects of relief excluded from twelfth-century Byzantine art. Nevertheless the Padua *Deposition* superseded the Byzantine version (by way of Cimabue), just as the Amiens *Annunciation* had superseded Byzantine versions of that theme by way of Romanesque sculpture. The fact that relief and uniform grounds were common to both arts has little importance. For Giotto broke both with the rigid correlation of the picture elements characteristic of the "sacred language" and with that aquiline, angular script which made it so frankly antithetic to appearance.

In this he resembled the great Gothics; but he did not carve cathedral porches, he painted *scenes*. Those at Assisi, to begin with. St Francis had been dead for seventy-five years, the same interval of time as that between Napoleon's death and Matisse's first paintings. The Franciscan Order had been founded. The Assisi frescos do not depict the *illuminato*, possessed by God-given joy; when they were made, St Francis' life had become no more than that of a great saint, one of the many figuring in the Golden Legend. Yet an elaborate theological system had been based on it. Exalting as it did a faith devoid of "concepts" against the legacy of Aristotelian philosophy, Franciscanism did not so much give the artist a directive as liberate him. But St Francis' immediate influence seems to have been relatively weak; though he preached a gospel of love, the figures at Assisi do not express love any more than do the French ivories. While the basic relationship of Man with God is obviously bound to have an effect on all religious arts, it *directs* only the arts concerned with public devotion. Gothic sculpture owed its triumphal progress to its insistent proclamation of Christ's victory by means of the Church—a victory in which the Prophets, the Apostles, and the Virgin in the portals were associated with Him. The purpose of the art which represented sacred events was to enable incidents that had taken place under mortal eyes to enter into the eternity of the divine; the scenes of the lives of Bishop Firmin at Amiens and Bishop Remigius at Rheims were subordinated (even as to the dimensions of the figures) to the statues whereby St Firmin and St Remigius joined the company of the Apostles in the City of God. The Franciscan Order prescribed the subjects of the Assisi frescos; it wished them to be edifying, but they were not required to voice any specific "message." The figure of Christ in the *Last Judgment* aspires to dominate the whole Scrovegni Chapel, but in vain; the scenes impose a world of their own making, even on the *Last Judgment*; with the result that Christ the Judge is neither more nor less impressive than the Jesus who is raising Lazarus from the grave.

Actually He "raises" no one, and judges but half-heartedly.

THE KISS OF JUDAS (DETAIL, REVERSED), XIIIth C.   SAN MARCO, VENICE

And the placid Madonna in the Uffizi does not bear comparison with the Virgin of the *Visitation* or the *Nativity*. The religious world that Giotto shows us is the world of a Christian familiar with that of Dante and with the writings, full of tenderness and human feeling, of the pseudo-Bonaventura : the world of anecdotal scenes which his century had inaugurated. Already in the Upper Church of Assisi the St Francis cycle had heralded the triumph of the fictionalized biography. Giotto depicted *events*, as did the narrative imagery soon to proliferate on choirscreens and altarpieces of the North. While we can trace a vague affinity between his *Kiss of Judas* and that at Rheims, it differs entirely from the Naumburg version; yet all three alike replace the symbolic representations of the same scene in the mosaics with a depiction of "what happened"—that story-telling art which Christendom was henceforth to prize so highly.

However, it was by no means self-evident in the early fourteenth century that painting was to become the most favored

THE KISS OF JUDAS, C. 1250.   ROODSCREEN, NAUMBURG CATHEDRAL

medium of this art of story-telling. The relief that Giotto, following Cavallini, imparted to his figures by the use of shading could not compete with sculptural relief and, moreover, nearly all the sculpture of the time was colored.

But the carved figures (like those of Byzantine murals) stood out against gold or anyhow abstract grounds. That of the Saviour in the *Appearances of Christ* in Notre-Dame of Paris (begun before the Scrovegni frescos, but completed only in 1351) is more illusionist than the Christ at Padua, but the scenes in the *Appearances* are much less so than Giotto's. The illusionism of the former is fragmentary and intentionally so; the sculptor is reproducing, not imaginary scenes, but the very Acts of Christ. He makes no effort to represent distant planes, as Ghiberti was to do. The undulating patterns of his grounds are not meant to produce the effect of sky; they *suggest* the world in which a sacred event that took place on earth is to be located, but *represent* nothing whatever. Each of the scenes at Notre-Dame is enacted in a setting of symbolic accessories and against an abstract background stemming from the supramundane grounds of the earlier period.

At Assisi the scenic accessories much resemble those of sculpture and the staffage of contemporary Byzantine scenes; we find the same conventional rocks, the same small trees acting as symbols of "real" trees and, if not the same architecture (for here it has become Tuscan), the same use of architectural motifs. Giotto's backgrounds come hardly nearer to representing what he would actually have seen had he been present on the spot, than do the backgrounds of the bas-reliefs. His towns, when isolated as details in color photographs, suggest a Cézannesque style directed to religious ends. But the relations between figures and their surroundings are quite different from those in sculpture for although, for the first time in Christian painting, they have affinities with carved figures, they are not detached from their backgrounds in the same way as are the figures in bas-reliefs. And even when bas-reliefs took to imitating painting, their figures never stood out from their grounds in the same way as Giotto's. When the sculptor of the *Appearances of Christ* replaced his gold ground by a blue, he nonetheless rendered *in true relief* his figures, rocks and trees, the effect being to isolate them from their ground, whereas Giotto's illusionist modeling unites them with it and thus imposes on the beholder a quite different kind of participation in the scene before him.

The practice of bringing out the solidity of figures was not altogether new in Christian painting; Carolingian historical illuminations—e.g., the Vivian Bible—had inherited it from Late Antiquity. But Carolingian painters used it merely as a means for giving a rudimentary effect of relief to figures telling out against a background hardly less abstract than that of sculpture, despite the fact that there was nothing sculptural about their works. Indeed these scenes are located in a sort of no man's land. Where, for example, is Count Vivian presenting his Bible to Charles the Bald? Not in the palace, nor outside the palace, nor yet in heaven. Here and there a figure in that Bible, and even in the Vienna Bible or the Rossano Gospels, may resemble a Giotto figure; but its background (in the Rossano Gospels the purple of the vellum) never resembles that of the Padua frescos—which abolish it as they did the grounds of Gothic bas-reliefs. It was the suppression of those backgrounds that led Renaissance artists to acclaim Giotto as their forerunner; for the Giotto who painted the *Madonna Gloriosa* or the *Death of the Virgin* on a gold ground was overshadowed by the supposed "inventor of the sky."

Actually Giotto did *not* "invent the sky"; all he did was to employ grounds of an opaque, intense blue like that employed by Cimabue in the Lower Church at Assisi (but for other ends) in the *Virgin with Angels and St Francis*. The habit of mistaking Giotto's backgrounds for imitations of blue sky has been furthered in a curious manner by the damaged state of his frescos. No one is misled by the flaking of the paint in the case of figures; but in the backgrounds at Assisi and Padua, when its effect has been to lighten the lower portions of the frescos (they have flaked away chiefly in places where the grounds touch the figures), we seem to have a suggestion of depth. Also, when the upper areas have grown lighter, for the same reason, we have

GIOTTO (AND ASSISTANTS). ST FRANCIS HONORED BY A SIMPLE MAN, BEFORE 1300. ASSISI

a vague suggestion of clouds, leading us to read into Giotto's
mottled blue grounds an anticipation of the skies of Fra Angelico
or Piero della Francesca. But those grounds which have stayed
intact or been restored make it clear that distance counted for
nothing in Giotto's art and that he neither anticipated nor
aimed at Leonardo's effects of deep recession. Needless to say,

he had no inkling of Quattrocento perspective; he was not only unaware of the architectonic value of an horizon line, but made no attempt to represent it. In the cases where he seems to do so, this is because, as the result of cleanings cut short just above the figures (for fear of damaging them), most of the backgrounds of his frescos have become paler and the untouched parts, remaining darker, give a suggestion of distance. (This is particularly evident in the famous *Preaching to the Birds*.) When figures are not separated from the blue "wall" by buildings or rock formations, this "wall" extends right down to their feet. The same is true of Giotto's air; it is not open space, it is a *plane*.

The men of the Renaissance were acquainted with only two kinds of painting. The first of these, which they disdained and whose significance was no longer understood, comprised that legacy of the "unenlightened" past in which Romanesque and Gothic frescos and Christian mosaics were lumped together indiscriminately. This was the two-dimensional painting which had liberated its figures from the world of men and was related solely to the world of God. The other kind of painting, which professed to imitate nature, was that of the Renaissance artists. They praised Giotto for having inaugurated this latter style of painting, since, to their thinking, nature imitation was the best, indeed the only way, of avoiding "Greek and Gothic uncouthness." But the arts of extinct cultures have made it clear to us that every figurative style is based on a *selection* from the elements of appearance; the wash-painting of the Far East, when it supplanted an art no less hieratic than Byzantine art, created a form of representation without volumes, diametrically opposed to *trompe-l'œil* verisimilitude. We know today that the spirit of an art is best evaluated in terms of the specific field of reference to which it is related, by its correlation of the elements employed, and not by the fidelity of its imitation or its achievement of illusionism. Thus we regard as merely incidental Giotto's presumed acquaintance with the fragments of the decorative painting of antiquity still to be seen in the Rome of his day, and the indifference of his contemporaries in this respect does not surprise us. This anyhow is certain: that they found his frescos "convincing." Similarly, the Persians of Isfahan and the Mussulmans of Akbar's court, the Chinese of the Sung dynasty and the Japanese of Kamakura found their artists' works convincing. But though the Indians were fully aware of the world of difference between Mogul miniatures and the Ajanta frescos, and the Japanese of that between Takanobu's great portraits and the Nara frescos (as we today can see what differentiates Giotto from the Roman frescoists)—though this was so, neither the Indians nor the Japanese regard their medieval painters as pioneers of illusionism. Giotto's art cannot be defined in terms of what the future was to read into it. He no more inaugurated a primitive illusionism than Chinese wash-drawings ushered in a primitive chromatism. The arbitrary correlations he invented were not means to any sort of illusionist realism, but to a rendering, in painting, of the Christian saga that had hitherto been expressed in sculpture.

For Giotto painted neither landscapes nor still lifes, neither his wife nor his children (he had eight), nor the magnates of Florence, and when Enrico Scrovegni figures in his painting, it is in the capacity of donor. Vasari might have better understood the spirit of his art if he had given less thought to "nature" and more to the theater.

That word can be misleading, since it may suggest the imitation of religious plays—and there is nothing of the sort in Giotto's art. The influence of mystery plays took effect much later; they had not come into existence in his time. As compared with his paintings, such religious drama as then existed was hardly less primitive than the *tableaux vivants* of the day: groups of people posing without backgrounds, on floats, which were driven through the streets under conditions that practically ruled out any dramatic action. Giotto's "actors" play their parts in the setting of a ceremonial theater amid "properties" hitherto of a somewhat hieroglyphic order. The dead trees in the *Deposition* do not imitate a landscape but form an accompaniment to the death of Christ; in the Assisi frescos Arezzo is not a portrayal or an emblem of a town as were the views of towns in Byzantine art and Gothic bas-reliefs—though it seems to hold a dialogue with

GIOTTO.   THE DEVILS CAST OUT OF AREZZO, BEFORE 1300.   ASSISI

the monk who is driving the devils out of it.   Giotto did not
imitate any existing theater; he invented an imaginary theater
which reflected the gradual transmutation of communal worship
into private worship, and of the liturgical drama into the mystery

335

play. The liturgical drama commemorated the Incarnation and the Resurrection, Christmas and Easter Day; it was in Giotto's time that there began to figure in the ritual—as in the tympana of cathedrals—first the Crucifixion, then scenes of the Passion of Christ. But the *Crowning with Thorns* was not regarded as a "Manifestation of God" in the same sense as the Nativity; for all such "Manifestations of God" were now by way of becoming *scenes of the life of Jesus.*

Nonetheless these biographical scenes retained their character of sacred events and Giotto made a point of rendering them as such. He sought to maintain the sanctity of Jesus as the Christ, of Mary as the Virgin, of Francis of Assisi *quâ* saint: not to imitate, but to convince. His illusionism takes very different forms, according as he is representing figures or merely their surroundings; for the figures are protagonists in the "action" of his sacred scenes, its "actors." He thinks up for them commanding gestures, makes them exchange glances; but he contents himself with a space that is restricted and is not—nor perhaps did he wish it to be—that of the world of appearance. This space, which has been described as scenic and contrasts both with the space of Gothic sculpture and that created in Byzantine mosaics by the gold grounds in which the figures seem to be embedded, is limited not by the artist's ignorance of perspective but by the exigencies of the world of God. To assume that Giotto aimed at making exact imitations of imaginary scenes in his frescos and that Dante and Petrarch regarded them as fragments of reality, we should need to believe in the alleged "naivety" of the Middle Ages. True, these scenes carried conviction to contemporary beholders, to Dante and to Petrarch, but in the same way that, for us, *Antigone* carries conviction, though we know the curtain will fall on the last act; or a black-and-white film carries conviction, though we know the world is not monochrome.

Giotto's conception of art as an emotive expression of the central episodes of the Christian saga was the same as that of the cathedral sculptors in their renderings of sacred scenes— from the "Annunciations" in the portals to the bas-reliefs in

Paris and Naumburg. But the Amiens *Annunciation* belonged to a world as remote from the workaday world as Sunday is from weekdays—because it was the world of the cathedral. Even when an *Annunciation* was executed in bas-relief and figured on a choirscreen or the periphery of a choir, it belonged directly to that world. Thus the shimmering backgrounds of the *Appearances of Christ* related them to the starry vault of Notre-Dame of Paris. Every cathedral, every church, served as the gold ground of its figures, just as every portal was the gold ground of its statues. Italy replaced this ground with a "backcloth" that, while it did not imitate the world of creation, tallied with it much as the blue of the Padua grounds tallied with the sky. Giotto did not copy the sky men see, but transmuted it, for the first time, into a sky charged with Christ's presence.

Thus he brought to painting a power that was new in Christian art: the power of locating without sacrilege a sacred scene in a world resembling that of everyday life. Untrammelled by any conventional arrangement of the elements of appearance, he handled them freely so as to express, through them, the Christian message latent in all the created world. This discovery of Giotto's is not to be regarded as a stage in the progress of nature imitation midway between Byzantine "formalism" and Masaccio's chiaroscuro; rather, it constitutes a landmark in the history of Christian expression, a drastic change on which there was no going back. For the first time sacred scenes related no less to the world of man than to the world of God.

As a result they ceased being fragments of a cathedral, even of a chapel. In that extraordinary "picture box," the Scrovegni Chapel, nothing remains of the earlier framework of gables and pinnacles. When we compare it with the liturgic sculpture of Amiens, the great tympana, or a sequence of bas-reliefs, we cannot but be struck by the creative power of the art which now brought into being an illusory world no less effectively than sculpture had bodied forth a vision of the City of God. Though, disposed on three registers, the scenes give the impression of a gigantic checkerboard, they conveyed to the Christian the reality of the events depicted, with an unprecedented actuality.

Giotto was well aware that his towns and trees and rocks were essentially emblems, and that his architecture played the part of a stage set. And his figures would belong to the same world of the imaginary as those of the Amiens sculptor if, like the latter, they were correlated with a cathedral. But the world to which they are related and which was now to replace that of the cathedral; the world of men which the Renaissance was to identify with "reality" was a world of—fiction.

Neither the climate of Italy nor her architecture, neither her mentality nor the temper of her faith, necessarily ruled out the stained-glass window. The window ascribed to Duccio is enough to prove this, as also the window in Florence Cathedral, made by Uccello in the mid-Quattrocento and rivaling the masterworks of Chartres. But the invention of the story-telling picture, as revealed in the œuvre of one of the greatest artists of all time, not only gave a sudden change of direction to Italian painting but set the course of all Christian painting in the years to come: a path without return. The reflux of transcendence had left its mark on the religious imagery of the age, from Moissac to the Amiens portals, then to the bas-reliefs on choir-screens, and had diverted religious sentiment from epiphanies of God the Father towards illustrations of the Life of Jesus. Pictorial fiction opened the eyes of western Christendom to a world it had vainly sought for in narrative sculpture. By bringing the divine on to a plane nearer that of man, by ceasing to be related to cathedral or church, and by drawing on the imaginary, this new art met the needs of fourteenth-century Christians, just as hieratic representation had satisfied their predecessors' craving for transcendence. It was this recourse to fiction that raised painting to the status of a major art and it was from this that Christian painting derived the special accent that distinguishes it from all other religious painting. The gulf between the Padua frescos and those of the thirteenth century is wider than that between the latter and the murals of Ajanta and even those in the Valley of the Kings. Nevertheless the Scrovegni *Visitation* is in the lineage of the Chartres *Visitation*, as the *Meeting at the Golden Gate* is in that of the Gothic bas-reliefs. We are intellectually

GIOTTO.   THE MARRIAGE OF THE ·VIRGIN, 1304-1306.   SCROVEGNI CHAPEL, PADUA

aware that stained glass is the "painting" of the great cathedrals, yet emotionally we are reluctant to admit this; whereas
we "feel" that the paintings at Padua are next-of-kin to the
statuary of Rheims.   When Giotto broke with Byzantine tradition
he made an end of it; but insofar as he broke with the Gothic
tradition he fulfilled it.

His *genius* is not to be identified with that fulfillment, nor
with the discovery that made it feasible; all this did was to make

of the Assisi painters a school of highly competent *imagiers*. Giotto's genius lay in his power of shaping the media of the theater into that sublime expression of the Christian drama which, until Masaccio, no other artist succeeded in achieving; and of creating a latent harmony between the actors in that drama, conceived in terms of an ideal statuary and an ideal edifice, no longer temple or cathedral, whose possibility had dimly haunted the mind of western man. His scenes are dominated by standing figures which sometimes seem to uphold that edifice, playing the role of caryatids. Though their faces convey emotion of a quality that has rarely been surpassed, they interpret the Incarnation with the solemnity of the masks of antique tragedy. His last frescos, despite numerous repaintings—e.g. the *Life of St Peter* and even the *Life of St Francis*—might be described as Canticles of Columns; perhaps, indeed, his genius, like that of Piero, consisted in his power of imparting to saintly figures the note of majesty which sculptors had sometimes given the figure of Christ in their renderings of the *Coronation*.

But it was not this that did away with Byzantine forms; it was the incursion of fiction into art. Fiction now became the common measure of all Italian, then of all Christian painting. If Giotto did not "invent painting" as Vasari thought, he invented a certain kind of painting; and though the mastery of illusion was not its *raison d'être*, its evolution, up to the end of the Baroque era, marched side by side with that of the mastery of illusion. With the introduction of the fictional into religious art, thanks to which the fresco now competed with bas-reliefs and statuary, and along with the new, momentous tendency to rank it higher than mosaics and stained glass, there began the form of art which was to bear the name of painting throughout Europe from the Renaissance onward.

This was inaugurated by the ateliers of Assisi, and Duccio, Giotto's contemporary, was in touch with them. Though he revered Byzantine art for its "noble style," he rejected the idea behind it, and the gold grounds in the scenes he painted do not so much express the supernatural as suggest a sort of sunset glow. When a scene is located within a building, gold is dispensed with, and it even ceases to be present by implication, despite the hieratic quality of the design.

Florence's victory over Siena was the triumph of the fresco over the Tuscan icon; of the blue over the gold ground. But already, even in Siena, the latter was being adapted to the demands of fiction. That Sienese masterwork in the Uffizi at Florence, Simone Martini's *Annunciation*, shows how this was done. Until quite recently it was styled "Byzantine" on the strength of its hieratic quality; today, in virtue of its smoothly flowing line, it is styled "Gothic." We can easily picture that shrinking movement which poignantly expresses the Virgin's awe-stricken response to the angel's message, figuring in a mosaic or an illumination; but the scene is not placed in the world of Santa Sophia or even Nerezi; nor, despite its obviously Gothic feeling, in that of the *Psalter of St Louis*. The hieraticism of Constantinople and Venice, the linear arabesque of Paris, the sentimental appeal of French ivories, the Tuscan mastery of volumes—all four were synthesized in the fiction which originated at Assisi, and which is still more in evidence in Sienese frescos; for Sienese art almost always tends to become Florentine to some extent, when fresco is its medium.

Thus Tuscan fiction supplanted Byzantine representation —and all previous representations. It became that new language of the Church to which Cennini was referring when he said that Giotto "translated painting from Greek into Latin." When he advised artists to "copy big stones full of cracks" and to study Giotto, this was in order to paint mountains *"in the good style"*—it was a question of style, not of illusionism. And though Giotto's followers lost sight of the purport of his dramatic effects, the underlying similarity of their frescos had nothing to do with nature imitation; what had happened was that a convention of modeling with shadows and binding forms with heavy outlines had replaced the conventions of Byzantine design. Art had far less discovered nature and a wider freedom than come under a new discipline.

But this was not confined to Giotto's immediate followers. Andrea da Firenze (in the Spanish Chapel of S. Maria Novella), Traini (in the Pisan Campo Santo) and (in North Italy) the

THE THEBAID (DESTROYED), XIVth C.   DETAIL.   CAMPO SANTO, PISA

"Padani" discarded the imaginary window in which Giotto
framed his scenes at Padua.   Andrea replaced this with architectural layouts and Traini with continuous narrative.   By an
amazing chance the 1944 bombardment brought to light sketches
made by the Campo Santo painters whose frescos it destroyed
—sketches to which corresponded, presumably, the lost sketches
of many other Giotteschi.   The Pisan artists blocked out in red
chalk the scenes they were to depict; then, far from using the
means of painting to heighten their illusionism, translated them
into the new "Church Latin," as their predecessors had translated
their sketches into "Greek."   But now this Latin was becoming
secularized.   Lorenzetti's "Good and Bad Government" frescos
were new developments, even if they owed something to

342

SKETCH OF THE FIGURE OPPOSITE, BROUGHT TO LIGHT BY THE 1944 BOMBARDMENT

343

FRANCESCO TRAINI (?).   THE TRIUMPH OF DEATH, C. 1360.   BEFORE

the (lost) frescos Giotto made for the Palazzo del Podestà at
Florence.   The spirit of courtly art—and its alter ego, the cult
of the fabulous—re-emerged and flowered in a series of works
of whose near-Persian arabesques there had been no intimation in the Padua frescos.   For it is often of a Persian art, as
yet unborn, that we would be reminded by those heraldic dogs
and horses, by the woodlands in the Avignon hunting scenes and
even by the delicate refinement of the new palette, were it not
that the huntsmen are treated like figures in the Scrovegni
frescos and the greyhounds given thick outlines like those of the
angels of religious art.   A counterpoint between all that associated

the forms of art with the world of everyday life and all
that dissociated them from it was now beginning to play in
painting the part it played in northern sculpture—vaguely
to begin with, then explicitly. (Before twenty years had passed
there had developed a "Giottesque Baroque.") Something
of that delicate stylization which was to affiliate Pisanello
and Botticelli to Gozzoli is already present in Traini's work on
the walls of the Campo Santo, where we also find, here and
there, Italian counterparts of Nordic fluting.

But whereas the backgrounds of the Avignon frescos belonged
to the allusive art of illumination and tapestry, the Pisan frescos

345

wholly belong to fiction. We are shown horses—put to the service of Dominican faith, not to that of the sophisticated taste of Pope Clement VI—bending their necks towards open coffins; thus fiction provided an outlet for the spectacular imaging which Assisi, like Byzantium, ruled out. The *Triumph of Death* is a Judgment Day, a new version of the nearby, traditional *Last Judgment*; yet it does not depict what will happen on the Last Day nor a scene of Incarnation (even were it viewed through human eyes alone). What it shows is the corpse-strewn streets of one of the Tuscan towns half whose population had been carried off by the Plague. When the Dominicans of Pisa commissioned this gruesome scene they wished it to be charged with a compelling monitory power : the power which, until then, had been confined to scenes of the world of God. For though the Byzantines had had experience of the Plague, graveyards never figured in their art, and the sole reminders of death in the cathedrals were the recumbent effigies on tombs. But, *Judgment* by *Judgment*—from Chartres to Bamberg, from Bamberg to Bourges, from Bourges to Padua—the world of God had been losing its instancy, and to the *Judgments* of Padua and Florence the Pisan Dominicans now added the grim "romance" of death.

It is significant that the chief group of frescos linking up the second half of the fourteenth with the next century should figure in a cemetery, not in a church; it was as though in both painting and sculpture the world of God needed to pass through death before it could join up with that of the living. The *Triumph of Death* does not represent the dead alone; we are also shown the music-makers of a "Court of Love." Both groups seem intended to convey a like message, under the auspices of Christ: "in the midst of life we are in death." But, if treated in the Byzantine style, the entire composition would have lost its eloquence. Could it have retained this, anyhow to the same degree, if the medium had been sculpture? It is difficult to imagine so vast a bas-relief existing outside a church. True, the makers of the Orvieto bas-reliefs combined previous tendencies in just this manner; but they still were working for a cathedral, and their Last Judgment was no romance. To render "the romance

of death" no other mode of expression could compete with that of pictorial fiction. That power implicit in the painter's art which so sharply differentiates the Pisan frescos from the Orvieto reliefs was now to differentiate Pisanello's "Princess" from the princesses in tapestries. It is this power which prevents our regarding the International Gothic of the century's end as a somewhat ambivalent phenomenon—no less a revival than an innovation—and it was this that made possible the Sienese combination of Giotto's volumes with French mannerism and German stylization, and also with the gold grounds of the past. Tending to recede as the landscape rises, the gold ground dwindles to a narrow strip suggesting a cloudless sunset, like that more vaguely hinted at in Duccio's grounds. Sometimes the Trebon Master and the anonymous master in the Mayer van den Bergh Museum replace the gold with red, while in the latter painter's *Nativity* the ultramarine around the figure of God seems to be crowding back the gold into the margin. Thus the "sacred" golden ground of Byzantium was ending, now in the faint glow of an earthly sunset, now in the limpid sheen of Paradise.

The Assisi painters were chary of dispensing with the "sacred ground." The opacity of their mineral blue was related

PISANELLO. ST GEORGE AND THE PRINCESS OF TREBIZOND, C. 1435. VERONA

to the vaulting of the chapels, and in the geometrical ornamentation of the backdrops placed behind the figures we recognize that of the *Nativity* in the dismantled choir screen at Chartres, and also, rendered on a different scale, the checkerboard or zig-zag patterns and interlaces that formed the backgrounds of illuminations in some psalters. Italian art was less inclined to abandon these abstract grounds than to give them meaning, and the transformation of the zig-zags into curtains similarly patterned symbolized the painter's new approach. The reluctance of the illuminators to follow this lead is naively revealing; throughout the Trecento one gets the impression that they are struggling to use the checkered or ornamented grounds in such a way as to adjust Italian volumes, which now were creeping into the art of the miniature, to an ambience akin to that of the stained-glass window. A miniature made in 1415, notable both for its quality and for its handling of light, shows the Duc de Berry, preceded by his mace-bearer, walking under a sky dappled with fronds of gold like that above the dramatic figures in the Rohan Hours. And perhaps the Limbourgs would not have dared to paint as they did the skies of their *Months*, had these not merged into the semicircles of the Zodiacs overhead.

The gradual stages by which painters substituted fiction for Gothic abstraction and adapted Giotto's religious stagecraft both to appearance and to a world of dreams are particularly evident in the treatment of religious architecture. The northern Gothics employed gables and pinnacles even more frequently than checkerboard and other abstract patterns. And just as what symbolized the Church had pertained to the sacred, so what represented it still belonged to God. Already the neo-Byzantines and, later, Duccio had seen that it came more naturally to replace the gold ground by a nave than by a landscape. Even Jean Pucelle, when he placed his figures in vaguely indicated sanctuaries, made them look like fragments of some Tuscan predella. In the works of Giotto's pupils and those of Altichiero, simulated religious architecture bulked ever larger and defined the picture space; the connecting link between the world of the cathedral and that of nature became, paradoxically enough, the representation of a cathedral interior.

An interior complemented by the domes and façades of imaginary buildings that associated the scenes with a supernal world of a more or less fabulous nature. When Pisanello painted his *St George and the Princess*, with its poetic vision of an imaginary Trebizond as background, was he appealing to religious faith alone? And when the Limbourgs and Gentile da Fabriano painted the *Adoration of the Magi*, were its values solely of a religious order? Ostensibly the Virgin justifies these cortèges, the horses whose heraldic splendor (a legacy of Pisa) so much delighted the ducal courts, and Jean de Berry's cheetahs which the Limbourgs—in whose *Adoration* the ox and the ass are omitted—painted as meticulously as the Duke's châteaux. Actually the feelings aroused by such scenes had less to do with the Adoration than with the fairytale world evoked by the artist. Not that religious feelings were submerged; but these were supplemented by the thrill of discovering an imaginary realm revealed by a power of the artist that differed from his power of representing scriptural scenes, in that it no longer called forth veneration, but—like the new sculpture—admiration. True, the biblical motif always makes its presence felt, but when we fix our gaze on the figures of the Magi, we feel it is hardly more than an allusion. And in the Limbourgs' *Meeting of the Kings* and Pisanello's *St George and the Princess* we can forget it altogether. This Princess calls to mind Andromeda; also, perhaps, the "Flora" in Botticelli's *Primavera*. Figures of pagan mythology are now forgathering with those of the Christian iconography of sainted women, which includes Isabella of Bavaria. As in some vast Pisan fresco, the living and dead and visions of a dreamworld—portrait, cadaver, and the towers of an imagined Trebizond—together make their entrance into art.

VI In Flanders the sacred figures had for backgrounds Gothic towns, not fabulous cities, and it was there that finally the world of men replaced the world of God. When they painted mountains, the Flemish artists did not copy pebbles. To the nineteenth century the term "realism" seemed to have been coined for their benefit. But to this realism there was superadded, in the religious pictures, a quality traditionally described as "mystical naturalism." On this view the *Madonna of Chancellor Rolin* was primarily a portrait of the Chancellor—to which Jan van Eyck thought fit to add a Madonna.

But the Madonna had figured in painting and sculpture long before there was any question of depicting donors. Then, from the Byzantine period on, she had "invited" them, turn by turn, into stained-glass windows, sculpture and the Tuscan "fictions." The Van Eycks did not regard the Ghent Altarpiece, that manifesto of the new painting, as a genre scene; its donors belonged (like Enrico Scrovegni) to the world of religious fiction; as did (like the cavalcades of the Limbourgs and Gentile da Fabriano) its "Knights of Christ," and (like Pisanello's "Trebizond") its vision of Paradise.

In contrast with the cathedrals, where the chief figures represented only divine beings or the Blessed—and even with the Campo Santo frescos—fifteenth-century painting gives the effect of celebrating the redemption of *all* Creation, a general amnesty in which trees of Flanders and Florentine streets take part in the procession following the Magi and join up with the saints and shepherds and the animals beside the Christchild's manger. But now it seems that the divine can no longer be expressed otherwise than by appearance. The reason why the Pantocrator of the Ghent Altarpiece, though towering above the meadow across which some hundred persons are advancing, resembles a human being is not so much the fact that He made man in his image, as that the barrier between the sacred and the created world had steadily been lowered; the basic Otherness of God—that Romanesque transcendence which had been gradually humanized in fourteenth-century Madonnas—had vanished from portrayals of the divine.

VISION OF THE THRONE OF GOD. FLEMISH APOCALYPSE, C. 1400. BIBLIOTHÈQUE NATIONALE, PARIS

This had come about almost imperceptibly; no proclaimer of God's eclipse had succeeded the preachers of his glory. Yet indulgences now formed part of religion as fines formed part of the penal code. From the fourteenth century on, criminals sentenced to death were refused absolution. And in the *Dances of Death* extinction carried on a furtive dialectic with eternity. The early fifteenth century witnessed the appearance—a startling innovation—of the genial or majestic Ancient of Days whose attributes were now those of the pope, now those of the emperor: that new image of God which marked a turning-point in the spiritual evolution of the West—for, needless to say, it signified, not the sudden entry of the Creator into the world of art, but his annexation by the world of man. God had once been represented only by symbols (for example, the Carolingian "Hand"), or allusively; He had created men through the intermediacy of the Word, and, even at Byzantium, Eve was shown coming forth from Adam's body in front of an effigy of Christ. The Flemish illuminator who made of the Apocalypse a *Vision of the Throne of God* confessed (unwittingly) that the saga begun at Moissac had become as unintelligible to him as Byzantine art had been to Boccaccio. True, this is a minor work, but the Ghent Altarpiece, too, is a metamorphosis of the *Christ of the Second Coming*; in it singing angels have replaced the music-making Elders and a "Paradise Garden" replaced the World of God. The realm of Archangels, Principalities and Powers was coming more and more to be identified with the Garden of Eden, the celestial with the earthly Paradise, and the garments of the saints were becoming like those of the ordinary Christian. Yet though St George might now resemble some rustic squire and St Crispin the local cobbler, these figures still breathed fervent faith. Nonetheless that profoundly religious work, the Ghent Altarpiece, testifies to the annexation of the world of God by that of man, and to the incursion of Time into eternity: that human Time which had never until now figured in Christian art, nor for that matter in the art of the ancient East, in Buddhist or Hindu frescos, or in the Moslem art of Persia and Bagdad. No religious art, as yet, had taken notice of the passing hour.

GIOTTO. THE CRUCIFIXION, 1304-1306. SCROVEGNI CHAPEL, PADUA

True, when artists depicted the Virgin as St Anne's little
daughter and, later, as the aging woman of the Crucifixion, Time
had already left its mark on certain holy figures. But the Time
in which the Virgin had grown old was imprecise. There was
no question of hours recorded by the clock; rather, of successive
phases of the day: morning, afternoon (vaguely indicated),
twilight and the darkness of the night-pieces that had figured
in illuminations long before Bosch invented those of hell. Yet
"on the day of the Nativity dawn came early," as darkness
did on that of the Crucifixion. Beginning with the Angelus,

FRA ANGELICO. THE DEPOSITION (DETAIL), C. 1440. CONVENT OF SAN MARCO, FLORENCE

church bells meted out the hours with reminders of the Gospel story. That Christian art escaped the thrall of Time was neither accidental, nor due to the artists' lack of skill; it was due to the fact that what it represented took place *also* in the world of the eternal. For the mosaics, the light was that of the church interior; for the stained-glass window, the living light of God, as it was also for the statues. But in the fifteenth century a fictive Time implemented fictive space; light passed from God's hands to the painter's. While in the Ghent Altarpiece the light bathing the Christian Hesperides, the Gothic town, the singing angels, and

355

cypresses like those of Siena and Fiesole, is a divine light (replacing the gold ground), it is also that of a certain hour of the day, and the whole scene, though oriented to the divine, takes place on earth. Thus art invented a Time that welcomed-in the figures of eternity, as Chancellor Rolin and his peacocks welcomed his celestial visitant—in a Space defined by light and shade.

This conception of Time was not borrowed from secular imagery, nor was it sponsored by artists unconcerned with the divine; for it made its appearance simultaneously in Italy and Flanders, in religious scenes. And Italy, which had had premonitions of it fairly early (in the margins of pictures, for example Gentile da Fabriano's predella) brought it to fruition in the art of the only painter beatified by the Church: Fra Angelico.

We must beware of limiting this sudden change that came over painting to a "discovery of light." True, Fra Angelico did not handle light in the same way as Giotto, or even Masaccio. But he did not set out to paint a light effect on ramparts serving, incidentally, as a background for a Deposition from the Cross, any more than Van Eyck set out to paint a garden in which, as an afterthought, he placed a "Mystic Lamb." It was in order to give more instancy to a religious scene, not to imitate the data of appearance, that both artists invented landscape and a light varying with the passing hours. Needless to say they did not forestall the Impressionists; the hour of day played quite a minor part in their works. But, though still dedicate to God, that hour sounded the knell of Eternity.

Flemish painting seems to celebrate a sudden, long-awaited triumph of appearance. Yet we cannot explain its emergence if we dissociate it from the already longstanding trend which gave rise to it; if, for example, we see in the *Madonna of Chancellor Rolin* a portrait of the Chancellor to which the painter has added the Madonna, and not a world pertaining to the Madonna into which the Chancellor has been admitted. For such pictures are as far from representing scenes of everyday life as were those preceding them. Despite its very real debt to the illuminated book, Flemish creative art (like Giotto's) developed in a close, if ambivalent, relationship with sculpture. The sculpturesque accent which, by way of the Flemalle Master's "hard relief," was taken over by Van der Weyden, left its imprint more emphatically than did Van Eyck's shading, on all Germanic painting, and yet more emphatically than the Gothic accent affected Tuscan painting. In the same way as the latter replaced or implemented with its fresco cycles existent bas-reliefs and cycles of statuary, so Flemish painting replaced or implemented carved retables and statues of the Madonna with its painted altarpieces and Madonnas. True, in some isolated cases we can see in a Van Eyck *Virgin* the imitation of a real or imaginary model (we sometimes find this, also, in Madonna statues); yet, even so, this *Virgin* belongs to a sequence of Madonnas, not to one of portraits. It is less the likeness of a woman than a statue transmuted into a picture, and none of the great Flemish (or German) painters abandoned altogether the characteristic flutings of sculptured drapery. To the contemporary *Krumlov Madonna* it adds an ambience of the imaginary world which painting now was substituting for that of the cathedral. And, indeed, it was the cathedral that in Van Eyck's *Madonna in a Church* was now by way of becoming "fictional" in its turn. The Krumlov Madonna *happens to be* in a church; Van Eyck's is *represented* in one because this serves the painter's turn; were she transposed into reality, she would become an absurdly gigantic figure. A successor of the sculptured Madonnas, she brings to them that quality of the fictional which they were inviting once they had quitted the church portals. The *Madonna in a Church* is generically akin to those Crucifixions paradoxically located in cathedrals which have perplexed so many commentators. Van der Weyden knew very well that Christ was not crucified in the nave of Sainte-Gudule, and he did not aim at representing the scene on Calvary but at vying with the carved Crucifixions figuring in churches. And the central panel of the *Altarpiece of the Seven Sacraments* is in fact a sculptured Crucifixion changed into a picture.

But though the Flemish painters' dialogue with the sculpture of the past was of the same order as Giotto's, their reaction to

the painting of the past was very different from his. Giotto
had broken with Byzantium, but they were far from breaking
with the fictional in religious art. The new trend away from
transcendence oriented their innovations and gained strength
from all; and when the Van Eycks planned their altarpiece, they
aimed at superseding all the painting previous to theirs, but in
the same way as Giotto had superseded sculpture—by *fulfilling* it.

When on the imaginary stage of Italian art men and women
enacted as convincingly as possible episodes of the lives of Christ,
the Virgin and St Francis, these had been given purely *allusive*
backcloths and settings; Giotto substituted for them fragments
of "nature," but without any attempt to correlate its elements.
The Flemish backgrounds replaced the Italian in the same
way as in our time the cinematic background replaces that of the
theater. The Flemish masters discovered the horizon, and in
their art towns were no longer emblems, nor did their architecture
seem like a stage set. Also, it was with reference to them that
there first was talk of artists "capable of painting to perfection a
square inch of skin." Hence their keen interest in developing
the oil technique—unlike Masaccio, who was little interested in
the physical properties of his medium. Like the film producer,
they concentrate on selected aspects of appearance, but they also
seem to bear in mind the correlation of the fragments, with the
result that the world of appearance represented in their pictures,
as in the cinema, seems all-inclusive. It was with reference
to the Flemings that art historians began to use the term
"reality," instead of "nature."
But reality was still far from entering into painting as the
compulsive model it was later to become; like the Space of the
Italian frescos it was treated as a means, not as an end. Though
most of its elements tally with the evidence of our senses, angels
do not seem out of place in Flemish art. Van der Weyden, who
in his early *Descent from the Cross* merely replaced the gold ground
by a gilt wall (like that of altarpieces), subsequently showed the
Baptism taking place in front of a portal opening on a river (as
on a church interior) and staged the Crucifixion in the nave of

Sainte-Gudule, with a priest officiating in the background. Landscape was substituted for the gold ground in the same way as the church interior. It was not in a neutral, stereotyped landscape that the painter located his *Nativity*, but in one appropriate to the sacred scene, as the bare trees in the Master of Flémalle's *Nativity* were attuned to the stable, and the interiors of the first Flemish "Annunciations" to the figure of the Angel —and the tree in Giotto's *Deposition* harmonized with its theme. The scene of St Joseph making mousetraps (a symbolical allusion in any case) in the right wing of the Mérode *Annunciation* does not convert the panel into a carpenter's shopsign. The Flemish Primitives were realistic in the same way as Kafka is realistic.

The Limbourg brothers did not "invent" landscape in the same sense that Monet can be said to have invented Impressionism. Our "Imaginary Museum" (to which belong the manuscripts all of whose illuminations cannot be exhibited simultaneously) often omits the "Zodiacs" above the "Months" in the *Très Riches Heures*, and necessarily isolates the "Zodiacs" from the *devotional* book containing them. They compose a *Calendar* and as such derive from the Gothic imagery of "Months" converted by fourteenth-century illuminators into scenes. But the Limbourgs had also a feeling for the picturesque qualities of architecture—the feeling we sense in Flamboyant Gothic— and their châteaux are romantic counterparts of those dream castles which Altichiero was to bequeath to the Veronese painters. Their owner, the Duke, commissioned "portraits" of his favorite residences, and the painter did not handle these as he handled the sacred edifices in the *Life of Jesus* which he painted afterward. They have *not the same value*, though they definitely have one and are, indeed, the protagonists of the *Calendar*.

Not always, however. Sometimes they are shown in the far distance, and there is none for February. But this art had no posterity. The Flemish masters did not take over its courtly elegance, and it was only much later they invented the "pure" landscape. Though they learned much from the art of the illuminators, the Flemings rejected its rich diversity of motifs —those hunts, scenes of peasant life or historical events and genre pieces which crowd the pages of illuminated manuscripts. Not until a century later were the motifs of illumination released from the manuscript book and from the text which justified their freedom. But Flemish large-scale painting did not take appearance as its model; what it sought for was the means of expression most suitable to renderings of religious "fiction." To Flemish artists Nature did not mean a landscape before which they set up their easels, but a thesaurus of aspects of the visible, some of which, after due selection, could be integrated into the religious world, so as to give figures of Christ, the Virgin and Saints a more vivid actuality. At the time when portraits of living persons, donors and others, were being given neutral or somber backgrounds, landscape or meticulously rendered interiors served as settings for the Madonna. It was for his Madonnas that Van der Weyden painted those views of public squares, framed in a window, which had been, it seems, "invented" by the Master of Flémalle. And though the Van Eycks may appear to have been trying to imitate appearance when they painted the vastest landscape of the age, their true purpose was to actualize the vision of a world-beyond-the-world in which Pilgrims, Just Judges and Knights of the Faith advanced with measured steps towards the Mystic Lamb.

Like the cathedral portals, Giotto's frescos had been *permanent* manifestations of Christian faith. But the Ghent Altarpiece displayed its *Adoration* and its *Angels* only when the wings were opened on great feast-days and, once the festival over, it closed them on this noble celebration of the spirit of the Crusades. Thus these fleeting disclosures had, for the congregation, the effect of sudden revelations and quickened feelings differing from those aroused by familiar portal statues, scenes on tympana and even the Italian frescos. Van Eyck was not admired *more* than Giotto, but for other reasons; the admiration he inspired came not only from his power of expressing the divine by means of appearance, but also from his introduction of appearance into a world that sublimated it and was other than that in which St Joseph seemed a simple carpenter. It was the world in which a carpenter could become St Joseph and Chancellor Rolin meet the Virgin. Far from accepting the supremacy of Nature, he exercised his power of bending appearance to his will and using it to express what had hitherto been kept apart from it. Our familiarity with fifteenth-century paintings blinds us to the amazing novelty of such an art as this, in which one of the painter's contemporaries is shown kneeling—in his house or in a church which might do duty for it—before the Virgin on whose head an angel sets a crown, while peacocks are walking on the terrace and two small nondescript figures idly gazing at the town below, bathed in mellow afternoon light. Never at Byzantium, never in any cathedral or even in the Scrovegni Chapel had any artist shown a donor meeting the Virgin in a world so much like that of living men. But, while this was no longer Giotto's world, neither was it that of Chancellor Rolin; it was *the world of painting*.

This new art was a successor of the "fictional" art of Italy, liberated from the place of worship. The fresco cycles had formed part of the sacred edifice (as did the portal statues), but (like the cult statue) the altarpiece was movable. Yet, though Italian altar-pictures could be moved, their gold grounds associated them with the church, as the blue "wall" of their skies bound the frescos to its walls. When in the fifteenth century the flat "wall" of sky was replaced by light-flooded vistas, painting was well on its way to independence. (Often it seems as though the function of the gables on the frames and the statues painted on the wings is to restore a link between the figuration and the cathedral.) Painters were discovering the means of imparting depth to their fictive, but still religious, space at the same time as architects were ceasing to create "real" religious space and to add new perspective vistas and ever longer avenues of shadow to the cathedrals. Yet the natural habitat of the Ghent Altarpiece was still a cathedral. And, if the *Madonna of Chancellor Rolin* figured in the Chancellor's oratory, this was simply because to display it elsewhere would have seemed in bad taste. But, actually, its proper place was—nowhere! This object of private devotion was no longer an icon, like the

Wilton Diptych. If we showed the latter to someone who knew nothing about painting and asked: "Where exactly do you suppose King Richard II is kneeling before the Virgin?" he would answer (as he would answer if one put him the same question apropos of Enrico Scrovegni): "Why, in heaven!" And if he was asked where the Chancellor, kneeling like King Richard, is gazing at the Madonna, he would answer: "In his own home." All the same he would not take the picture for a family group; grandfather, mother and child. Nor did spectators of the time, or the Chancellor, or the painter, take it for anything of the sort. They would have admitted that the Virgin might, conceivably, have deigned to appear to Rolin (though the Chancellor would surely have shown surprise at her appearance). The true scene of their meeting is the world of painting, as that of Macbeth and the witches is the world of poetry, and the scene of the meeting of Rastignac and Vautrin, the world of the novel. Balzac's novel resembles reality, but does not coincide with it; if it did, it would affect us in a different way and we would cease admiring it. The early masters of what came to be called realism—rather to point a contrast with idealization than with any reference to illusionism (in point of fact the near-immobility of its imagery used to pass for "primitive")—these early masters, from Campin to Bouts, from the Van Eycks to Fouquet, painted pictures which resembled real scenes, but it is not this resemblance we admire today. For they also painted something that we can admire: that something else which differentiates their pictures from the scenes that they resemble. They demonstrate their skill by lifelikeness, but their genius by that difference; by the creation of that uncharted world towards which all great painters are forever groping their way when they express themselves by means of illusionism. That world is never one of mere *trompe-l'œil* and what severs it from reality is the creative power itself, the very act of painting.

This becomes clear if we try to imagine the *Madonna of Chancellor Rolin* or the scenes of the Ghent Altarpiece changed into tableaux vivants, and it is even truer of the illustrations in Fouquet's *Jewish Antiquities*, whose gold highlights so patently

JAN VAN EYCK.   THE MADONNA OF CHANCELLOR ROLIN, 1436.   LOUVRE

dispel any notion of illusionism.   Indeed the miniatures are
more significant in this respect than the *Chancellor Rolin*—if
only because far more minor works have survived in the form of
illuminations than in that of large-scale pictures.   For the term
"realism" applies more accurately to these than to the large

works, not because their illusionism better conveys the data of reality—actually it conveys them less well—but because, being conceived exclusively in terms of reality, they throw light on all that in such major works as the Ghent Altarpiece and the *Antiquities* does not stem from it. In these last-named works the divine, incarnated in the imaginary, merges into the real sublimated into the imaginary, as when the Madonna meets the Chancellor in the world of painting; that is to say, when painting is freed from the thrall of representation and becomes "art." When an inferior illuminator paints the Virgin with a Chancellor, they meet on earth, and when he paints an "Adoration of the Lamb" the setting ceases to be Paradise. This applies even to non-religious scenes; if he paints one in *trompe-l'œil*, there is no *picture*; and if he paints a face with photographic accuracy, no *portrait*. For what portrait is solely the imitation of a face?

It has long been usual to see in the Flemish portrait the Christian painter's first act of submission to reality and a symbol of "fidelity to nature." But what the Flemings discovered was not the physiognomy of their contemporaries; what was novel was their practice of isolating faces and separating donors from the saints escorting them or from the Virgin before whom they were kneeling.

Individual faces had long been depicted, but always in the service of God; cathedrals, illuminated books, International Gothic had teemed with them. Those of the Knights of the Faith in the Ghent Altarpiece had had precursors in Gentile da Fabriano's altarpiece; when we look at the panel containing the likeness of the donor of the Ghent Altarpiece, Joos Vydt (styled "Jodocus Vyd"), we are reminded of the Knights and their companions and of the statue of Philip the Bold in the Champmol portal; but hardly of the *John the Good* in the Louvre.

The *Man with a Red Turban* and the *Jean de Leeuw* are in the spirit of the *Leal Souvenir* (or *Tymotheus*), said to be a likeness of Van Eyck's friend Gilles Binchois, the composer, which in turn has a spiritual kinship with the *Joos Vydt* portrait. For portraits of the living still were justified by an association, explicit

H. AND J. VAN EYCK.   JOOS VYDT AND ST JOHN.   GHENT ALTARPIECE, 1422-1432.   ST BAVO'S, GHENT

or implied, with the divine, and they retained over a long period an accent never to be recaptured by the so-called realistic portrait.   Though Cardinal Albergati was not a donor, he has a family likeness with Canon van der Paele, who was one.   In Fouquet's portrait of Charles VII, *"très-victorieux roi de France,"* the king has the humility of Etienne Chevalier (in the Melun diptych).   And though the *Madonna of Chancellor Rolin* is not a portrait of the Chancellor to which a Madonna has been added, all Van Eyck's portraits are in a sense donor portraits from which the Madonna is omitted.   They may appear to modern eyes the acme of illusionism, but to the eighteenth century they seemed "wholly without depth," and Far Eastern artists (who regard photographs as infallible) find a distinctive "spirituality" in all European portraits, from Van Eyck to Fouquet, and look on *Margaret van Eyck* much as we look on Buddhist frescos or portraits of shoguns.

In the same way as Titian took as his point of departure the face of Francis I, known to him only through miniatures and medallions, but also that world of the unreal into which he wished to introduce it; in the same way as Cézanne bore in mind not only his wife's face but all the possible means of introducing it into the world of painting—so Van Eyck took account not only of the faces of his sitters but also of a world that pre-existed them.   Margaret van Eyck joins company with the donatrices and minor female saints of the altarpieces, and his Virgin with the Madonnas of sacred art, thus becoming other than a good-looking young Flemish woman.   The portrait differs from the "real" Margaret as does that of Jean de Leeuw from its model: by all that assimilates them to the portraits of Joos Vydt and his wife and the other figures in the Ghent Altarpiece; in the same manner as the living woman Isabella of Bavaria differed from the statue, in respect of all in it that likened her to the saints, and the Emperor Augustus differed from his effigies, in respect of what was godlike in them.

Portraits of *living* persons were, strictly speaking, incompatible with the sacred, since they enabled man to "escape from Time." Both Christianity and Judaism saw in Time an outcome of original sin; indeed all religions regard it as a penalty of the human situation. The sacred arts of the past had released from Time only those effigies which participated in the sacred (images of priest-kings and the dead) and Christian art exempted from it only those which belonged to God. There is no knowing whether any Christian painter before Van Eyck had felt moved to make a likeness of his wife. Were it not that some of the potsherds used by Egyptian artists for their preliminary sketches have survived, we should never have guessed the amazing liberties they took when making them. The sketches of many cultures have disappeared with them and, though Giotto did not make paintings of his children, there is nothing to prove that he never amused himself making drawings of them. Had paper been invented sooner, how many more sketches would have come down to us! When Van Eyck painted his wife's face, this was not because it had caught his fancy and he had discovered means of imitating it, but because he had discovered means of causing it to enter, through the medium of painting, into a world that welcomed its inclusion and justified its existence. Once the Crucifixion entered into Time, portraits won their entry into painting; if artists were to paint faces emancipated from the divine, perhaps it was needful that the image of the Creator in the Ghent Altarpiece should, first, have become a "portrait of God."

Thus it is not irrelevant to cite, apropos of Jan van Eyck, such works as *John the Good*, *Rudolf the Founder* and the lost portraits that formed a link between them and *Joos Vydt*. Or to observe that these were likenesses of monarchs.... But the emergence of the Flemish and Italian portrait was not a mere episode in the history of the imitation of individual faces; besides the recognition of a new power vested in the artist, it heralded yet another metamorphosis of the role of art.

Though not in any sense a religious picture, the double portrait *Arnolfini and his Wife* retains an atmosphere of piety; this is due to its subject (it commemorates a wedding), to the symbolism of its accessories—the "fruit of Paradise" on the windowsill, the small dog, emblem of fidelity, and so forth—and to the sculpturesque fluting of the garments and the harmony between the attitudes of the married couple and a "dim religious light." Never before used in Christian painting, this curious half-light is not found in any painting outside Europe. It was not just an illusionist device, it was something *invented* by the painters, for outside pictures it does not exist. In *Eve*, in *Adam* and the two donor portraits of the Ghent Altarpiece, in the *Man with a Red Turban* and *Jean de Leeuw*, this faintly tinted haze *represents* literally nothing. It is quite different from Giotto's light and from Fra Angelico's. Angelico's light records on his sacred figures the passing of the hours, whereas Van Eyck's dusk seems to transpose his *Adam* and his portraits into a timeless world. And when from those glimmering shadows which were now replacing the black grounds, as the sky replaced the bright grounds of the past, there emerges the face of the turbaned man or Jean de Leeuw's, it is evident that a change is coming over art; for whereas Van Eyck painted the living persons who figure in the altarpiece explicitly in their capacity of donors, neither the turbaned man or Jean de Leeuw had "donated" anything. Nor had the Arnolfinis.

These pictures were not made for churches. Nor for Bibles, like the Carolingian portraits (always donor portraits); nor even for Books of Hours. Though stemming from religious imagery, they no longer derived their value from the service of God. Nor from what they represented, for their subjects interested only a few people; nor from their illusionism alone. Actually *trompe-l'œil* effects play no greater part in *Jean de Leeuw* than they do in *Monna Lisa*. Yet, even assuming that the former was relatively little like its model, it would still suggest to contemporaries an attempt to vie with the forms of the created world—and this even without Van Eyck's skillful shading, since portraits by the Flémalle Master and Van der Weyden reveal a similar attempt. Donors had always been shown gazing towards Christ or the Madonna, but the eyes of Jean de Leeuw and the man with a turban are turned *toward the painter*. Once Christ and the Virgin were omitted, the world of painting could find place for Van Eyck's wife and the Arnolfinis (even for their bedroom), just as the cathedral had given access to saints and

JAN VAN EYCK.   THE GOLDSMITH JAN DE LEEUW, 1436.   VIENNA MUSEUM

effigies of dead men, Giotto to the sky and the Ghent Altarpiece to Joos Vydt and his wife. What painters were now in process of discovering, marginal to religious figuration, was in fact the easel picture.

In this respect the Italian portrait followed suit with the Flemish. But though they developed simultaneously, they have neither the same scope nor quite the same significance. Deprived of its portraits Flemish painting would seem a truncated art; this is not true of Italian painting. The Italian portrait stemmed less from donor portraits than from the cortèges in religious pictures such as depictions of the Magi. True, Piero della Francesca's *Malatesta with Saint Sigismund* is in the lineage of Pisanello's *Lionello d'Este*; but the latter's *Ginevra* was primarily a successor of the "Princess of Trebizond," as other portraits are of Masolino's *Salome*. Relatively minor works; for it was outside the portrait proper that Italy achieved that image of Man which it was to impose on the Western world. It is not the single portrait by Masaccio which has come down to us (the one in Washington) which we compare and contrast with the *Man with a Red Turban*, but that magnificent self-portrait in *The Tribute Money*, which purports to represent an apostle. As against the major creations of the first generation of Quattrocento painters, their portraits—charming as these sometimes are— seem no more than the work of often highly skilled craftsmen and a brilliant legacy of courtly art. But they are nonetheless portraits and in them the artist's power of transmuting a living being into a painted image is even more evident, if in a more superficial manner, than in Petrus Christus' famous *Young Girl*.

Already, when the Duke of Berry commissioned Pol de Limbourg to illuminate the *Très Riches Heures*, it was not merely because this artist could be depended on to record more faithfully than any other the splendors of the Duke's banquets and cavalcades. The esteem that Christendom accorded to outstanding works of art now was tinctured with an admiration of that mysterious power which the development of non-religious painting was making more and more apparent. At the time when polyphony was coming into vogue in convents and nuns were confessing to Denis the Carthusian the "lasciviousness of heart" they felt when joining in such chants, the reservations voiced by certain austere Christians as regards the Ghent Altarpiece were doubtless due to the fact that it aroused in them a similar "lasciviousness of heart"—meaning their admiration for the Van Eycks' paintings as works of art. For the Ghent Altarpiece aroused the same uneasy consciousness of an attempt to vie with God's creation as that produced by contemporary portraits. Gothic art had not aroused such feelings and Giotto's personal creative power had been less in evidence, since he exercised it almost always in the service of God alone.

Yet the domain in which this power was then, and thereafter, exercised remained strangely circumscribed. Though many of the non-religious works are lost, we are sufficiently familiar with Flemish painting by and large to know that this domain covered a much narrower field than illumination, or even tapestry— probably Cranach's art gives a fair idea of its extent. If this painting is "a mirror held up to life," as used to be said, it is evident that, from Van Eyck to the early work of Bosch, the mirror always reflected much the same objects, though not always in the same manner. When there is talk of the growth of Flemish realism in the fifteenth century, what is meant is the change that came over the figures in religious pictures, not a discovery, like Bruegel's, of scenes of daily life. It is known that Jan van Eyck painted hunting scenes, a money-changer and a woman bathing *(The Toilet)*. Why of all the scenes that met their eye and all that figured in illuminations, did Flemish painters retain just these scenes, and over so long a period? Was it not that Van Eyck's money-changer was (like so many other "money-changers" of the period) a Saint Eligius? And did his hunting scenes owe nothing to the Magi's cavalcades, and his woman bathing to the nudes in "Last Judgments" or to the "Bathsheba" motif? Even in the very poor extant copy of *The Toilet* we seem to see an after-image of the Ghent *Eve*. And it is still the art of that *Eve*, not the imitation of any living model, that we find in the nude figures of Van Eyck's followers and the little sorceress of *The Love Charm*.   One gets an impression that these men were on the brink of making good the autonomy of scenes of everyday life, and a new, secular fiction. What mysterious power held them back?

Once the Age of Enlightenment decided that the preternatural was a province of the imaginary, the Middle Ages came to be regarded as a period when the latter reigned supreme. But for medieval man the preternatural was an aspect of *reality*; he was no more surprised by angels than by elephants—indeed angels were more familiar since he saw more of them.   True, the elephants were "emissaries" of some Saracen monarch, whereas angels were those of God (and the demons, Satan's). But though angels and demons did not form part of the terrestrial world, they formed part of Creation, on the same basis as elephants—and man.

To medieval thinking the imaginary was never something that could not exist.   It was something that existed by the will of God; perhaps in faraway lands such as that of Singing Trees and the dogheaded men who were St Christopher's forbears; or simply "somewhere else," in a land where knights slew giants and dragons: a wonderland whose frontiers were still uncharted. A dragon might be merely some so far unknown species of elephant.   But the dragon-slayer was a real knight, one of God's creatures—another Ulysses, perhaps, but not, like Achilles or Hercules, a descendant of the gods.

Heroic deeds were, so to speak, only the small change of miracles, their *value* was always relative, and medieval fiction always somewhat childish.   Not that Christianity itself was naive; but it made over to secular fiction only its more childish traits.   The military character of feudalism tends to make us forget that the Bible is a sacred book *without a hero*.   Foreign to the New Testament by his very nature, the hero plays a very small part in the Old, which ascribes less importance to the Maccabees than to the prophets.   Compared with Brunhild, Esther and Judith cut dim, unimpressive figures.   If we imagine an Israelite "hero" we think of David, whose name Charlemagne adopted. David owed his victories to God's will; Charlemagne is renowned for his famous conquests, but the legendary Charlemagne would have been defeated, had God so willed. Neither conquests nor exploits suffice to make the hero; his personality stems from the unreal and from an appeal to the human instinct for the more-than-human; an instinct that he whets because it has given birth to him. The courage of a Roland or a Perceval enables him to overcome obstacles or baneful spells; the superhumanity of Hercules and Prometheus leads them to challenge the whole scheme of things. From the Church's point of view a conflict with the scheme of things can mean only a struggle against Original Sin, or else Satanic pride; the only superhumanity recognized by the Church is sainthood, and there can be no sainthood without Grace. The hero is always attempting to free himself, more or less, from the human condition, that condition which Christ deliberately took upon himself. The romances of chivalry are tales of adventure, hardly to be taken seriously; the tragic doom of Tristan and the fate-fraught saga of the Nibelungs are utterly unlike them. When the story-tellers made use of the Grail theme in order to associate God with their romantic fictions, the Church took alarm and instituted the Feast of Corpus Christi to combat the Grail. For she knew how hard it is to convert adventurers into Christian knights, and she counted more on St Michael than on Sir Galahad. By way of heroes she countenanced only champions of the Faith. The cathedrals, which ignored Tristan and Siegfried and mistrusted Roland, did not welcome even Perceval within their walls. And though their artists lent an accent of spirituality to even the humblest saints, none of them thought of inventing an "heroic" accent for King Arthur.

Thus in the sculpture of the age of the Crusades no place had been found for Godefroy de Bouillon, for Richard Cœur de Lion or for the Leper King, and the spirit of chivalry was given expression only through its saints. The few knights figuring on the walls of churches (in front of which their deeds were chanted) and the painted knights in Templars' Chapels seem like mere shells of armor, untenanted. The effigies of *Courage* in them are

R. LOISEL AND T. PRIVÉ.   TOMB STATUE OF DU GUESCLIN (DETAIL), 1397.   SAINT-DENIS

as paltry as the *Courage* in Notre-Dame of Paris. Those great *Founders* at Naumburg are not heroic figures; nor are the monumental effigies of the Black Prince and Bertrand du Guesclin. And though some English statues show touches of a fleeting grandeur, the knights who fought in the Crusades, on making their entry into the world of God, dwindle into conventional effigies, as the knights of the old legends dwindle into allegories.

This is illustrated also by the practice of the illuminators. Some strange compulsion, like that forbidding Mahometans to represent

COURAGE, XIIIth C.   NOTRE-DAME, PARIS

Sindbad, seems to force them to transform Perceval and all the heroes of the Breton legends into robots. How does one of these marionettes in armor suggest the "real" Perceval? Simply by brandishing a sword and, explicitly, because the text tells us who he is. Without inscriptions these legendary exploits would pass for unidentifiable scenes of knights in combat. "But," the illuminator might protest, "how could Perceval raising his sword, with his visor down, fail to look like any other knight wearing the same armor? Or even, for that matter, with his visor up?" In the mid-fifteenth century the illuminator of the *Cœur d'Amour Epris* (King René, by all accounts), though capable of giving a dreamlike accent to firelight, handles knights in the same way as trees or tents; or, thinking to transfigure them, converts them into beetles. (Already Minnesinger manuscripts were being illustrated with the would-be heroic antics of big insects in courtly raiment.) For, to the thinking of the age,

VENUS, JUNO AND PALLAS, C. 1500.   FOLIO 198 (DETAIL) OF "LES ECHECS AMOUREUX."
BIBLIOTHÈQUE NATIONALE, PARIS

admiration was not wholly justifiable unless the acts represented related to the service of God. From the thirteenth to the fifteenth century the Church was so much against tourneys as to contemplate refusing the last unction to those who fell in them. Only by participation in the spiritual could earthbound man be sublimated; unless he were a St George, no knight could be more than an effigy in armor, even if he were combating malefic sorcerers. For the domain of art in which he could figure as a "hero" had not yet come into being.

Hence the manner in which scenes of mythology and folklore now were treated. From the Byzantine period, when angels were shown driving away cloven-footed gods, until the fourteenth century when Saracen centaurs were depicted carrying off Deinairas guarded by helmeted archers, the Fable had never quite disappeared from illuminated manuscripts. In them Mercuries in the garb of bishops or pipers, turbaned Dianas and Saturns plying sickles forgathered with Mars-like figures in carts and Vulcans wearing farriers' aprons. Illuminators had no more given up painting Venus on the pages of medieval books—whether as planet or as chatelaine, in zodiacs or in gardens—than they had given up reading Latin. But now that she had ceased being a planet or a malign demon (only satirical renderings of demons were known to medieval art), she had become a "character" in folk-tales. Thus by the end of the fifteenth century Venus was being depicted in garden closes with trimly laid-out flower-beds—still somewhat allegorical and precursors of those "paradise gardens" where we see the Virgin teaching the Christchild to play the cithara. But though the painter saw in his goddesses symbols of contemporary mores he depicted Venus merely as a naked woman (direct descendant of the naked women risen from their graves on Resurrection day), and could make known the identity of the Lady in the Garden only by inscribing her name above her. In what world of painting could she become anything other than a naked woman, or a sister of the Proserpines and Plutos satirically represented in their "Courts" with lute-players making music? It was just as impossible for a painter to find a place for

377

THE HOUSE OF HADES, C. 1500. "LES ECHECS AMOUREUX." BIBLIOTHÈQUE NATIONALE, PARIS

Venus, pictured as a "glamorous" nude or a pagan queen, in the world of forms created by Van Eyck as for a sculptor to place her among the saints in the Chartres portal. She would seem an interloper in the Ghent Altarpiece, and when she figures (discreetly) in the Arnolfini's room, Van Eyck represents her merely as a naked woman, like the one figuring in *The Toilet*. It was only thus that she could find a place in Flemish painting, which confines itself to what *exists* and treats the supernatural as a fragment of the real world whose spiritual significance it is the artist's duty to reveal. Van Eyck painted his (lost) *Huntsmen*, as he painted the Arnolfini couple, because they existed— and Eve, the Virgin and the saints because they existed *even more*.

But Italy was now to paint Venus *because she did not exist*.

Regrettable as may have been the part played by fashion in pre-Raphaelitism, neither this nor the modern antipathy for the nineteenth-century notions of the Renaissance can alter our conviction that art underwent an abrupt mutation during the second half of the fifteenth century. In 1450 Roman painting did not surprise Rogier van der Weyden, nor did his art seem strange to the Italians. We can easily imagine him exchanging ideas with Piero della Francesca. But would this have been possible for Memling and Botticelli? Despite some affinities between their portraits and their religious works, it is clear that what Botticelli set out to create in his *Birth of Venus* was radically different from all that Memling was creating, from all that Van Eyck had created and from all that Van der Goes had in mind when he painted *The Adoration of the Shepherds* which, however, was commissioned for a church at Florence (and now cuts the figure of a "hostage" in the Uffizi). And it differed no less from what all Christian artists aimed at creating prior to the emergence of the Tuscan "mythologies." For the *Birth of Venus* opened up a new domain so far untouched by any Christian art: that of the Unreal. This was quite other than the innocent Never-never land where the dreams of paganism had been given the childish accents of the fairytale; it was a realm in which a Christian artist now dared, for the first time, to pit the images of his dreams against those of the world of God.

Masaccio's *Virgin* was no less—perhaps even more—"the Virgin" than Van Eyck's, and both painters solved the problems of representation on similar lines. However, we can hardly

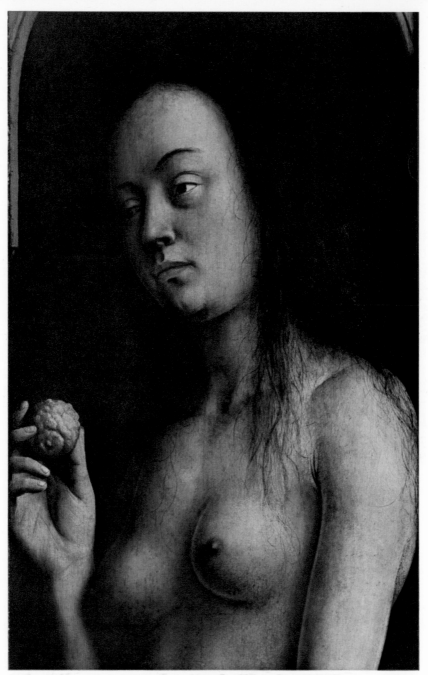

H. AND J. VAN EYCK. EVE (DETAIL). THE GHENT ALTARPIECE, 1422-1432. GHENT

BOTTICELLI. THE BIRTH OF VENUS (DETAIL), C. 1485. UFFIZI, FLORENCE

imagine the august gesture of the Florentine "Christ" figuring in the Ghent Altarpiece.

Masaccio's feeling for antiquity was, by way of Giotto, in the direct line of the Christian tradition that had begun with the *Coronation of the Virgin*. Giving rein to his personal genius, and adding some imperatorial gestures, Masaccio carried a stage further the scenic art of Padua (whose backgrounds he seemed to pulverize in *The Tribute Money*). His successors built up a space of their own and a new colorism; it is a far cry from Giotto to Piero. Yet Piero's knights, like Van Eyck's, are no more "heroes" than are the Gothic knights. In virtue of its monumentalism his *Queen of Sheba* falls in line with its predecessors in the cathedrals; it does not point the way to Venus. For Piero's figurations of the imaginary, like Van Eyck's—also like Giotto's and those of the cathedrals—are based on *Truth*. A whole world of the spirit passed away with the Arezzo Master, and it was one of his frescos in the Vatican that Julius II caused to be effaced so as to make way for Raphael's *Liberation of Saint Peter*.

There is no denying that Flanders and Italy had discovered simultaneously a light of a new order, as well as forms and layouts that made all preceding them seem obsolete; also that Van Eyck's shading and Masaccio's chiaroscuro stood for a decisive break with all that is connoted by the term "International Gothic." But Masaccio's genius would have blazed a trail solely for Piero's, as Van Eyck's genius prepared the soil for the flowering of Antonello da Messina's art and that of Bosch, were it not that Italy now made the discovery of a world of pictures in which Venus could meet on equal terms the Virgin, nymphs compete with angels—and the Unreal with the City of God.

SYNOPSIS

SYNOPSIS

PART ONE : INTRODUCTION

The mysterious power of the work of art, enabling it to transcend history, 1. — For many millennia art's function was to represent the gods, 1. — The significance of art in the first culture that is trying to discover the significance of man, 2. — To Baudelaire our museums would seem to be invaded by an art that was not an end in itself. The meaning of the word "art" has changed with our new conception of art's function. Sacred arts refuse to submit their images to the evidence of our senses, 3. — Sacred sculpture and architecture, 4. — At Gizeh, as in our cathedrals, we sense the presence of another world, 6. — Egyptian art does not record *that which was*, it gives the dead man access to the eternal and transmutes appearance into Truth, 9. — The "Architect with a Plan": at once worshiper, god and temple, 10. — Ellora proclaims that a truth exists beyond appearance. Against appearance is set up something that transcends "concrete" reality, 13. — The legend of Narada, 14. — All that reflects a consciousness dominated by Time is—appearance, 16. — Sacred architecture created with its ziggurats, pyramids, Egyptian temples, places where chaos becomes cosmos, 17. — The sacred statue is a figure liberated from appearance, as the temple is a place liberated from the surrounding world, 19. — The arts of the early (historical) civilizations were means whereby contemporary man gave visible form to his world of Truth, 20. — The art of a culture is both the art it creates and the repertory of figures that voice its message. Idols have become works of art by entering into a world of art unknown to any civilization before ours. Europe "discovered" Negro sculpture when Europeans saw it in the context of Picasso and Cézanne; the metamorphosis of the past began with a metamorphosis of our way of seeing, 21. — Art museums transform the work of art into an "object"; our "Imaginary Museum" includes the cathedrals, tombs, grottos, etc. that no real museum could house. In it European art becomes but one great art among others, as European history has become, for us, but one history among others, 22. — Since world art came on the scene appearance has come to mean no more than the inexhaustible libretto of an interminable opera, 24. — If man had not set up against appearance his successive worlds of Truth, he would have not become a rationalist, but another ape, 25. — Artists of the static civilizations of the East relate their work to a continuum *outside* "history"; medieval artists (like the Greeks) were conscious of an historical evolution, 27. — Christian art lost sight of eternity only when Italy discovered immortality. Michelangelo felt sure of achieving it since beauty is immortal. But gradually the meaning of the word "beauty" changed, ceasing to signify that which ensures immortality to a work of art, 28. — The Egyptian sculptor believed he was releasing his model from the thrall of time, Vermeer sought to release his *picture* from it, 29. — The world of art implies the presence in our midst of what would, normally, belong to death, 31. — A "discontinuous" history of cultures substitutes a discipline of the mind for sentimental notions of the "noble savage," and treats the past as a sequence of "interrogations." We ask the history of extinct civilizations to tell us what man is when he is not like ourselves. But also in what ways he resembled us, 33. — The ineluctable "nevermore" of dead civilizations is challenged, enigmatically, by the living presence of their works, 33. — Our "cities of art" attract more pilgrims than Rome attracted in Holy Year. A host of visitors from all countries (hardly aware of their fellowship) seems to ask the art of all ages to fill a void they vaguely sense within them, 34. — The aim of this book is to reveal the significance of the fact that man has always sought an answer to the problem set by the spark of eternity implicit in him: a problem of a new complexity in our modern culture, first to realize its ignorance of man's significance, 35.

PART II : THE DIVINE

I A fragile art of daylight, gods fated to perish with the nightfall, 40. — The art of Mycenae was far from symbolizing liberty, 41. — In the last holy place of Persia, Behistun, we sense the same virile fraternity as on the high cliffs of Taygetus, 41. — From Asia Minor to Etruria we encounter not the accent of the East but that of "white barbarians," 44. — Around 550 B.C. all arts were hieratic. Fifty years later man had lost touch with the sacred, 44. — Hieratic art involves rejection of the profane. The independent figure in Greek art did not herald the triumph of imitation but art's liberation from the sacred, 47. — In sacred arts representation always means translating into the language of a supramundane world. Eastern painters and sculptors knew the possibilities of the independent figure but ruled it out as incompatible with the purport of their art, 50. — The ritual gesture of Greece was not obeisance but the presentation of offerings, 50. — The myths are not to be confused with "biographies" of gods, or the gods with their effigies, 52. — For Greece, the "sacred" in its full sense did not exist, but neither did the wholly profane, since immanent in every form of life was an element of the divine, 52. — Greece did not "invent" joy or youth, but she was the first to celebrate their splendor, 56. — The Greek hero was an object of admiration, not of adoration. These heroes who vied with the immortals could be born only of a soul unmindful of an Almighty God, 57. — A sense of the divine, like that of the sacred, is innate in mankind, 58. — The Erinyes became the Eumenides, and the last version of the Medusa's face showed a sleeping goddess. The Greeks set up against the hierarchy of the Absolute the prestige of the imaginary and concentrated their efforts on *doing* all that could be done to harmonize themselves with their loftiest ideals, not on *being* as they should be so as to attune themselves to the eternal, 59. — Greek art isolates and manifests the "divine" element of the cosmos by liberating it from appearance. The sacred is replaced by the sublime, the supernatural by the marvellous, and Destiny itself by tragedy, 59. — Greek Tragedy, though related to a sacrifice, does not stem from this but from the art of poetry, and Greek poetry challenged Destiny on equal terms, 63. — Tragedy did not imply submission to the tragic but a victory over it, 63. — In all the arts deriving from Athens, though human figures might resemble gods, gods were never quite like mortals, 63. — The Olympian Games played the same part in the world of the Divine as the great religious festivals in that of the Sacred. The Greek sculptor sought in what he borrowed from appearance means for expressing the divine, 66. — The symbolization of cosmic forces played a relatively small part in Greek art, 69. — The "Greek miracle" was the creation of forms expressing the divine; it was by these forms, not by any idealization of appearance that the sculptor achieved "beauty," 72. — A work by Pheidias does not aim at imitation but at winning a place for itself in a world beyond appearance. The most skillful forger could not insert an illusionist face in the Parthenon frieze, 78. — The sacred style seemed like an emanation of the sacred; the divine seems to emanate from its form. The forms the artist was called on to invent corresponded to the spirit of enquiry basic to Greek thinking, 79. — The gods of Greece took form through art, as light through all that which it illuminates, 80. — After Delphi the only surviving element of the sacred in Greek art was the divine. The end of "the gods worshiped in darkness," 81.

II Greece had recognized Athena in the *Parthenos* and Apollo in his statue at Olympia; she did not recognize him in the *Apollo Belvedere*; "makers of gods" were now becoming makers of statues, 87. — The Olympians were no longer gods of a religion but gods of a culture. The ebb tide of Olympus left high and dry a company of figures exemplary but no longer numinous, 91. — With Lysippus, regarded by the Hellenistic age as its greatest sculptor, ended the creation of the divine, 92. — Athena had been a divine figure, the *Charioteer* a votive offering; henceforth a *Youth in Prayer* ranked as an "object of art." The new beauty was not that of living beings, but a quality *suggested* by the statues admired by Hellenistic connoisseurs and, from the artist's viewpoint, all that superadded the illusion of life, 95. — Idealization had begun, and with it appearance entered into sculpture, 95. — From the end of the ivth century until that of Rome the theatrical was supplanting the divine, 96. — Yet it was from the gods, not from men, that second-century sculpture derived its final accents.   Alexandria regarded this art as outlandish, not to say barbaric, and elected for the sculpture Rome was to make world-famous, 99. — In Rome art was regarded as imitation or idealization of appearance; the work of art was justified by the object represented, and the object by its function, 100. — The "fictions" into which the sculptors of Antioch and Alexandria transposed reality meant nothing to the Romans —except as elements of decoration.   Before Rome took over the Hellenistic portrait, her own tradition in this field was well established, 102. — It was in Rome that for the first time the order of appearance ranked as the order of the universe, and appearance as *the real*.

PART III : THE AGE OF FAITH

I Byzantium replaced gesturing statues by static figures, 113. — The "Imaginary Museum" of the fourth century is a compendium of rebels, among which Christian art is merely the most successful, 116. — When Christian forms were in the making, men's eyes were drawn towards the East; hence a style embodying the rejection of appearance characteristic of the East, 120. — The Fayum portraits, "children" of the Roman portrait, were parricides. On the eve of Constantine's triumph all arts concerned with the Other World disdained decorative or realistic art, 121. — The art of the Peace of the Church, which arose throughout the Empire, derived its accent from the Christian basilica, that "temple turned inside out," 126. — The antique forms in Christian art are neither those of Praxiteles, nor even clumsy copies of them; they are always forms drained of their significance. There could be no question of a "continuity of forms" now that the function of art had changed. If mosaics were once considered a decorative art this was because no one understood their language, 128. — The Church did not relegate its images to tombs; they were intended to be seen by generations as yet unborn. The mosaicists did away with the Space suggested by our senses; they did not try to give their figures depth but only (as in bas-reliefs) to combine them with a *ground*, 129. — Christian mosaics linked up with Late Antiquity, through the medium of the illuminated book, but this affected only the element of representation, and mosaic broke with it once it became an art in its own right, 130. — The great mosaicists brought to the Christian congregation a vision of the world of Truth (as Pheidias brought the Greek gods to the city); but they did not bring Jesus to it, 132. — Christ's "Revelation" was summed up in the words "God is love";

but the mystery of Godhead remained intact, 134. — The Ravenna mosaicists *spoke* the language their predecessors had been groping for, 136. — The Fayum portrait ended in the icon and the Palmyra bas-reliefs in figures of apostles, 140. — Mosaics took the place of sculpture, not that of painting; they stood in the same relation to the church as statues had to the colonnade, 140. — Christian creative art functioned on a plane above Byzantine luxury; it enabled man to rise above his earthbound self and to commune with his Maker. Imperial art was not "an expression of the Empire," 144. — The Byzantine sanctuary was not "propagandist," but a manifestation of the world of God, 146. — Christian imperial art was not an illustration of the Life of Jesus but a theological exposition of His nature. The Eastern Church would have stigmatized as profanation any religious art resembling fifteenth-century Gothic painting. The function of sacred art was to depict the sign, not the event, and solely in a transcendent world symbolizing the world of God, 147.

II By the eighth century Arianism had died out in Western Europe, but idols and sacred trees began wherever the Christian armies halted their advance, 150. — In the culture Charlemagne sought to introduce into his empire the classics played a minor role; his main endeavor was to propagate the Truth, 150. — The establishment of workshops of illuminators was part of a set program; not a single Carolingian illumination was made outside a monastery, 151. — The term "decoration" does not explain the reactions of the Carolingian monasteries to insular illumination. The Book of Kells was not intended to dazzle bibliophiles with its gorgeousness; its function was to celebrate God's glory, 154. — The absence of a major art gave illuminators a free hand in inventing forms that would have been excluded had their art been subordinated to another, 156. — Around 850 we find in the *Massacre of the Innocents* and the *Crucifixion* (both from Metz) an accent as foreign to Byzantium as that of the Ebbo *Saint Luke*, 160. — Perhaps this art stemmed more from S. Maria Maggiore than from Ravenna; for it is not an imperial art; it belonged to the Old Testament, as did the world in which it arose. Once exhibitions and reproductions have made artists as familiar with the painting of "the centuries without painting" as we now are with Byzantine mosaics, its fundamental unity will be as evident as the infinite diversity of its forms, 164. — When the holocausts of the invasions were rekindled, what remained of western culture was enshrined in the illuminated book, which was treasured like a sacred relic, 166. — Every great sacred art had been intended for the community at large; the art of the illuminated book was largely directed to a book-loving élite. Carolingian painting was in some ways an art for initiates, like much modern art, 168. — Following the decline of the illuminated book, the Church built up its own "imperial" art in the renascent West, 173. — The order of Christendom was beginning, 174. — Not a single Romanesque masterpiece owes its *art* to an illumination; illuminations did not furnish sculptors with *models* of expression or illusionism, but set *standards* of perfection, a frame of reference, 178. — The Saint-Benoît sculptor was, artistically speaking, unschooled; not so the Moissac sculptor; stone-carving was now becoming an "historical" art, 179. — Three centuries of forms simultaneously confronted Romanesque creative art, 182. — This sculpture was born of a metamorphosis; at its inception Romanesque sculpture, like the mosaics, was a kind of "super-painting," 183. — Polychrome sculpture brought relief effects to painting by bringing to it shadows; these had disappeared from art over five hundred years before, 184. — Thanks to the bas-reliefs Christ now figured *outside* the church, 185. — The Western Church desired to have its Christ, and the artists theirs—the same. Byzantium had been fascinated by God's inscrutable remoteness; Rome saw God's presence in all things, and this was the leit-motiv of the preaching of the age, 186. — It is not Jesus who presides over the Moissac tympanum, but Christ the Lord, 187. — Romanesque art broke with the images preceding it, working at once within their context and against it, 193. — What differentiates the art of Moissac from the Byzantine soliloquy is that its great tympana introduce Man into the world of God. The "Bible of the Illiterate" is a misnomer; *all* sacred arts are intended to appeal to the simple in heart, and none is illusionistic, 199. — Until the fifteenth century the Roman Church endorsed the rejection of appearance as wholeheartedly as does the Orthodox Church today. Like all who see their religion as a *living* reality, the nations of the West insisted on their artists' locating sacred scenes exclusively within a sacred world, 199. — The Church called every man to a crusade against his "heathen" self, so as to offer to Christ a Christendom true to its name, 200. — Innocence for Gislebert was a gleam of Christ lighting a human face, 202. — Reverting to Suger's themes, the Royal Portal of Chartres associates with God the whole world He has created, and redeemed, 206. — The elongation of figures was not suggested by the columns, but preceded them; it *ceased* with the coming of the heaven-aspiring urge of Gothic art, 206. — The function of architecture at the time was to create forms of stone capable of grasping the inapprehensible, 208. — The Romanesque masters created figures set free from appearance; all are symbols, since they signify something other than what they represent, as the fish signified Christ in the Catacombs. And the fish was solely a sign, 211. — The purpose of Romanesque art, like that of all arts of the sacred, was to transform signs into symbols of the inexpressible, 212. — No other art in any other civilization caused the sacred to embody so much of the human, and so fully expressed the sacred by way of the human.

III Romanesque art confined itself to the apostles; saints had no place in it. The saints of Gothic art link man up less with God the Father than with Jesus, 216. — Western Christendvm was now to celebrate in noble works of art the transformation of the Logos into Jesus; of the Mother of God into Our Lady, 218. — The "Christ" of the Royal Portal at Chartres was the first challenge to Romanesque symbolism. This break with the past was definitive; henceforth renderings of "scenes" superseded the creation of symbols, 218. — Gothic lay piety replaced the dictum "God is Love" by "God is Jesus," 219. — The successor of the Romanesque tympanum was not the Gothic tympanum but the porch itself, 223. — The Heavenly Father of Assisi replaced the God of the Burning Bush, and trust replaced obeisance, 224. — Through the teachings of St Francis and the art of the cathedral builders, adoration became communion. The saint depicted in sculpture was always a dead man, 226. — Where the Incarnation ended began an art of benediction, 228. — The cathedral is a mirror of the world or, rather, shows the world reflected in a divine mirror, 232. — The immense influence of Gothic architecture on sculpture (like that of Romanesque) was still of a spiritual order, 233. — Authentically Gothic sculpture symbolized the spirit of the cathedrals, as the gigantic *Saviour* had symbolized the spirit of Romanesque, and the nude was to symbolize that of the Renaissance, 235. — At the time when Gothic art was in the making an actor played the part of God in front of the church and anathematized Adam in French. The imaginary was expressed by representation, as the sacred had been by the symbol: *Mistère* (the old name of the mystery play) did not mean "mystery" but representation. To us the "imaginary" suggests fiction, but this was an imaginary *based on Truth*, 240. — All civilizations discover their secular art when they come to regard art as a value in itself. The aim of the sculpture in the cathedrals was not to idealize or spiritualize appearance, but to transmute the sacred into the imaginary as seen through Christian eyes, 243. — The art that gave form to this imaginary became one of the most potent elements of the communion that now took the place of adoration, 249. — This art cannot be understood if we disregard its accent of discovery; for it revealed, for the first time, the City of God, 250. — While offering to Christ the forms of his kingdom, sculpture also presented to men the forms of their sublimest dreams, 251.

IV It is not at Rheims, where the art of the *Coronation* lasted on until the end of the century, but in the Sainte-Chapelle that we find the artist asserting his personality in his work. Henceforth the term "beautiful" is applied not to the figure itself, *quâ* manifestation of the supernal, but to the statue *quâ* work of art, 272. — Hieraticism becomes calligraphy and "Church Latin" a "modish" idiom. Many Psalters vouch for the triumph of Chrétien de Troyes over the simple poetry of the Psalms, 274. — The incorporation of statues in the sacred edifice, their spiritual affiliation to the cathedral, ceased, and renderings of the Truth in terms of the imaginary no longer figured in monumental sculpture, 280. — In fourteenth-century religious sculpture the term "realism" applies only to *fragments* of each work, 280. — Sculptors now resort to stylization (which has ceased to mean, for them, a sacred language) as a means of integrating their religious figures into the world of God, 282. — The cathedrals were associated with the transition from a feudal hierarchy to an urban civilization, 284. — Christ no longer spoke to all men, but to the individual believer, and the chief aim of piety was a secret, intimate contact with the divine, 286. — In the side-chapels men prayed with their backs turned to the nave. With the coming of the Gothic ivories, stylistically so foreign to Romanesque, begins the "sentimental" icon of the West, 286. — In the spiritual world of private worship the transcendence of the Cross was now to signify compassion. But for thirteen centuries the Church had been preaching Faith, not compassion, 293. — While public worship was giving place to private devotion, the transcendent world of the Almighty was being replaced by a world in which the Mother gazes at her dead Son, 296. — In Christian imagery Love and Sorrow figure side by side, 296. — The treatment of emotive themes not as symbols but as representations suggests the search for a God who is withdrawing himself, 299. — This new style no longer conveyed the spiritual implications of the sacred narrative; once saints became "statues," spirituality was dying out of art, 300. — Fictionalized biography replaces the Gospel story, as the "scene" replaces the symbol, but this biography is not a Renanesque *Life of Jesus*; it is the work of an inventive Fra Angelico who puts his illusionism to the service of the supramundane, 308. — Sculpture ceases to be anonymous; the atelier is now the headquarters of a Master, 312. — The sculptor is no longer a revealer of the Divine City, but a man gifted with a mysterious power, and art acquires a demiurgic quality, ultimately leading to the creation of "profane" figures, 312. — The architect adapts to his patron's whims figures conceived for the service of God, 318. — It was not the château that ousted the cathedral; it was that realm of fiction whose most favored form of expression was no longer sculpture, but the art that for a century had been challenging it in Italy: the art of painting.

V Giotto's art broke not only with the *maniera greca* but with all previous Christian painting. The surprising thing is not that Byzantine art was swept away so suddenly, but that the change came so late; that for so long Franciscan prayers were addressed to icons, 322. — The Renaissance saw in Giotto an artist of genius but a clumsy executant and ascribed to his genius all that made for illusionism and to incompetence all that departed from it in his art, 323. — In the history of forms the art current which flowed from Compostella to Paris and from Paris to Rheims ceases at Rheims; in that of Christian inspiration it seems to make its way, underground, as far as Florence, 327. — Giotto's art must not be appraised in terms of what the future was to read into it. His arbitrary correlations were not means to *trompe-l'œil* effects but to an expression, in painting, of the Christian saga hitherto expressed by sculpture. He invented an imaginary "theater," which had a share in the conversion of communal into private worship, 335. — Manifestations of God were becoming scenes of the Life of Jesus, but these still were viewed as sacred events and Giotto rendered them as such, 336. — He brought to painting a power that was new in Christian art: that of locating, without sacrilege, a sacred scene in a world resembling the world of men, 337. — The world of men in which the Renaissance was to see "reality" was one of "fiction," and it was this discovery of pictorial fiction that gave Italian painting a new direction, modified the course of all subsequent Christian painting, and elevated painting to a major art. When Giotto broke with Byzantinism he made an end of it; insofar as he broke with Gothic tradition he fulfilled it, 339. — Florence's victory over Siena was that of the fresco over the Tuscan icon; of the blue ground over the gold ground, 341. — Tuscan fiction superseded all previous modes of representation, 341. — The frescos at Pisa dealt exclusively in fiction and illustrated scenes that were ruled out at Assisi, as at Byzantium, 346. — For rendering "the romance of Death" no other art form could vie with that of pictorial fiction, 347. — The gap between nature and the world of the cathedral was bridged by the depiction of cathedral interiors, or the façades and domes of an imaginary edifice, 350. — As in some gigantic Pisan fresco, the living and the dead and visions of a dreamworld, together made their entrance into art.

VI In Flanders Gothic towns, not legendary cities, serve as backgrounds for the sacred figures; for now the world of men is coming to replace the world of God, 351. — That profoundly religious work, the Ghent Altarpiece, testifies to the invasion of Eternity by human Time; no previous religious art had recorded the passing hours, 353. — Art invented a Time that welcomed the figures of Eternity into human Space, rendered in light and shade, 356. — Flemish art, like Giotto's, developed in a close if ambivalent relationship with sculpture. Van Eyck's "Virgin" has a place in a sequence of Madonnas, not in one of portraits; it is less the likeness of a woman than a statue transmuted into a picture, 357. — The Flemish Masters discovered the horizon, 358. — Landscape or church interiors now replaced the earlier gold grounds, 359. — Flemish Primitives are "realistic" in the same sense as Kafka is "realistic," 359. — Their painting does not go to appearance for its models, but seeks for the most telling means of rendering religious "fictions," 360. — Far from accepting the paramountcy of Nature, Van Eyck discovered his power of bending appearance to his will and used it for expressing what had hitherto been isolated from appearance. Never at Byzantium, nor in any cathedral, had an artist shown the Madonna meeting a donor in a world so much like that of living men as the setting of the *Madonna of Chancellor Rolin*. But it was *the world of painting*, 361. — Though the masters of so-called realistic painting, from Campin to Bouts, from the Van Eycks to Fouquet, painted pictures that looked like real scenes, it is not this resemblance we admire in them, but all that separates them from the "real" scenes they look like, 362. — The *Madonna of Chancellor Rolin* is not a portrait of the Chancellor to which the Madonna has been added; and all Van Eyck's portraits are in a sense "donor portraits" with the Madonna left out, 366. — Van Eyck takes account not only of the faces of his sitters but also of a world pre-existing them, 366. — Once the Crucifixion had entered into the world of Time, portraits entered into painting; thus the image of the Almighty in the Ghent Altarpiece has become "a portrait of God." The rise of Flemish and Italian portraiture heralded a metamorphosis of the role of art, 367. — Painters were discovering, marginal to religious figuration, not reality, but the easel picture, 370. — Van Eyck painted his (lost) *Huntsmen*, as he painted the Arnolfini couple, because they *existed;* his Eve, the Virgin and the saints, because they *existed even more.* But Italy was to paint Venus because she does not exist. The Florence *Venus* opened up a domain hitherto unknown to Christian art: that of *the Unreal.* For the first time a Christian artist dared to pit the images of his dreams against those of the world of God.

First Part

LIST OF ILLUSTRATIONS

LIST OF ILLUSTRATIONS

I

Black and white

II

Folding pages

III

Sepia

IV

Full color

Works of sculpture are reproduced in black-and-white, drawings in facsimile, paintings in full color, except in the case of (a) works no longer extant or impossible to photograph, (b) works compared with these, and (c) pictures that are compared with sculpture.

FOR THIS EDITION OF
THE METAMORPHOSIS OF THE GODS
THE TEXT WAS PRINTED BY IMPRIMERIE GEORGES LANG IN PARIS
AND THE COLOR GRAVURE BY DRAEGER FRERES AT MONTROUGE
FOR DOUBLEDAY & COMPANY, NEW YORK
MAY 1960